HISTORICAL DICTIONARIES OF RELIGIONS,
PHILOSOPHIES, AND MOVEMENTS
Edited by Jon Woronoff

1. *Buddhism,* by Charles S. Prebish, 1993
2. *Mormonism,* by Davis Bitton, 1994
3. *Ecumenical Christianity,* by Ans Joachim van der Bent, 1994
4. *Terrorism,* by Sean Anderson and Stephen Sloan, 1995
5. *Sikhism,* by W. H. McLeod, 1995
6. *Feminism,* by Janet K. Boles and Diane Long Hoeveler, 1996
7. *Olympic Movement,* by Ian Buchanan and Bill Mallon, 1995
8. *Methodism,* by Charles Yrigoyen Jr. and Susan E. Warrick, 1996
9. *Orthodox Church,* by Michael Prokurat, Alexander Golitzin, and Michael D. Peterson, 1996
10. *Organized Labor,* by James C. Docherty, 1996
11. *Civil Rights Movement,* by Ralph E. Luker, 1997
12. *Catholicism,* by William J. Collinge, 1997
13. *Hinduism,* by Bruce M. Sullivan, 1997
14. *North American Environmentalism,* by Edward R. Wells and Alan M. Schwartz, 1997
15. *Welfare State,* by Bent Greve, 1998
16. *Socialism,* by James C. Docherty, 1997
17. *Bahá'í Faith,* by Hugh C. Adamson and Philip Hainsworth, 1998
18. *Taoism,* by Julian F. Pas in cooperation with Man Kam Leung, 1998
19. *Judaism,* by Norman Solomon, 1998
20. *Green Movement,* by Elim Papadakis, 1998
21. *Nietzscheanism,* by Carol Diethe, 1999
22. *Gay Liberation Movement,* by Ronald J. Hunt, 1999
23. *Islamic Fundamentalist Movements in the Arab World, Iran, and Turkey,* by Ahmad S. Moussalli, 1999
24. *Reformed Churches,* by Robert Benedetto, Darrell L. Guder, and Donald K. McKim, 1999
25. *Baptists*, by William H. Brackney, 1999
26. *Cooperative Movement*, by Jack Shaffer, 1999
27. *Reformation and Counter-Reformation*, by Hans J. Hillerbrand, 1999

Historical Dictionary of Zionism

Rafael Medoff and Chaim I. Waxman

*Historical Dictionaries of Religions,
Philosophies, and Movements, No. 31*

The Scarecrow Press, Inc.
Lanham, Maryland, and London
2000

SCARECROW PRESS, INC.

Published in the United States of America
by Scarecrow Press, Inc.
4720 Boston Way, Lanham, Maryland 20706
http://www.scarecrowpress.com

4 Pleydell Gardens, Folkestone
Kent CT20 2DN, England

British Library Cataloguing in Publication Information Available

Library of Congress Cataloging-in-Publication Data

Medoff, Rafael, 1959–
    Historical dictionary of Zionism / Rafael Medoff and Chaim I. Waxman.
        p. cm. – (Historical dictionaries of religions, philosophies, and
        movements ; no. 31)
    Includes bibliographical references.
    ISBN 0-8108-3773-0 (alk. paper)
        1. Zionism—History—Dictionaries. 2. Israel—History—Dictionaries.
    I. Waxman, Chaim Isaac. II. Title. III. Series.

    DS149 .M375 2000
    320.54'095694'03—dc21   99-087955

♾™ The paper used in this publication meets the minimum requirements of
American National Standard for Information Sciences—Permanence of
Paper for Printed Library Materials, ANSI/NISO Z39.48-1992.
Manufactured in the United States of America.

Contents

Editor's Foreword

Over the past half-century, literally dozens of independent states have been created or re-created. In most cases, this involved a long and bitter struggle for statehood; but in no case were the odds against success quite as steep as for the state of Israel. Independence was sought by a movement that was long regarded as more visionary than practical and was fought for by a rather small Jewish minority in a largely Arab territory ruled by the then-still-solid British empire. Yet more exceptional, for many decades in the Diaspora Zionism was not even supported by the majority of Jews for whom the state was intended. It was only due to some of the most tragic events in human history that Zionism became widely accepted, within the Jewish community and further afield, and that it achieved its goals. Even then, Zionism was not a united, let alone monolithic, movement—a fact that should be borne in mind because although the state has been created, unlike nearly all others it remains contested.

This *Historical Dictionary of Zionism* is useful as a source of information on Zionism, its founders and subsequent leaders, its various strands and organizations, major events in the struggle, and its present status. By showing the movement's strengths and weaknesses, this book can also be a corrective to overly idealistic comments by Zionism's supporters and the wilder claims of its opponents. A much more realistic understanding is offered in the introduction, which presents and explains the movement; the chronology, which shows its historic progression; the dictionary, which includes numerous entries on crucial persons, organizations, and events; and the bibliography, which points the way to further reading.

This volume was written by Rafael Medoff and Chaim I. Waxman. Both are eminent scholars on Jewish studies, the former presently at Purchase College, the State University of New York, and the latter at Rutgers University. Both men are also leading authorities on Zionism, having written numerous articles and several books each on the subject. And both are keenly interested in the state of Israel, which grew out of the efforts of the Zionist movement. Thus, they see Zionism more broadly than most people do and they place it in its historical context, realizing that history does not just stop at an arbitrary date but is always with us. This viewpoint is particularly important at a time when, far from being forgotten, the debate on Israel, its origin and future, and the relationship of the Jews to Israel is increasingly vigorous.

Jon Woronoff
Series Editor

Acronyms and Abbreviations

AACI	Anglo-American Committee of Inquiry
AIPAC	American Israel Public Affairs Committee
AZC	American Zion Commonwealth
AZEC	American Zionist Emergency Council
AZF	American Zionist Federation
AZM	American Zionist Movement
AZMU	American Zionist Medical Unit
CCAR	Central Conference of American Rabbis
CJFWF	Council of Jewish Federations and Welfare Funds
DPs	Displaced Persons
ECZA	Emergency Committee for Zionist Affairs
FAZ	Federation of American Zionists
HMO	Hadassah Medical Organization
IZL	Irgun Zvai Leumi
JCA	Jewish Colonization Association
JDC	American Jewish Joint Distribution Committee
JDL	Jewish Defense League
JNF	Jewish National Fund
JTO	Jewish Territorial Organization
JV	Judische Volkspartei
Lehi	Lohamei Herut Israel
Mapai	Mifleget Poalei Eretz Israel
Mapam	Mifleget Hapoalim Hame-uhedet
NJA	New Jewish Agenda
NRP	National Religious Party
NZOA	New Zionist Organization of America
PAI	Poalei Agudat Israel
PLO	Palestine Liberation Organization
UHR	United Hebrew Resistance
UIA	United Israel Appeal
UJA	United Jewish Appeal

UPA	United Palestine Appeal
UN	United Nations
UNSCOP	United Nations Special Committee on Palestine
UTJ	United Torah Judaism
WZO	World Zionist Organization
ZOA	Zionist Organization of America

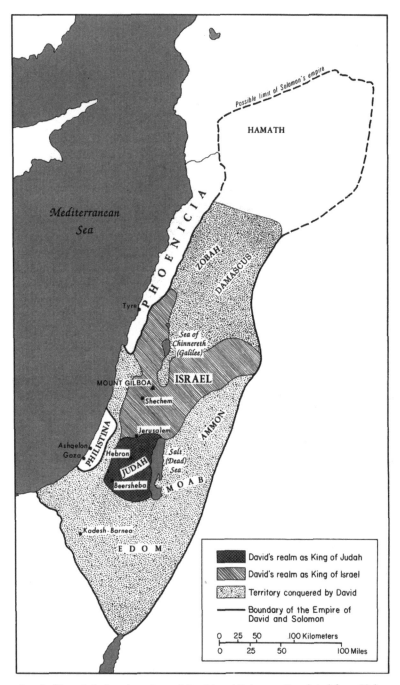

Land of Israel during the reigns of David and Solomon. Reprinted from Helen Chapin Metz, *Israel: A Country Study*, United States Government as represented by the Secretary of the Army (Washington, D.C., 1990).

Mandate of Palestine. Reprinted from Helen Chapin Metz, *Israel: A Country Study*, United States Government as represented by the Secretary of the Army (Washington, D.C., 1990).

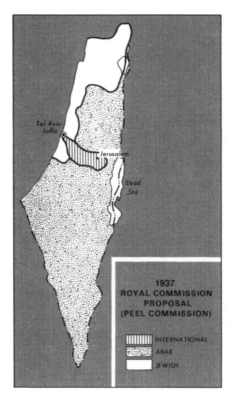

1937 Royal (Peel) Commission proposal.
Reprinted from Helen Chapin Metz, *Israel: A Country Study*, United States
Government as represented by the Secretary of the Army
(Washington, D.C., 1990).

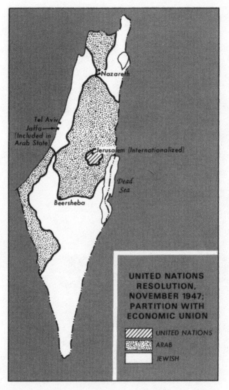

United Nations Resolution, November 1947.
Reprinted from Helen Chapin Metz, *Israel: A Country Study*, United States
Government as represented by the Secretary of the Army
(Washington, D.C., 1990).

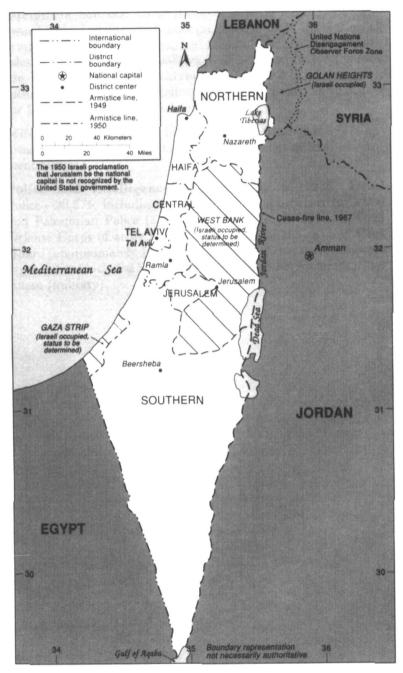

Israel. Reprinted from Helen Chapin Metz, *Israel: A Country Study*,
United States Government as represented by the Secretary of the Army
(Washington, D.C., 1990).

Chronology

1700s B.C.E.—Abraham emigrates from Ur to Canaan.

1600s B.C.E.—Jews migrate from Canaan to Egypt.

1200s B.C.E.—Exodus from Egypt.

1250 B.C.E.—Jewish conquest of Canaan.

1025–1006 B.C.E.—Kingdom of Saul.

990–968 B.C.E.—Kingdom of David.

968–928 B.C.E.—Kingdom of Solomon.

940 B.C.E.—First Temple is built.

928 B.C.E.—Division of Jewish kingdom into separate states of Israel/Samaria and Judea.

722 B.C.E.—Assyrian conquest of Israel/Samaria.

586 B.C.E.—Babylonian conquest of Judea and destruction of First Temple.

538 B.C.E.—The first exiled Jews return from Babylonia.

515 B.C.E.—Construction of Second Temple is completed.

167–164 B.C.E.—Maccabean revolt; reestablishment of Jewish sovereignty.

63 B.C.E.—Roman occupation of Jewish kingdom.

66–70 C.E.—Jewish revolt against Rome; Roman destruction of Second Temple.

73 C.E.—Mass suicide of last Jewish rebels against Rome, atop Masada.

132–135 C.E.—Bar Kochba revolt.

135—Romans rename Jerusalem "Aelia Capitolina" and change the name Eretz Israel to "Syria-Palaestina."

637—Muslim conquest of Eretz Israel.

1099—First Crusaders conquer Palestine.

1187—Muslims, led by Saladin, defeat the Crusaders and occupy Palestine.

1211—Three hundred French and English rabbis settle in Acre and Jerusalem.

1267—Nachmanides settles in Jerusalem.

1517—Ottoman Turks conquer Palestine.

1665—Shabtai Zvi, in Jerusalem, declares himself to be the messiah.

1700—A group of Polish Hasidim settle in Jerusalem.

1862—Moses Hess writes *Rome and Jerusalem;*
    Rabbi Zvi Hirsch Kalischer writes *Drishat Tzion.*

1870—Mikveh Israel Agricultural School is founded near Jaffa.

1878—Petah Tikvah is founded.

1882, September—Leo Pinsker's *Auto-Emancipation* is published.

1882—Bilu movement is founded.

1882–1904—First Aliya.

1885—American Reform rabbis adopt anti-Zionist "Pittsburgh Platform."

1886—"Hatikvah," later to become the Zionist anthem, is published in Jerusalem.

1889—Ahad Ha'am founds the Benei Moshe society.

1891—Christian Zionists' Blackstone Memorial petition is delivered to U.S. president Harrison.

1894, December—Captain Alfred Dreyfus is convicted of treason in France.

1896, February—Theodor Herzl's *Der Judenstaat* is published.

1897, August 29–31—First Zionist Congress is held in Basle.

1898, July 4—Federation of American Zionists (Zionist Organization of America) is founded.

1903, April 6–7—Kishinev Pogrom.

1903, August 23–28—Sixth Zionist Congress endorses Herzl's proposal to explore the Uganda Plan.

1904–1914—Second Aliya.

1905, July 27–August 2—Seventh Zionist Congress rejects all proposals for settling Jews outside of Palestine.

1907—First world union of Labor Zionists is founded.

1909—Tel Aviv is founded; Deganya, the first kibbutz, is founded.

1912—Hadassah, the U.S. women's Zionist organization, is founded.

1913—Hashomer Hatzair is founded.

1913–1914—"Language War" in Palestine.

1914, August—Louis D. Brandeis becomes the leader of the American Zionist movement.

1915—The Palestine Jewish espionage group Nili is founded.

1917, August 23—The Jewish Legion is founded.

1917, November 2—The Balfour Declaration is issued.

1917, December 11—British conquest of Jerusalem.

1919–1923—Third Aliya.

1920, February—Haganah is founded.

1920, December—Histadrut is founded.

1920, March 1—Yosef Trumpeldor is killed at Tel Hai.

1920, April—Palestinian Arab mob violence against Jews in Jerusalem.

1920, April 25—League of Nations, meeting in San Remo, awards Palestine Mandate to Great Britain.

1921, May—Palestinian Arab mob violence against Jews in Jaffa.

1922, September 16—British announce severance of Transjordan from Palestine Mandate.

1923—Betar Zionist youth movement is founded in Riga.

1924–1931—Fourth Aliya.

1925, April 1—Hebrew University of Jerusalem opens.

1925—Revisionist Zionist movement is founded.

1928—Soviet Union establishes an alternative Jewish homeland in the Siberian region of Birobidzhan.

1929, August 23–26—Arab riots throughout Palestine.

1931–1939—Fifth Aliya.

1931—Irgun Zvai Leumi is founded.

1933, January 30—Adolf Hitler becomes chancellor of Germany.

1933, June 16—Labor Zionist official Haim Arlosoroff is killed in Tel Aviv.

1936, April 15—Palestinian Arabs launch a general strike and mass violence.

1937, July—British Peel Commission recommends the partition of Palestine.

1938, November 9–10—*Kristallnacht* pogrom.

1939, May 15—British White Paper restricts Jewish immigration to Palestine.

1939–1948—Sixth Aliya.

1940, February 28—British restrict Jewish land purchases in Palestine.

1940, July—The militant underground later known as *Lohamei Herut Israel* (Lehi) is founded.

1940, November 25—Sinking of the Jewish refugee ship *Patria.*

1942, February 24—Sinking of the Jewish refugee ship *Struma.*

1942, May 11—American Zionists adopt Biltmore Program.

1942, December 17—Allies confirm Nazi genocide.

1943, April 19—Warsaw Ghetto revolt erupts.

1943, August—Abba Hillel Silver becomes the leader of the American Zionist movement.

1944, February 1—Irgun Zvai Leumi launches a revolt against the British in Palestine.

1944, June—Hannah Senesh is captured by the Nazis in Hungary.

1944, September 20—Jewish Brigade is founded.

1944, November 6—Assassination of Lord Moyne by Lehi.

1946, October–July 1946—Joint Haganah-Irgun-Lehi revolt against the British.

1946, April 20—Anglo-American Committee of Inquiry on Palestine recommends United Nations trusteeship.

1946, July 22—Irgun bombing of British headquarters in the King David Hotel, Jerusalem.

1947, May 4—Mass escape of Irgun and Lehi members from Acre Prison.

1947, July—Voyage of the *Exodus.*

1947, July 30—Irgun's retaliatory hanging of two British soldiers.

1947, November 29—United Nations General Assembly recommends partition of Palestine.

1948, May 15—State of Israel is born.

1948—Left-wing Zionist factions unite to form Mapam, the United Workers Party.

1948–1951—330,000 Holocaust survivors emigrate from Europe to Israel; 600,000 Jews who were expelled from Arab countries immigrate to Israel.

1950—Israel enacts the Law of Return, granting automatic citizenship to Jewish immigrants.

1950s—96,000 Romanian Jews and 45,000 Polish Jews immigrate to Israel.

1951—Twenty-Second World Zionist Congress adopts the Jerusalem Program.

1952–1964—200,000 Moroccan Jews immigrate to Israel.

1956—Mizrachi and Hapoel Hamizrachi unite to form the National Religious Party.

1961—The General Zionists and the Progressive Party unite to form the Liberal Party.

1965—Herut and the Liberal Party unite to form the Gahal bloc.

1969—The Labor Party and Mapam unite to form Ma'arah (Alignment).

1971–1978—Over 100,000 Soviet Jews immigrate to Israel.

1972—28th Zionist Congress is embroiled in controversy over a resolution requiring Diaspora Jewish leaders to make *aliya* after two years in office.

1973—Gahal bloc and allies unite to form Likud.

1974—Gush Emunim movement is created to establish Jewish communities in Judea-Samaria/West Bank and Gaza territories.

1983—Sephardi activists break from Agudat Israel to form the Shas Party.

1984–1992—30,000 Ethiopian Jews immigrate to Israel.

1988—Degel Hatorah Party is established by dissident Agudat Israel faction.

1990–1998—600,000 Jews from the USSR and former Soviet Union immigrate to Israel.

1992—Degel Hatorah and Agudat Israel unite to form the United Torah Judaism Party.

1992—Mapam, Shinui, and the Citizens Rights Movement unite to form the Meretz Party.

1993—Israel and the Palestine Liberation Organization sign the Oslo Agreement.

1995—Prime Minister Yitzhak Rabin is assassinated by an opponent of the Oslo Agreement.

Introduction

The Jewish attachment to Zion is many centuries old. Although the modern Zionist movement was organized little more than a century ago, the roots of the Zionist idea reach back nearly 4,000 years to the day that the biblical patriarch Abraham left his home in Ur of the Chaldees to settle in the Promised Land, where the Jewish state subsequently arose.

When the Jewish kingdom was destroyed and its populace taken captive to Babylonia in 586 B.C.E., the exiles' passion to return to Zion was never quelled. It permeated their prayers, their works of religious scholarship, and their popular culture. Less than fifty years later, the return to Zion had begun and the reconstruction of the Temple was under way.

The destruction of the Second Temple and the loss of Jerusalem to Rome in 70 C.E. resulted in the end of Jewish sovereignty in the Holy Land and the onset of the dispersion of Jews and Jewish communities to distant countries throughout the world. Nevertheless, Eretz Israel was never far from the consciousness of Jews during the subsequent 1,878-year absence of Jewish sovereignty in the land. Throughout that period, Eretz Israel continued to play a central role in traditional Jewish culture. Small Jewish communities persevered in such cities as Jerusalem and Safed, aided by contributions from Diaspora Jewish communities. Some Diaspora Jews visited Eretz Israel, while others actually managed to move there on a more permanent basis. For Jews around the world, the Holy Land and the dream of return were embedded in daily religious rituals and prayers, as well as in law and lore. Each day, in the morning, afternoon, and evening prayers, as well as in the blessings recited after each meal, Jews prayed for their return to Zion and the rebuilding of Jerusalem. In the Jewish ritual calendar, three days each year are set aside as fast days commemorating aspects of the destruction of the Temple and the loss of the Holy Land. Likewise, the loss of Jerusalem is symbolized in the rituals of the Jewish marriage ceremony. The daily prayers are recited facing east, toward Jerusalem. The service at the Passover feast, the Seder, concludes with the prayer "Next year in Jerusalem!" These served as constant reminders and sustained the persistent yearning for both being in Eretz Israel and the ultimate messianic redemption.

Talmudic lore is replete with statements affirming the superior status of the Holy Land, the obligation for Jews to live there, and the absolute faith in the ultimate collective return of the Jewish people to their rightful land. Thus, the Talmud states, "One should always live in Eretz Israel, even in a city in which the majority of the population is gentile, and one should not live outside of the Land, even in a city in which the majority is Jewish. . . . Whoever lives outside of the Land is as if he were committing idolatry." Aggadic literature describes prominent rabbinical sages in the Diaspora tearing their clothes in mourning over their failure to remain in the Land of Israel, an obligation that they characterized as being "equal to all of the commandments in the Torah."

Abraham Joshua Heschel eloquently put it this way:

> Throughout the ages we said "No" to all the conquerors of Palestine. We said "No" before God and man emphatically, daily. We objected to the occupations, we rejected their claims, we deepened our attachment, knowing that the occupation by the conquerors was a passing adventure, while our attachment to the land was an eternal link. The Jewish people has never ceased to assert its right, its title, to the land of Israel. This continuous, uninterrupted insistence, an intimate ingredient of Jewish consciousness, is at the core of Jewish history, a vital element of Jewish faith. How did the Jews contest and call into question the occupation of the land by the mighty empires of the East and West? How did they assert their own title to the land? Our protest was not heard in the public squares of the large cities. It was uttered in our homes, in our sanctuaries, in our books, in our prayers. Indeed, our very existence as a people was a proclamation of our link to the land, of our certainty of return. [Abraham Joshua Heschel, *Israel: An Echo of Eternity*]

Part and parcel of this attachment to Eretz Israel was the strong religious rejection of the Diaspora, *Galut* (exile), which was a major theme of most Jewish philosophers. While there were differences among rabbinical scholars in terms of the degree to which they explicitly emphasized the negative nature of Diaspora existence or the drive to return to Eretz Israel, there was virtually no Jewish religious authority until the modern era who even remotely suggested *Galut* existence as an ideal. Without exception, *Galut* was defined as an ultimately negative existence; Zion was the unequivocal ideal. Not surprisingly, during periods in which the physical conditions of Jewish life in the Diaspora deteriorated, there was usually an increased emphasis upon and yearning for Eretz Israel. However, despite periodic fluctuations in the extent of emphasis upon the theme of Eretz Israel, traditional Judaism throughout the history of the dispersion resolutely expressed the supreme holiness of and love for Eretz Israel.

Despite the unwavering centrality of the return to Zion in Jewish thought and culture over the centuries of exile, relatively few Jews personally settled in the Holy Land. For the overwhelming majority of Jews, the reference was to one of a heavenly or spiritual Zion rather than Eretz Israel as a material reality. The occupation of Eretz Israel by hostile forces, the harsh conditions in the desolate Jewish homeland, and the primitive state of international transportation made *aliya* an unrealizable dream for all but a fortunate few.

During the early nineteenth century, however, a coalescence of factors fostered a more realistic notion of return. Among Jews, this desire to move to Eretz Israel was largely in reaction to catastrophes, rampant anti-Semitism in Europe, the infamous blood libel and subsequent pogrom in Damascus in 1840, and a particularly devastating earthquake in Safed in 1837, which destroyed most of the homes in the city and resulted in the deaths of some four thousand Jews and about a thousand others. These events led to heightened messianic anticipation and the emergence of a movement to return to the Holy Land. What was unique about the movement was that it spurned the popular perception that the physical relocation of the Jewish people to Eretz Israel must await the prior miraculous arrival of the Messiah. Instead, these early pioneers regarded the return to Zion as a human act that is part of a natural process of redemption or even that is a prerequisite for messianic redemption. A significant number of the forefathers of Hibbat Zion, the first European Zionist movement, such as Rabbis Yehuda Alkalai and Zvi Hirsch Kalischer, viewed the resettlement of the Jewish people in Eretz Israel as an initial step in a natural messianic process. Although this idea was initially opposed by the majority of the Orthodox rabbinate as an unfounded secularization of the traditional belief about the Messiah, a growing number of rabbis and a much larger lay following accepted what they viewed as the legitimate adaptation of traditional notions to contemporary conditions. In their view, it was the responsibility of the Jewish people to prepare themselves and Eretz Israel for the Messiah's arrival. Their resettlement efforts were assisted by a corresponding growth in Christian Zionist sentiment, propagated by Christian millenarians in Great Britain and the United States. The Christian Zionists anticipated a Second Coming, to be preceded by the return of the Jews to the Holy Land. Accordingly, the noted British Christian millenarian Laurence Oliphant and others undertook efforts to create a Jewish state in Palestine.

These settlers were followed by those of Bilu, a pioneering settlement movement initiated by Russian Jewish students after the pogroms of 1881. With no previous agricultural experience or familiarity with the local environment and in the face of highly adverse conditions, members of this movement went to Palestine and established settlements, most of which succeeded and became a model and a source of inspiration for other young Jews in Eastern Europe.

Zionism as an organized political movement did not emerge until the second half of the nineteenth century, when the forces of anti-Semitism and modern nationalism converged. In Germany and the Austro-Hungarian empire, these forces manifested in the emergence of overtly anti-Semitic political parties. In Russia, the assassination of Czar Alexander II in March 1881 sparked nationwide pogroms as well as severely discriminatory legislation. The combination of economic, political, and physical persecution led to two major types of movements among Eastern European Jews, one geographic and the other political. The geographic movement consisted of a massive emigration of Jews from Eastern Europe, the overwhelming majority of whom immigrated to the United States, with much smaller but not insignificant numbers choosing Palestine. The political movement gave rise to organized Zionism.

The emergence of organized Zionism was also a consequence of a number of developments within European Jewry during the second half of the nineteenth century. The traditional Jewish community in Eastern Europe had experienced the processes of modernization and secularization. Likewise, the relationship between the community and the larger society was in a state of flux. Until the nineteenth century, Eastern European Jews lived in communities that were predominantly isolated from the larger societies and cultures of the countries in which they dwelled. People in those Jewish communities, to a great extent, lived separately from the non-Jewish population. In Russia, Jews were restricted to the "Pale of Settlement," an area of 386,000 square miles spanning the territory from the Baltic to the Black Seas and comprising ten Polish and fifteen Russian provinces. Jews not only formed a majority of the population in many *shtetlach,* or towns and hamlets, as well as a considerable percentage in the bigger cities, but the Jewish sections in these settlements were often exclusively Jewish. The interaction of Jews with non-Jews, to the extent that it happened at all, was usually of the most formal type. Accordingly, along with their physical isolation, Jews were culturally isolated. In these communities, Jewish traditionalism, including religious observance and Jewish values and attitudes, prevailed, and there was a strong sense of kinship with Jews elsewhere.

This tightly integrated community was, however, in the process of breaking up, coinciding with larger societal changes that Europe experienced in the course of modernization. When a society is transformed from traditional to modern, it undergoes rationalization and secularization. Among Europe's Jews, one manifestation of this was the *Haskala*, the Jewish Enlightenment movement, which attracted ethnically Jewish but religiously alienated Eastern European Jewish intellectuals. The growing Hibbat Zion movement became the organizational expression of deep Jewish ethnicity. Simultaneously, in Western Europe, those Jews who had sought to assimilate or, at least, integrate into modern Western European society but were rebuffed, redirected their energies to the new Jewish nationalism.

The Zionist movement was comprised of many philosophies and wings, as will be discussed further on. Socialist Zionism was among the earliest and largest of these groups. Socialist Zionism was a manifestation of the secularization that invariably accompanies modernization and was an attempt to replace the previous religious universalist-particular synthesis inherent in Judaism. Socialism was the universalistic aspect, Zionism the particularistic. This modern secular synthesis was a major reason for the overwhelming rejection of modern Zionism by the Orthodox rabbinical elite in the nineteenth and early twentieth centuries. It was not the nationalism, per se, to which they reacted. On the contrary, those rabbis would have been the first to assert the national component of being Jewish. The notion that Judaism is solely a religion, in the Western nonethnic sense, with no national component is a modern one, most characteristic of "classical" Reform Judaism of the nineteenth and early twentieth centuries. The traditional self-definition is that a powerful historical and cultural interrelationship exists between Jewish religion and Jewish nationalism.

Although Zionism emerged during the era of European nationalism, it differed from other modern nationalisms in many important respects. Other national movements arose within the state of a nation. In some cases, the movements strove for national unity and in others they sought recognition as a nation, but always within the state from which the movements emerged. Zionism was unique in that it emerged among a people who were scattered and not in the national homeland. In fact, there was no consensus on the issue of a homeland. As will be discussed further on, some among the early Zionist ideologues did not even consider Eretz Israel—or Palestine, as the Romans dubbed it—an objective.

Our describing the Zionist movement as organized is not meant to suggest that the Zionist movement was united on all issues. In fact, numerous deep ideological divisions manifested themselves on a variety of issues. In particular, there was a fundamental disagreement between those who placed primacy on the land and those who placed primacy on the people. Theodor Herzl and Leo Pinsker, for example, placed primacy on the people and initially sought a haven for the Jewish refugees regardless of its location. Indeed, this was a source of contention at the very beginning of the Zionist movement, in the struggle over the Uganda Plan. Herzl and his followers urged the adoption of the plan as a temporary measure, while opponents refused to even consider any place other than Eretz Israel.

Socialist Zionism was only one of many streams of thought in the movement and was itself divided into a myriad of factions, some of them passionately Marxist, others less so. Religious Zionists, for whom the rebuilding of Eretz Israel was a religious act as well as part of the messianic process, longed for a state based on the principles of Jewish tradition. Revisionist Zionists emphasized the need for Jewish military might and the territorial integrity of the Jewish state-to-be. Cultural Zionists were less interested in the prospects for Jewish sovereignty than in the intellectual and cultural climate of the *yishuv.*

But beyond the specific factions of the Zionist movement were three broad approaches to the question of how a Jewish state could be attained. For many, settlement was the key. The painstaking creation of a modern community, built from the ground up, would establish Zionism as a physical reality that could not be budged. The slogan "one more cow, one more *dunam*" symbolized this approach, particularly in the early decades of the modern *yishuv* when agricultural settlements were a central component of the Zionist enterprise. The rapid growth of Palestine's urban areas, especially as a result of the German Jewish immigration of the 1930s, somewhat altered the character of this nation-building process but not its central theme.

The movement had its settlers and builders, but it also had its diplomats. For some people, diplomacy, not settlement, was the crucial factor. In their view, the great powers' endorsement of Jewish statehood would, more than anything else, decide the fate of Zionism. Farms and factories had their place, but without internationally guaranteed political sovereignty the *yishuv* would end up as just another Jewish minority community living at the sufferance of others. Securing international support for the Zionist cause became the Jewish diplomats' overriding ambition.

A third approach championed the idea of armed revolt. Support for the use of force to attain Jewish statehood intensified in response to the persecution of European Jewry and Britain's refusal to open Palestine to refugees fleeing the Holocaust. By the mid-1940s, all factions in the *yishuv* had joined the armed struggle against the British Mandatory authorities. In the end, however, no single approach prevailed. It was, rather, a combination of all three approaches that made the Jewish state a reality.

Although more than fifty years have now passed since the establishment of the State of Israel, the most basic questions of the state's identity and purpose, which have vexed the Zionist movement since its emergence a century ago, remain unsettled. An extraordinary variety of political and religious factions, representing an array of conflicting values and strategies, are still alive and well throughout both Diaspora Jewry and modern Israel. For more than one hundred years, these factions have struggled with each other, with many of these struggles manifesting themselves in some of the basic rifts in contemporary Israeli society. The struggle may well continue for another century. No one can say for certain if Israelis today are essentially united, despite their differences, or essentially different, despite all that unites them. What has been remarkable is that in spite of these differences and tensions, Zionism succeeded in fashioning an underlying sense of ethnicity and kinship among Jews that made it possible for them to unite in the successful battle to reestablish the Jewish state after nearly two thousand years of exile. It is our hope that this dictionary, by helping to clarify the terminology, concepts, factions, and major events of Zionism, will make some small contribution to an increased appreciation for both the diversity and the consensus that characterize the Zionist experience.

The Dictionary

-A-

AARONSOHN, AARON (1876–1919). The Zionist inventor and activist Aaron Aaronsohn was born in Bacău, Romania, and immigrated to Eretz Israel with his parents in 1882. He was educated in the newly established settlement Zikhron Ya'akov. In 1896, after completing his studies at the agricultural college at Grignon, France, Aaronsohn was appointed agricultural instructor at Metullah, under the auspices of Baron Edmond de Rothschild.

Between 1902 and 1915, Aaronsohn participated as a geologist and botanist in a series of research expeditions in Eretz Israel, Syria, and Transjordan, under the geological tutelage of Max Blankenhorn and the botanical tutelage of Rachel Rogov-Joffe, sister of the noted malaria specialist Dr. Hillel Joffe. Joffe, who served as chairman of the Hovevei Zion executive committee, had established a regional hospital and medical center in Zikhron Ya'acov and was instrumental in the planting of a forest of eucalyptus trees in the swamps of Hadera as a means of combating malaria there. Aaronsohn's agronomic reputation was greatly enhanced by his discovery of a species of wild wheat in the Galilee in 1906, leading to an invitation from the U.S. Department of Agriculture to meet with American agricultural experts. During his visit to the United States in 1909, Aaronsohn also met with such leaders of American Jewry as Julius Rosenwald, Julian Mack, and **Judah Magnes** about his ideas and plans for agricultural experiments in Eretz Israel. Aaronsohn succeeded in enlisting their support and in 1910 opened an experimental station at Atlit, near Haifa, which housed a laboratory for testing crops and an impressive technical library, as well as collections of geological and botanical specimens. Aaronsohn was a nonconformist who sometimes clashed with prevailing notions. For example, he advocated the employment of Arab workers, a position that conflicted with that of the established Zionist leaders.

When World War I broke out, almost all of the work of the experimental station came to a halt, and it was obvious that there was almost no chance for Zionist development under the Turks. Aaronsohn therefore enlisted the help of an assistant at the experimental station, Avshalom Feinberg, and organized a group of friends and family members, which they named **Nili**, for the purpose of spying on the Turks and providing secret information to the British officials in Egypt. In 1916, Aaronsohn visited London and promoted the idea of a Jewish National Home in Eretz Israel as part of British policy in the region.

After the war, Aaronsohn was appointed a member of the **Zionist Commission** headed by **Chaim Weizmann**, and he returned to Palestine where he found himself shunned by many because of his Nili activities. Weizmann, however, continued to support him and in 1918 gave him the task of traveling to the United States to enlist American Jewish support for the Zionist cause. Aaronsohn was a member of the Zionist delegation to the Paris Peace Conference and participated in designing recommendations for the borders of Palestine. He died in an airplane accident over the English Channel, on a flight from London to Paris. His pioneering work on the flora of Eretz Israel was published posthumously.

ACHOOZA SOCIETIES. Achooza Societies were Zionist organizations established in the United States in the early 1900s for the purpose of purchasing cultivable land in Palestine. The first Achooza (Hebrew for "estate" or "holding") group was created in St. Louis in 1908 at the initiative of Simon Goldman, a local Zionist activist and former Palestine resident. Each Achooza member was required to pay $1,400 in installments over a ten-year period, in return for 12.5 acres of land planted with almonds, grapes, or olive trees, on which he was expected to settle after five years, when the trees began to yield fruit. Fourteen additional Achooza societies, patterned on the St. Louis model, were organized in cities across the United States and Canada and reached a peak combined membership of about five hundred in 1915. The outbreak of World War I dealt the Achooza movement a serious blow. Wartime conditions impeded the acquisition of land and the economic downturn in the United States discouraged potential investors. The Achooza groups declined rapidly. They were supplanted by the **American Zion Commonwealth**, created by the national **Federation of American Zionists** to purchase land in Palestine that would be settled by Eastern European immigrants—perhaps a more realistic goal than that of Achooza, given the limited interest among North American Jews in the idea of personally relocating to Eretz Israel. The Achooza movement's practical accomplishments, although falling short of its leaders' goals, were by no means insignificant. The St. Louis and Chicago Achooza societies established the towns of Poriya (1910) and Sarona (1913); the New York branch established Ra'anana (1921) and Gan Yavneh (1931).

AGRON (AGRONSKY), GERSHON (1893–1959). Zionist journalist Gershon Agron (née Agronsky) was born in the Ukraine and came to the United States in 1906. A professional journalist, he edited Jewish newspapers in Yiddish and English. In 1918 he went to Palestine and served with the **Jewish Legion**. After his return to the United States, Agron was a journalist with the press bureau of the **Zionist Commission** in 1920–1921. He then became editor of the Jewish Telegraphic Agency and also served as correspondent for the London *Times* and the *Manchester Guardian*. In 1932 Agron founded the *Palestine Post,* which, after the creation of the state, became the *Jerusalem Post* and was for many years Israel's only English-language daily newspaper. During the pre-state era, the paper served as a quasi-official Zionist organ for the non-Hebrew–speaking public, including mandatory officials. In 1945 Agron served as part of the **Jewish Agency** delegation to the United Nations conference at San Francisco. In 1949–1951, he served as director of the Israel Government Information Services and from 1955 to 1959 as mayor of Jerusalem.

AGUDAT ISRAEL. Agudat Israel is a worldwide movement of Orthodox Jews that was founded in Katowice, Poland, in 1912 and guided by the Council of Torah Sages (*Mo'etzet Gedolei Hatorah*) as its religious authority on all political matters. Agudat Israel opposed secular Zionism and the **World Zionist Organization**. It initially consisted of three major groups: German sectarian Orthodox followers of Rabbi Samson Raphael Hirsch, the Lithuanian yeshiva world, and Polish Hasidic rabbis and their followers, especially the Gur Hasidic group. It sought to create a structure that would act as the collective voice of Orthodox Jewry and provide a range of religio communal services that would strengthen the Orthodox community.

Agudat Israel established itself independently of the organized Jewish community in Palestine, but in 1933, despite its ideological opposition to secular Zionism, it entered into an agreement with the **Jewish Agency**, according to which it received 6.5 percent of the immigration permits that the agency received from the British Mandate authorities. In 1947 Agudat Israel entered into an even more comprehensive agreement that has come to be known as the "status quo letter." This document guaranteed basic religious interests in Israel and also served to legitimize Agudat Israel's inclusion in the government-in-formation and the initial 1949–1951 government coalition. Agudat Israel subsequently left the government in protest of the government's decision to draft females into military service. In 1977, it supported the Likud-led coalition and joined the national unity government. Since 1984, it has joined in every government although it has consistently refused a ministry.

Agudat Israel experienced a number of internal rifts that came to a head in the 1980s. In 1983, due to long-simmering resentment over the absence of Sephardi leadership in the party, the Jerusalem Sephardi members of Agudat Israel broke away and established the Shas Party (Shas is an acronym for Sephardim Shomrei Torah, or Sephardi Torah Guardians party). Shas was so successful in the October 1983 municipal elections in Jerusalem that it ran a national slate in the 1984 Knesset elections and won four seats, establishing itself as a force to be reckoned with. At the same time, a years-old conflict between the Hasidic and Lithuanian-type yeshiva elements within Agudat Israel, represented by the Hasidic rabbis of Gur and Vizhnitz, on one side, and Rabbi Eliezer Shach, the head of the Ponevez Yeshiva in B'nai Brak, on the other, reached new heights and culminated in the formation of Shach's Degel Hatorah (Torah Flag) party, just prior to the 1988 national elections. In 1992 Agudat Israel joined forces with Degel Hatorah to form the United Torah Judaism Party (UTJ). Despite this new union, it won only four seats, as compared to 1984 and 1988, when Aguda and its partners had eight and seven seats, respectively. Despite their adamant rejection of secular Zionism and the religious significance of the state, they participate in all aspects of Israeli society, including the political sphere, where their power has increased since the days of early statehood. As with the other *haredi* parties, Agudat Israel concentrates on all matters of domestic policy that it perceives as affecting religion, especially the educational institutions. Although the leadership is officially nonnationalistic, there is a very strong nationalist sentiment among the rank and file. *See also* POALEI AGUDAT ISRAEL.

AHDUT HA'AVODA. Immigrants of the Third **Aliya**, together with Palestinian Jewish workers who were dissatisfied with the country's existing political parties, established Ahdut Ha'avoda, the United Labor Party, in February 1919. The founders of the new group hoped to bring the two main workers' factions, **Poalei Zion** and **Hapoel Hatzair**, into their ranks, but personal and ideological differences kept Hapoel Hatzair from joining the new alliance. The rivalry between Ahdut Ha'avoda and Hapoel Hatzair continued and intensified throughout the ensuing decade.

As followers of **Nahman Syrkin**, the ideological pioneer of **Socialist Zionism**, Ahdut Ha'avoda advocated the development of a Jewish national home in Palestine in accordance with socialist principles such as class struggle, nationalization of the means of production, and the creation of workers' collectives (kibbutzim and *moshavim*). To protect the growth of the Jewish sector's economy, Ahdut Ha'avoda promoted the "**Hebrew Labor** only" campaign to persuade Jewish employers to refrain from hiring Arabs.

During the early 1920s, under the leadership of Berl Katznelson, David Ben-Gurion, and **Yitzhak Tabenkin**, among others, Ahdut Ha'avoda promoted the Gedud Ha'avoda workers' brigades; established the **Histadrut** labor union and Histadrut Hanoar Ha'oved youth movement; and played a major role in the creation of the **Haganah** self-defense militia and the Labor Zionist daily newspaper *Davar.* In 1930 Ahdut Ha'avoda united with Hapoel Hatzair to become Mapai, the Eretz Israel Workers Party. Mapai was the nucleus of what is today the Israeli Labor Party.

A left-wing faction within Mapai broke away in 1944 to become the Tenua le-ahdut Ha'avoda (Movement for a Unified Labor), merged with another small faction and changed its name to Ahdut Ha'avoda-Poalei Tzion in 1946, then merged with the radical **Hashomer Hatzair** youth movement in 1948 to become Mapam, the United Workers Party, and became a partner in many Labor-led Israeli governments.

ALIYA. Eretz Israel is considered the highest spiritual place on earth, and going to the Holy Land, therefore, is termed *aliya,* which in Hebrew means "going up." When Zionists speak of moving to Israel, they do not speak of it as "immigration," *hagira,* but *aliya.* Conversely, leaving Israel is not simply emigration, but *yerida,* "going down." In Zionist ideology, *aliya* is a core ideal, and *yerida* is a moral blemish, if not a catastrophe.

Part and parcel of the attachment to Eretz Israel was the strong religious rejection, or negation, of the Diaspora, *Galut,* which was a major theme of most Jewish philosophers. While there were differences among rabbinical scholars in terms of the degree to which they explicitly emphasized the negative nature of Diaspora existence and, concomitantly, the degree to which they emphasized the drive to return to Eretz Israel, there is virtually no Jewish religious authority until the modern era who even remotely suggested *Galut* existence as an ideal. Without exception, *Galut* was defined as an ultimately negative existence; Zion was the unequivocal ideal.

Despite the strong religious link to Eretz Israel and the moral rejection of the Diaspora, there have historically been variations in the degree to which the link was overtly expressed, and it appears that an important variable in determining the emphasis placed upon Eretz Israel was and is the degree of security experienced by the Jews in the Diaspora. During periods in which the physical conditions of Jewish life in the Diaspora deteriorated, there was typically an increase in emphasis upon and yearning for the Holy Land. Historians commonly divide the modern waves of immigration that preceded the establishment of the State of Israel into six periods, or *aliyot*.

The First Aliya, from 1882 to 1904, consisted of some 30,000 to 40,000 Jews from Eastern Europe, primarily Russia and Romania, who sought to escape persecution by fleeing to Turkish-ruled Palestine. Many were members of the early Russian Zionist movements **Bilu** and **Hibbat Zion**. With aid from Baron Edmond de Rothschild, the immigrants of the First Aliya established a number of agricultural communities, including Petah Tikvah, Zikhron Ya'akov, Rehovot, Hadera, and Rishon le-Zion. At about the same time, some 2,500 Jews from Yemen also immigrated to Palestine.

The Second Aliya came in response to the Russian pogroms of 1903–1904 and lasted until the outbreak of World War I (1914). Many of the 35,000–40,000 immigrants of the Second Aliya were militant advocates of **Socialist Zionism**. They initiated the first **kibbutz** (Degania), the **Hashomer** self-defense group, and an array of publications, labor organizations, and political factions. They also played a leading role in a series of bitter struggles over workers' rights and employment conditions. A substantial number of those who arrived with the Second Aliya—no precise statistics were maintained—returned to Europe in disillusionment over the intra-Jewish struggles in Palestine as well as over the various hardships imposed on the *yishuv* by the Turkish authorities.

During the Third Aliya, which took place from 1919 to 1923, more than 35,000 Jews, primarily from Russia and Poland, reached Eretz Israel. This wave was ignited by the excitement generated by the **Balfour Declaration** (1917) as well as by the turmoil surrounding the Russian Revolution (1918), the Russian civil war (1918–1920), and the Russo-Polish war (1919–1920). The Third Aliya was hampered in part by restrictions on immigration imposed by the British Mandate authorities in response to Palestinian Arab violence in 1920 and 1921. The immigrants of the Third Aliya, many of whom were deeply idealistic, established the "labor battalions" that played a crucial role in the *yishuv*'s early pioneering efforts, as well as the **Histadrut** labor union and the first *moshav* (Nahalal, 1921).

The Fourth Aliya, dated by some as 1924–1928 but by others as extending to 1931, comprised some 80,000 Jews, mainly from Poland. This *aliya* was also popularly referred to as the Grabski Aliya, because many of the immigrants left Poland in response to a series of severe taxes imposed on the Jews there by Polish prime minister Wladislaw Grabski. The adoption of strict immigration quotas by the United States in 1924 made Palestine a likely destination for Polish Jewish emigrants during the late 1920s. More than 80 percent of the Fourth Aliya immigrants settled in Tel Aviv and other major cities.

The Fifth Aliya encompassed much of the 1930s and involved some 225,000 Jews. (Historians date the Fifth Aliya as beginning in 1929 or 1931 and continuing until 1936 or 1939.) Despite the Palestinian Arab violence that claimed 133 Jewish lives in 1929 and the growing British tilt against Zionist political aspirations, immigration quotas were increased and 45,000 German Jews reached Palestine following Hitler's rise to power in 1933. The majority of immigrants who arrived during the 1930s were from Eastern Europe, but the Fifth Aliya came to be known as the German Aliya because of the impact of the German immigrants, many of whom were highly educated professionals and industrialists. The capital that the immigrants brought, including that which was facilitated by the **Ha'avara**, or transfer agreement between the *yishuv* and the German government, was a significant asset to the country's economic development. Renewed Arab violence in 1936, which continued until 1939, brought about the British **White Paper** of 1939, which curtailed Jewish immigration to a maximum of 15,000 per year for the five years to follow. The Sixth Aliya took place against the backdrop of the Holocaust. During the period of the war, some 62,000 refugees from Hitler reached Palestine—50,000 with British immigration certificates and the remainder through clandestine operations by Zionist emissaries. From 1946 until the establishment of the State of Israel in May 1948, when the Sixth Aliya officially came to a close, an additional 60,000 Jews reached Eretz Israel.

The high priority that the Zionist movement assigned to the concept of *aliya* was given formal expression by the Knesset's passage, in July

1950, of the **Law of Return**, granting automatic citizenship to Jewish immigrants.

There have been a number of major waves of *aliya* to Israel. Some 330,000 European Holocaust survivors left their postwar **Displaced Persons** camps and immigrated to Israel during 1948–1951. About 600,000 Jews were driven out from Arab countries during the same period. To escape growing anti-Semitism and the civil strife of the struggle for Moroccan independence, over 200,000 Jews emigrated from Morocco to Israel between 1952 and 1964. During the late 1950s, the Romanian authorities permitted Jews to emigrate to Israel, and 96,000 did so. Some 45,000 Jews emigrated from Poland to Israel during the late 1950s as part of the Gomulka Aliya, named after the Polish Communist leader whose decision to permit Polish nationals in Russia to return to Poland enabled the Jews among the returnees to emigrate. Clandestine Israeli rescue operations brought over 30,000 Jews from Ethiopia to Israel during the mid-1980s and early 1990s. Over 100,000 Jews from the Soviet Union were permitted to emigrate during the early and mid-1970s, following worldwide protests on their behalf. Some 600,000 more left during 1990–1998, beginning in the waning months of the Soviet Union's existence and continuing after the collapse of the Union of Soviet Socialist Republics.

Ideological post-Zionists have called for abandoning the term *aliya* and replacing it with "immigration." *See also* ALIYA BET.

ALIYA BET. This is a term used to connote unauthorized immigration to Palestine, as distinct from ordinary *aliya*, which refers to immigration to **Eretz Israel** with the permission of the ruling authorities.

There were many instances of individuals entering Palestine illegally during the period of Turkish rule, but "Aliya Bet" is ordinarily used to refer to the organized efforts to bring groups of Jews to Eretz Israel in defiance of the immigration quotas imposed by the British. Some Aliya Bet immigrants reached Palestine by overland routes, but the majority arrived by sea. In 1937, the **Revisionist Zionists** began sending shiploads of European refugees to Palestine. This operation, under the direction of Vienna attorney William Perl, brought tens of thousands of Jews—the exact number is unknown—to Eretz Israel prior to the outbreak of World War II. The **Labor Zionist** leadership opposed Aliya Bet, for fear of harming Zionist relations with the British and because of what they claimed was the inclusion on Revisionist transports of individuals who were physically unsuited for life in Palestine.

Wartime conditions made further Aliya Bet voyages nearly impossible; the number of such ships dwindled to a handful during 1940–1943. Beginning in mid-1944, the **Haganah** organized its own series of Aliya Bet ships, this time with the blessing of the Labor Zionist leaders, whose views on the subject had been radicalized by the Holocaust and Britain's continuing refusal to permit more than a small number of Jews to legally enter Palestine.

After the war, the Haganah intensified its Aliya Bet activities. Most of its transports were intercepted by the British, and more than 50,000 passengers on those boats were taken to detention camps in Cyprus. Even the intercepted ships played an important role in the Zionist effort, however, as the international publicity surrounding their capture—as in the case of the famous **S.S. *Exodus***—increased pressure on the British to withdraw from Palestine.

Altogether, more than 100,000 Jews were brought to Eretz Israel in Aliya Bet ships from the 1930s until the establishment of the State of Israel.

ALIYA HADASHA. German and Austrian immigrants to Palestine who were uncomfortable with the existing political parties created their own party, Aliya Hadasha ("New Immigration"), in October 1942. Emphasizing the need for a more efficient society, greater integrity in public life, and early national elections, Aliya Hadasha did well in the communal elections of 1943. The following year, Aliya Hadasha won eighteen seats—about 10 percent of the vote—in the elections to the national **Va'ad Leumi**.

During the late 1940s, Aliya Hadasha aligned itself closely with **Chaim Weizmann**'s cautious approach to relations with the British and the Arabs, strongly opposing any use of force by Palestine Jewry. It was also careful to use the phrase "Jewish national home" rather than "state." Although many of its members sympathized with the idea of a binational Jewish-Arab state, the party leadership endorsed the 1947 United Nations plan for partitioning Palestine.

In the summer of 1948, Aliya Hadasha merged with a faction of the **General Zionist** party to become the Progressive Party, which won five seats in the first Knesset elections (1949). The political career of Shimon Siegfried Kanowitz, an Aliya Hadasha founder and later a Knesset member for the Progressives, summarized his movement's legacy: the phrase "Kanowitz law," which became part of the Israeli political lexicon, refers to a law that sounds good but cannot be enforced, such as Kanowitz's legislation against pollution.

ALKALAI, YEHUDA (1798–1878). One of the earliest advocates of modern **Religious Zionism**, Yehuda Alkalai was born in Sarajevo, Serbia, which was then under Turkish rule and where his father, Shlomo Hai, was a teacher. Alkalai was a student of *Midrash* (homiletics) and Kabbalah (Jewish mysticism), which he apparently learned from his major teachers, Rabbi Yaacov Finzi and Rabbi Eliezer Pappo, as well as from his travels throughout the large Sephardic communities in the Balkans.

Alkalai began his adult life in the footsteps of his father, by becoming a congregational "reader" (*hazan*) and a teacher. He developed a strong interest in Hebrew grammar and wrote a summary of the rules of Hebrew grammar in Ladino for the Sephardic community in which he was then serving. Subsequently, in 1839, Alkalai published his first book, *Darkhei Noam* ("Pleasant Ways"), on Hebrew grammar.

In the introduction to his next book, *Minhat Yehuda* ("The Offering of Judah"), published in 1843, Alkalai wrote lavish praise of **Sir Moses Montefiore** and stressed that the redemption will not come suddenly but in stages. He was one of the earliest advocates of a return to Hebrew as *the* language of the Jewish people, a theme that he reiterated in his later works. He also emphasized that Jewish tradition forecasts a heroic military leader known as Messiah, Son of Joseph, who will serve as a precursor to the arrival of the full-fledged Messiah, known as Messiah, Son of David, and that human action can hasten the arrival of the precursor. Therefore, he argued, due recognition should be given to the efforts of the Rothschild family and others, and everyone should contribute his or her own funds to the settlement of the Land.

In his next book, *Kol Korei* ("A Beckoning Voice"), first published in 1848, Alkalai offered a somewhat radical interpretation of the mitzvah of *teshuvah*. In place of the traditional understanding of *teshuvah* as "repentance," Alkalai interpreted the term literally, to mean "return," that is, to return to the Land. In 1871 Alkalai himself went to live in Jerusalem, where he continued his efforts to organize Jewry for the support of the rebuilding of **Eretz Israel**. In an article written that same year, he related his success in organizing Ashkenazi and Sephardi leaders of Jerusalem for the establishment of a branch of the **Alliance Israélite Universelle** ("*Kol Israel Haverim*"), an organization founded in Paris in 1860, of which Alkalai was an enthusiastic supporter. The Jerusalem branch had as its explicit objective assisting the poor in the settling and building of the Land. Likewise, he was an avid supporter of the Society for the Colonization of Palestine in Frankfurt on the Oder and of the agricultural school Mikveh Israel.

ALLIANCE ISRAÉLITE UNIVERSELLE. The Paris-based Alliance Israélite Universelle, created in 1860, was the first modern international Jewish organization. Its establishment was stimulated in part by the 1858 controversy over the abduction of an Italian Jewish child, Edgardo Mortara, by the papal police. The Alliance undertook diplomatic efforts on behalf of persecuted Jews in various countries, including some of the earliest initiatives to aid Jews in Ethiopia (1868) and Yemen (1908). By the 1890s, the Alliance began to concentrate on educational activities, setting up schools in Jewish communities in the Balkans, North Africa, and the Middle East.

In its early years, the Alliance refrained from endorsing Zionism, although some members of its Central Committee were Zionists. Alliance spokesman (and future president) Sylvain Levi testified against Zionist aspirations when he appeared before the Versailles peace conference in 1919. After the Holocaust, the Alliance began to express more sympathy for the Zionist enterprise.

Nevertheless, the Alliance established a network of Jewish schools in Palestine during the late 1800s. The agricultural training school it created near Jaffa, Mikveh Israel, was the first of its kind, and its graduates played an important role in the agricultural developments that so dramatically changed the face of the country during the ensuing decades. The original language of instruction in the Alliance schools in Palestine was French, but Hebrew soon played an important role as well. Indeed, the father of modern Hebrew, **Eliezer Ben-Yehuda**, first taught Hebrew in the Alliance school in Jerusalem in the 1880s. After World War II, the Alliance established secondary schools in Haifa, Tel Aviv, and Jerusalem that it continues to support and administer.

ALTALENA AFFAIR. In late 1947, American supporters of the **Irgun Zvai Leumi (IZL)** purchased a ship, which they named *Altalena* after one of the pen names of Revisionist Zionist founder **Ze'ev Jabotinsky**, for the purpose of bringing weapons from France for the Jewish fighters in Palestine. Arms negotiations between IZL representatives and the French authorities proceeded throughout the spring of 1948. Shortly after the establishment of Israel that May, with the IZL and the **Haganah** already in the process of merging forces, IZL chief **Menachem Begin** proposed that the Haganah and IZL bring the *Altalena* to Israel jointly.

David Ben-Gurion, still suspicious of the IZL after more than a decade of tension and rivalry with the militants, rejected the offer.

On June 11, having received the long-awaited French approval, the *Altalena* set sail for Israel with 900 volunteer soldiers, 5,000 rifles, 4 million rounds of ammunition, and assorted other weapons and supplies. Begin informed senior Haganah officials of the ship's imminent arrival, and Ben-Gurion authorized talks with the IZL on the disposition of the arms, 20 percent of which Begin wanted set aside for the effort to capture Jerusalem and for IZL units that were under-equipped. When no agreement was reached, Begin assumed the Haganah would simply refrain from assisting the landing. The ship reached its destination, the coastal village of Kfar Vitkin, on June 21, and local Haganah officials initially offered to help unload the vessel. Unbeknownst to Begin, however, Ben-Gurion had decided to use force against the *Altalena,* fearing that the IZL secretly intended to use the arms from the ship to overthrow him.

All but fifty of the men on board disembarked at Kfar Vitkin, and the unloading of the weapons began, but Haganah forces soon surrounded the beach and demanded that the IZL surrender the weapons. Begin refused; the Haganah opened fire. Six IZL men and two from the Haganah were killed before a cease-fire could be arranged. The Haganah seized the arms that had already been unloaded, while the *Altalena,* still carrying the bulk of the weapons, headed south toward Tel Aviv.

When the *Altalena* began unloading on the Tel Aviv beachfront on the morning of June 23, Haganah units under the command of Yitzhak Rabin launched a full-scale assault. Ten IZL men swimming for shore were shot dead, many others were wounded, and Begin himself narrowly escaped being hit. Intent on avoiding a civil war, Begin ordered his men to refrain from shooting back. Rocked by Haganah shells, the ship went up in flames, and most of the arms it was carrying were lost. Two cabinet ministers resigned in protest over the killings, but Ben-Gurion insisted that the use of force against the *Altalena* was justified because of what he said was the threat posed to the government by the continued existence of the IZL as a separate Jewish militia. The affair remains to this day a source of bitter controversy between the Labor and Likud camps. *See also* REVISIONIST ZIONISM.

AMERICA-ISRAEL CULTURAL FOUNDATION. Established in 1939 by the American Jewish philanthropist Edward A. Norman, the American Fund for Palestine Institutions changed its name to the America-Israel Cultural Foundation in 1957. It provides grants to Israeli cultural and educational institutions, scholarships to young musicians and artists, and fellowships to teachers and professionals in the arts.

AMERICAN COUNCIL FOR JUDAISM. Worried by the growing popularity of Zionism in the American Jewish community in general and within the Reform rabbinate in particular, several dozen Reform rabbis and lay leaders established the American Council for Judaism in 1942. Through lectures, publications, and contacts with government officials, the council sought to persuade American Jewry and the United States government to oppose Zionism.

Although its membership remained small, the council enjoyed a notoriety out of proportion to its numbers because of its close relationship with State Department officials and the prominent coverage it received in certain media outlets, particularly the *New York Times.* The council's activities were strongly criticized by mainstream Jewish organizations. The council's primary argument, that the citizenship or legal status of American Jews would be endangered by the creation of a Jewish state, proved unfounded, and the organization faded into obscurity soon after Israel was established.

AMERICAN ECONOMIC COMMITTEE FOR PALESTINE. Robert Szold and Israel Brodie, longtime associates of American Zionist leader **Louis Brandeis**, established the American Economic Committee for Palestine in 1932 to aid the country's economic development. The committee was their response to the Passfield **White Paper**, a British policy statement challenging future Jewish immigration to Palestine on the grounds that the country lacked the room and resources to absorb large numbers of newcomers. The American Economic Committee provided potential immigrants and investors with detailed information on the country's economy, job market, industrial needs, and the like. The committee's reports played an important role in the establishment of many factories in Palestine during the 1930s. Later, the committee focused on assembling technical data to help farmers and manufacturers improve the production and marketing of their goods. After the creation of Israel, the American Economic Committee became a part of the **Jewish Agency**'s Economic Department in New York. The committee was formally disbanded in 1954.

AMERICAN EMERGENCY COMMITTEE FOR ZIONIST AFFAIRS. *See* AMERICAN ZIONIST EMERGENCY COUNCIL.

AMERICAN ISRAEL PUBLIC AFFAIRS COMMITTEE (AIPAC). Known as the American Zionist Public Affairs Committee when it was created in 1954, the American Israel Public Affairs Committee is the largest registered pro-Israel lobbying organization in Washington. It has played a crucial role in securing U.S. aid for Israel and encouraging the passage of pro-Israel legislation. Although AIPAC is prohibited from contributing directly to political candidates because of its status as a registered lobby, its reputation as the primary spokesman for American Jewry on Israel affairs has earned it significant clout in Washington.

AIPAC's annual guidebook, *Myths & Facts,* was long considered the bible of pro-Israel activists. Although *Myths & Facts* was discontinued in 1992, AIPAC's biweekly newsletter, *Near East Report,* remains an important source of Israel-related information for public officials and the Jewish community alike.

AMERICAN JEWISH COMMITTEE (AJCommittee). The American Jewish Committee was established in 1906 for the purpose of defending the rights of Jews around the world through diplomatic intercession and education. Its founders, primarily wealthy American Jews of German descent, frowned upon Zionist ideology and the idea of a Jewish state, but many of them sympathized with the notion of Palestine as a haven for Jewish refugees. They expressed "profound appreciation" for the 1917 **Balfour Declaration** on the grounds that "there are Jews everywhere who, moved by traditional sentiment, yearn for a home in the Holy Land for the Jewish people."

American Jewish Committee president Louis Marshall successfully negotiated with **World Zionist Organization** president **Chaim Weizmann** for the creation, in 1929, of the enlarged **Jewish Agency** for Palestine, bringing into its fold a large contingent of non-Zionists. Marshall himself was named chairman of the agency's American wing and was succeeded, after his death in late 1929, by fellow AJCommittee leader and non-Zionist **Felix Warburg**.

The AJCommittee opposed the 1937 **Peel Commission** plan for partitioning Palestine, since it would have included the establishment of a sovereign Jewish state. At the same time, the committee consistently opposed British restrictions on Jewish immigration to Palestine during the 1930s and 1940s.

A series of conciliation meetings between AJCommittee leaders and **David Ben-Gurion** in Connecticut during 1941–1942 ended unsuccessfully because of opposition both from Zionists who would not permit Ben-Gurion to compromise on the goal of Jewish statehood and from those elements within the AJCommittee who opposed cooperation with the Zionist movement. Joseph Proskauer, an avowed anti-Zionist who became president of the AJCommittee in early 1943, strove to put further distance between the organization and Zionism. The AJCommittee participated briefly in the August 1943 **American Jewish Conference**, but withdrew after the conference endorsed the goal of a Jewish commonwealth in Palestine.

In the wake of the Holocaust, the AJCommittee gradually embraced the idea of creating a Jewish state in Palestine, and it endorsed the 1947 United Nations partition plan. After the establishment of Israel, AJCommittee leaders tangled with Prime Minister Ben-Gurion over his remarks urging American Jews to immigrate to the Jewish state. In 1950 and again in 1961, protests by AJCommittee president Jacob Blaustein persuaded Ben-Gurion to issue public statements affirming American Jewry's exclusive loyalty to the United States and backtracking on his suggestions that U.S. Jews had a religious obligation to immigrate to Israel.

While differing on occasion from specific Israeli policies, the AJCommittee today is supportive of Israel, issues pro-Israel publications, organizes visits to Israel by American academics, and maintains a liaison office in Jerusalem, in addition to its primary activities, which focus on international Jewish concerns and interfaith relations.

AMERICAN JEWISH CONFERENCE (AJConference). In an effort to achieve American Jewish unity in dealing with matters of pressing concern, in January 1943 **B'nai B'rith** president Henry Monsky organized a meeting of representatives of major Jewish organizations in Pittsburgh. While remaining noncommittal on the future of Palestine and other issues, the meeting's attendees resolved to organize a national, democratically elected American Jewish Assembly, later that year, to consider problems facing world Jewry.

The **American Jewish Committee** objected to the term "Assembly," fearing it emphasized Jewish separateness and worried that votes taken by an "Assembly" would be binding on all its participants. In deference to the committee's concerns, the organizers agreed to change the name of the gathering to the American Jewish Conference and guaranteed the right of participants to dissent from the conference's decisions. Local elections in various Jewish communities were planned for June, and August 29 was selected as the date for the convening of the AJConference in New York City. All Jewish organizations were permitted to take part in the elections, except for the **Revisionist Zionists** and two Jewish Communist groups.

More than 80 percent of the delegates elected or appointed to the conference represented Zionist organizations or their allies, and passage of a strong Palestine resolution seemed certain. But one faction of prominent Zionists, led by **Stephen Wise**, sought to soften the conference's stand on Jewish statehood, in the hope of assuaging concerns expressed by State Department officials and the American Jewish Committee. The Wise faction sought to broker a deal by which the Palestine resolution would make no reference to a Jewish state or commonwealth, in exchange for the support of the AJCommittee and other non-Zionists for language favoring unlimited Jewish immigration to Palestine. But a groundswell of pressure from the delegates, coupled with a fiery speech by **Dr. Abba Hillel Silver**, resulted in the passage of a strongly pro-Zionist resolution by a margin of 497 to 4, with only the 3 AJCommittee delegates and 1 other opposing. Two months later, the AJCommittee formally withdrew from the conference.

During the Zionist lobbying efforts in Washington in the years that followed, the AJConference's Palestine resolution was frequently cited as evidence that virtually all of American Jewry endorsed the Zionist platform. The AJConference itself, however, played only a minor role in organized Zionist activity, and it never evolved into a significant force in the Jewish community. Some of the conference's member-organizations favored turning the conference into a permanent body to act as the spokesman for American Jewry. But internal rivalries and a feeling among most of the groups that with the creation of Israel, the conference had outlived its usefulness, resulted in the decision in early 1949 to dissolve the organization.

AMERICAN JEWISH CONGRESS (AJCongress). Jewish activists, many of them Zionists, convened the first American Jewish Congress in 1918, as a democratically elected, grassroots alternative to the established Jewish organizations. The 400 delegates, most of them chosen by over 300,000 voters in Jewish communities around the United States, endorsed the **Balfour Declaration** and resolved to send representatives to take part in the Paris Peace Conference and to press for Jewish rights in postwar Eastern Europe.

Organized as a permanent body in 1922, the AJCongress addressed a broad range of Jewish concerns, domestic and international, and spearheaded the boycott of German goods during the 1930s. It also played a prominent role in Zionist educational and lobbying activity, and its presidents frequently served simultaneously in the leadership of the American Zionist movement.

Focusing increasingly on domestic issues in recent decades, the AJCongress has become particularly well known for its legal action on behalf of church–state separation and consequently regards itself as "the Attorney General for the Jewish Community." The AJCongress also played a prominent role in the fight against the Arab boycott of Israel during the 1970s and 1980s and sponsors an extensive travel program to Israel and other countries.

AMERICAN JEWISH JOINT DISTRIBUTION COMMITTEE (JDC). In an effort to aid European and Palestinian Jews suffering from the ravages of World War I, American-Jewish philanthropists brought together several disparate U.S. Jewish relief groups in 1914–1915 to form the unified Joint Distribution Committee.

Postwar travails and anti-Semitic persecution in Eastern Europe convinced the JDC to continue its activities even after the initial war crisis had passed. Although the JDC's leadership and major donors were primarily American Jews of German origin who were less than enthusiastic about the Zionist goal of Jewish statehood, they favored developing Palestine as a haven for Jewish refugees and provided considerable aid to the *yishuv* during the interwar period.

Much to the dismay of the Zionist movement, the JDC also took a strong interest in the settlement of Russian Jews in Soviet-sponsored agricultural colonies in the Crimea region of the Union of Soviet Socialist Republics, beginning in the 1920s. Later, however, the Soviet authorities changed their minds, abandoned the scheme, and forced the JDC's Agro-Joint agency to leave the country in 1938.

Tensions between the Zionist leadership and the JDC over its aid to Jews settling outside of Palestine persisted during the 1930s. The persecution of Jews in Nazi Germany, however, galvanized the JDC and its chief fundraising rival, the **United Palestine Appeal**, to join forces in 1939 and raise funds together as the **United Jewish Appeal**, although disputes over the division of the funds persisted.

During the Holocaust, the JDC provided funds for a variety of rescue and relief activities in Europe, although its efforts were sometimes hampered by Allied opposition to sending money into Nazi-occupied territories. The JDC also helped organize and finance the mass Jewish immigration to Israel from Arab countries during 1948–1950. The JDC continues to function today as the primary overseas relief agency of American Jewry, providing aid to immigrants and the underprivileged in Israel, as well as to needy Jews around the world.

AMERICAN JEWISH LEAGUE FOR ISRAEL. Members of the **Zionist Organization of America (ZOA)** who opposed its affiliation with the **General Zionist** Party in Israel broke away from the ZOA to establish the American Jewish League for Israel in 1957. Several prominent Zionist figures were among its founders, including veteran ZOA leaders Louis Lipsky, Isidore Breslau, and Louis Levinthal, but the league never attracted significant membership, and its current activities are limited to occasional meetings and a small newsletter.

AMERICAN PALESTINE COMMITTEE. Emanuel Neumann, an American member of the World Zionist Executive, established the American Palestine Committee in 1932 as a vehicle for attracting prominent non-Jews to support the Zionist cause. Although the committee was quickly endorsed by a number of leading public figures and its inaugural dinner was a singular success, its potential was left unrealized when Neumann relocated to Palestine later that year. After Neumann returned to the United States and became director of public relations for the **Emergency Committee on Zionist Affairs** in 1941, he revived the American Palestine Committee. During the ensuing five years, the committee attracted to its ranks thousands of national and state officials, prominent intellectuals, and other public figures. The committee's work played a crucial role in the effort to win American public support for Zionism.

In 1946 the American Palestine Committee merged with the Christian Council on Palestine, an organization of pro-Zionist Christian clergy, intensifying its public information efforts as the American Christian Palestine Committee. After the establishment of Israel, the committee continued to spread its message through radio broadcasts, sermons, and its publication *Land Reborn.* The committee disbanded in 1961. *See also* CHRISTIAN ZIONISM.

AMERICAN ZION COMMONWEALTH (AZC). Bernard Rosenblatt, a leader of the **Federation of American Zionists**, established the American Zion Commonwealth in 1914 for the purpose of acquiring plots of land for settlement in Palestine. Unlike its predecessor, **Achooza,** the AZC did not require its members to personally relocate to **Eretz Israel** but instead focused on purchasing land for European Jews to develop.

The 30,000-plus acres of real estate the AZC purchased during 1914–1931 included the land on which the towns of Balfouriya (1919), Herzliya (1924), and Afula (1925) were established. During the late 1920s, financial difficulties experienced by the group's Polish-Jewish investors led to the demise of the AZC. Most of its assets were purchased by the **Keren Hayesod**, and the AZC disbanded in 1931–1932.

AMERICAN ZIONIST COUNCIL. *See* AMERICAN ZIONIST EMERGENCY COUNCIL.

AMERICAN ZIONIST EMERGENCY COUNCIL (AZEC). On the eve of World War II, the **World Zionist Organization** established the Emergency Committee for Zionist Affairs (ECZA) in the United States, expecting it to assume Zionist functions in the event of war-related restrictions or hardships on the Zionist centers in London and Jerusalem. Officially, the ECZA was an umbrella group for U.S. Zionist organizations, but in practice the **Zionist Organization of America**, by far the largest and most influential of American Zionist groups, dominated the new agency.

The ECZA was slow to get off the ground, due to financial difficulties, intraorganizational rivalries, and the reluctance of many U.S. Zionist leaders to criticize Great Britain while the British were fighting Hitler. A turning point came with the hiring of the activist-oriented **Emanuel Neumann** as director of the ECZA's new Department of Public Relations and Political Action in early 1941. As part of the ECZA's campaign to win over American public opinion to the Zionist cause, Neumann organized two effective Christian Zionist groups, the **American Palestine Committee** for laymen and the Christian Council on Palestine for clergy. In May 1942, the ECZA convened the **Biltmore Conference**, which brought together six hundred Zionist delegates from around the country to call for the establishment of a Jewish commonwealth.

Tensions steadily mounted within the ECZA leadership between moderates such as ECZA chairman **Stephen Wise**, who opposed confrontations with the Roosevelt administration over its Palestine policy, and activists such as Neumann who favored more forthright tactics. Neumann's resignation in late 1942, coupled with grassroots pressure for more activism, convinced **Chaim Weizmann** to make the dynamic **Abba Hillel Silver** co-chair alongside Wise. The ECZA, which had added the word *American* to its name after the bombing of Pearl Harbor in order to emphasize the organization's patriotism, now shortened its name to the American Zionist Emergency Council, undertook to raise a substantially larger budget, and hired a staff of lobbyists, publicists, and organizers to develop a national network of Zionist activists. By contrast with Wise, who was a Roosevelt loyalist, Silver lobbied Republicans as well as Democrats and sought to use congressional action as a means of pressuring Franklin D. Roosevelt toward a more pro-Zionist stance.

The hostility between Silver and Wise reached a boiling point at the end of 1944, with Silver resigning from the AZEC over Wise's opposition to a pro-Zionist congressional resolution. By the spring of 1945, however, a groundswell of grassroots Jewish pressure, galvanized by revelations of the full extent of the Holocaust, swept Silver back into power, this time as the AZEC's sole leader. Silver's renewed national campaign of rallies, lobbying, and political pressure during 1945–1948 helped win congressional and public sympathy for the Zionist cause, blunted the State Department's attempts to turn President Harry S. Truman against Zionism, and added to the international pressure on Britain to pull out of Palestine.

With the establishment of Israel, the AZEC's primary task was complete. Dropping the word *Emergency* from its name, the AZC continued functioning as a coalition of leading U.S. Zionist groups engaged in pro-Israel information efforts. After the establishment of the **American Israel Public Affairs Committee** (1954) and the **Conference of Presidents of Major American Jewish Organizations** (1955), the AZC's influence and level of activity steadily waned. It was eventually revived and reorganized in 1970 as the **American Zionist Federation**.

AMERICAN ZIONIST FEDERATION. *See* AMERICAN ZIONIST MOVEMENT.

AMERICAN ZIONIST MEDICAL UNIT (AZMU). Hadassah, the American women's Zionist movement, organized the American Zionist Medical Unit in 1916 to aid the Palestine Jewish community, which had been ravaged by cholera and typhus epidemics and a shortage of medical facilities. Hadassah's leaders saw the unit as "an embryonic Department of Health" for Palestine Jewry. Delayed by Turkish opposition, the AZMU finally reached Palestine in August 1918 after the British conquest. The forty-five doctors, nurses, social workers, and administrators set up clinics or hospitals in Haifa, Safed, Tiberias, Jaffa, Tel Aviv, and Jerusalem; sent health inspectors to schools and orphanages; ran a rural medical service for outlying communities; provided medical attention to newly arriving immigrants; established schools for training nurses in Jerusalem and Safed; and played a key role in early anti-malaria efforts.

In 1921, the AZMU was renamed the Hadassah Medical Organization (HMO). Asserting itself as a permanent part of the *yishuv* rather than a wartime emergency project, the postwar HMO expanded the scope of its activities, establishing infant welfare stations in various cities, building the Straus Health Centers in Tel Aviv and Jerusalem, and setting up the first milk-pasteurization plant in Palestine. The HMO's crowning achievement, the Hadassah hospital and medical school on Mount Scopus, affiliated with Hebrew University, opened in 1939.

AMERICAN ZIONIST MOVEMENT (AZM). Implementing the decision of the 27th **World Zionist Congress** (1968) to establish Zionist Federations in every country, the American Zionist Council was reorganized in 1970 as the American Zionist Federation (AZF), to serve as the umbrella group for major U.S. Zionist organizations. The AZF began with eleven member-organizations and expanded to sixteen by the 1990s. It provides Israel-related speakers, programming, and informational material to local Zionist groups.

In 1993, the AZF changed its name to the American Zionist Movement and began soliciting individual memberships in addition to organizational memberships. Three of its Orthodox member-organizations, and three nationalist ones, withdrew from the AZM in 1994 and 1995 over policy differences with the AZM leadership concerning its positions on religious pluralism and the Oslo process.

AMERICANS FOR PROGRESSIVE ISRAEL (API). Established in 1952 to serve as the American wing of Israel's Mapam party, Americans for Progressive Israel promotes the principles of **Socialist Zionism**. API publishes a quarterly magazine, *Israel Horizons;* sponsors U.S. speaking tours for Israeli Mapam representatives and kibbutz movement officials; and maintains small local chapters in various cities. *See also* GORDONIA; HACHSHARA; HALUTZ; HAPOEL HATZAIR; HEHALUTZ; HISTADRUT; KIBBUTZ.

AMIT. Originally known as American Mizrachi Women, Amit was established in 1925 as the U.S. women's division of the **Religious Zionist** movement. Its 425 chapters in the United States and Israel comprise a membership in excess of 80,000. Beginning with its sponsorship of the Beit Tzei'rot High School in Jerusalem in 1933, Amit has focused on educational projects in Israel and today oversees an array of religious vocational high schools, youth villages, community centers, and children's homes. In 1981, Amit was designated as the Israeli Education Ministry's authority for religious secondary technological education. *See also* MIZRACHI.

ANGLO-AMERICAN COMMITTEE OF INQUIRY (AACI). The British and American governments announced the creation of the Anglo-American Committee of Inquiry in November 1945, for the purpose of examining the Palestine problem and the demand by Holocaust survivors in European **Displaced Persons (DP)** camps to be permitted to immigrate to Palestine. The committee was co-chaired by an American, Judge Joseph C. Hutcheson, and an Englishman, Sir John Singleton. The other American members were James G. McDonald, the former League of Nations high commissioner for refugees; *Boston Herald* editor Frank Buxton; attorney Bartley C. Crum; veteran diplomat William Phillips; and Dr. Frank Aydelotte, director of Princeton's Institute for Advanced Study. The other British representatives were members of Parliament Richard H. S. Crossman, Major Reginald Manningham-Buller, and Lord Robert Morrison; economist Wilfrid Crick; and labor mediator Sir Frederick Leggett.

The AACI held hearings in Washington in January 1946, at which a variety of Jewish and Arab witnesses gave testimony. The committee then traveled to Europe for further hearings and meetings in London, Warsaw, and several of the DP camps. The AACI delegates continued their work in the Middle East, visiting Palestine as well as Egypt, Syria, Jordan, Lebanon, Saudi Arabia, and Iraq.

The AACI's final report, issued in April 1946, recommended temporary continuation of the British Mandate in Palestine, followed by a United Nations trusteeship over the country, with no Jewish or Arab state to be established; canceling the restrictions imposed by the British in 1940 on Jewish land purchases in Palestine; and the immediate granting of permits to 100,000 DPs to enter Palestine. While unhappy with the trusteeship proposal, Zionist organizations hailed the AACI's recommendations concerning immigration and land purchases, as did President Harry S. Truman. The Arabs and the British, however, rejected the AACI's proposals. Although the AACI's plan was never implemented, the attention that was focused on the proposal for 100,000 immigrants helped intensify the growing international criticism of British policy in Palestine.

ARLOSOROFF AFFAIR. Haim Arlosoroff (1899–1933), a senior **Labor Zionist** official, was shot and mortally wounded while strolling with his wife on the Tel Aviv beach on the evening of June 16, 1933. Just two days earlier, Arlosoroff had returned from negotiations with Nazi German officials over the **Ha'avara** agreement to facilitate the transfer of German-Jewish assets to Palestine by using them to purchase German goods. The agreement had been vigorously denounced by the **Revisionist Zionists** as a violation of the international Jewish boycott of Germany, prompting some Labor Zionist leaders to publicly claim that Arlosoroff must have been the victim of a Revisionist assassin.

Despite Arlosoroff's own statement, as he was dying, that his assailants were not Jews, and despite his widow's initial statements to the police that the attackers were Arabs, the British police arrested Revisionist activists Avraham Stavsky and Zvi Rosenblatt as suspects in the assassination. In a police line-up arranged under questionable circumstances, Arlosoroff's widow, Sima, identified Rosenblatt as the killer and Stavsky as the accomplice who had shone a flashlight on her husband just before he was shot. Abba Ahimeir, leader of a militant Revisionist faction and a particularly vehement critic of Arlosoroff, was indicted on the charge of inciting the murder. The Revisionists claimed that Labor officials, hoping to undercut their political rivals, had prevailed upon Mrs. Arlosoroff to identify Revisionists as the killers.

The arrests ignited a bitter and sometimes violent campaign by Labor Zionists against the Revisionists in Palestine and in Europe. Labor newspapers declared the suspects guilty even before their trials, and the Revisionist movement as a whole was accused of having inspired the murder. The controversy affected the outcome of the 1933 elections to the World Zionist Congress, with Labor's share of the vote increasing to 44 percent from its previous 29 percent, while the Revisionists dropped from 21 percent to 14 percent.

Before the trials got underway, Abdul Majid, a Palestinian Arab in jail on a different murder charge, confessed to killing Arlosoroff. Aspects of Majid's statement to the police and evidence found in his home seemed to substantiate the confession. Majid soon recanted, however, and the trials of the Revisionist suspects proceeded.

During the trials, medical evidence and testimony by a number of police officers cast doubt on some of Mrs. Arlosoroff's statements, and on the witness stand she was caught in contradictions on more than one occasion. Despite Mrs. Arlosoroff's identification of Rosenblatt, he was proved to have been in a different part of the city at the time of the murder. Both Rosenblatt and Ahimeir were acquitted, but Stavsky was convicted and sentenced to death. Shortly after the conviction, Abdul Majid again confessed to the Arlosoroff murder, this time to an attorney associated with Mrs. Arlosoroff, insisting that his previous recantation had been false. The Supreme Court refused to accept Majid's confession but overturned Stavsky's conviction on the grounds that there was no evidence to corroborate Mrs. Arlosoroff's claims. Labor Zionist leaders refused to accept the acquittals and continued to urge the excommunication of the Revisionists from *yishuv* society.

Years later, additional evidence emerged. In 1955, Yehuda Tannenbaum, the police officer in charge of the initial investigation, revealed that he had compiled a lengthy report concluding that Mrs. Arlosoroff and the prosecutors had fabricated evidence against the defendants, but his superiors responded by dismissing him from the case. In 1973 two Jewish members of the British police force, Yehuda Arazi and Tuvia Arazi, stated that their investigation in 1933 had identified two Arabs as the killers, but their report was ignored by their superiors.

An official Israeli government Commission of Inquiry, established in 1982, reexamined the controversy. It concluded, in a report issued in 1985, that there was no persuasive evidence against the Revisionist defendants, but that the identity of the actual culprits could not be determined.

ASEFAT HANIVCHARIM. Shortly after the British conquest of Palestine in World War I, leaders of the *yishuv* began preparations for the establishment of a democratically elected representative body of Palestine Jewry. The first nationwide elections to the Asefat Hanivcharim, or "Elected Assembly," were held in April 1920, with 77 percent of eligible voters casting ballots. The principle of woman's suffrage was upheld despite ultra-Orthodox (*haredi*) opposition, leading to the eventual secession of the *haredi* delegates from the assembly, although other Orthodox delegates opted to remain. Defining itself as "the autonomous national leadership of the Jews of Palestine," the Asefat Hanivcharim served as Palestine Jewry's official representative in dealings with the British ruling authorities, supervised the *yishuv*'s annual budget, and helped oversee the community's religious, educational, and social welfare spheres. By providing a forum for *yishuv* leaders to debate domestic and foreign policy issues, the Asefat Hanivcharim helped lay the groundwork for the future of Israeli parliamentary democracy.

Elections to the Asefat Hanivcharim were held again in 1925 and 1931. The Palestinian Arab violence of 1936–1939, followed by the eruption of World War II, delayed the subsequent elections until 1944. The **Labor Zionist** bloc won a plurality in each of the elections. The **Revisionists**, who competed for the first time in the 1925 election and won about 7 percent of the vote, increased their total to 21 percent in the 1931 election but boycotted the 1944 contest. The Asefat Hanivcharim was abolished in early 1949, following the establishment of the State of Israel.

AVUKAH. Avukah ("torch" in Hebrew), a national network of American Zionist college students, was established in 1925. It sponsored campus lectures and study groups in Jewish history, culture, and the Hebrew language. Avukah's leaders played a key role in the successful 1929–1930 campaign to have Hebrew accepted as a language to be studied in New York City public schools. In addition to promoting cultural and educational activities on campuses, during the 1930s Avukah established summer schools for training in Zionist organizing and ideology in New York and Michigan. It published a newsletter, the *Avukah Bulletin,* as well as two editions of a Zionist anthology, the *Brandeis Avukah Annual.*

With the ascension of Zelig Harris to the presidency of Avukah in 1934, the organization aligned itself closely with the League for Labor Palestine and the Marxist-Zionist youth movement **Hashomer Hatzair**. The increasing appearance in Avukah literature of denunciations of "imperialist war" and Avukah's advocacy of what it called "a non-minority center for Jews in Palestine," rather than explicitly calling for creation of a Jewish national home, aroused the ire of mainstream Zionist organizations.

By 1939, Avukah boasted sixty-five chapters and several thousand members. Many of Avukah's leaders and prominent members were drafted for service in World War II, leading to the dissolution of the organization by 1943. *See also* ZIONIST ORGANIZATION OF AMERICA.

-B-

BACHAD. The Brit Halutzim Dati'im ("Union of Religious Pioneers"), known by its acronym Bachad, trained young Orthodox Jews in Hungary and Czechoslovakia in the 1930s for a future of Religious Zionist pioneering in Palestine. Additional training centers were later established in Italy, Denmark, France, and the Netherlands. Bachad's activity in Germany was initially tolerated by the Nazi authorities because it helped facilitate the emigration of German Jews. After the November 1938 *Kristallnacht* pogrom, thousands of Bachad activists relocated to Great Britain, where fourteen training farms were established. Jewish refugees from other European countries were also brought to the Bachad centers in Britain. Numerous Bachad activists settled in religious kibbutzim in **Eretz Israel**, and a Bachad group was responsible for the establishment of Lavi, a religious kibbutz near Tiberias, in 1949. *See also* MIZRACHI; RELIGIOUS ZIONISM.

BALFOUR DECLARATION. On November 2, 1917, the British foreign minister, Arthur James Balfour, sent a note to Baron Lionel Walter Rothschild, in which he conveyed the following declaration of sympathy with Zionism:

> I have much pleasure in conveying to you on behalf of His Majesty's Government the following declaration of our sympathy with Jewish Zionist aspirations which has been submitted to, and approved by, the Cabinet.
>
> "His Majesty's Government view with favour the establishment in Palestine of a National Home for the Jewish people, and will use their best endeavours to facilitate the achievement of this object, it being clearly understood that nothing shall be done which may prejudice the civil and religious rights of existing non-Jewish communities in Palestine, or the rights and political status enjoyed by Jews in any other country."
>
> I should be grateful if you would bring this declaration to the knowledge of the Zionist Federation.

The sources of the government's action lay in its attempt to win the support of Russian Jews to prevent the use of Russian resources by Germany, with whom the Allies were at war. It was also believed that the declaration would muster the support of large numbers of American Jews who heretofore had not been staunch supporters of the Allied effort. In addition, the British were aware of rumors that Germany might seek the support of the Zionist movement by issuing a pro-Zionist declaration.

In 1922 the declaration was incorporated in the British Mandate on Palestine by the League of Nations. The precise meaning of the phrase "the establishment in Palestine of a national home for the Jewish people" became the source of controversy among Jews with differing conceptions of Zionism, as well as among non-Jews. The clause "that nothing shall be done which may prejudice the civil and religious rights of existing non-Jewish communities in Palestine, or the rights and political status enjoyed by Jews in any other country" also gave rise to a series of debates that have not yet been fully resolved.

The Arabs viewed the Balfour Declaration as an act of perfidy, especially because they had cooperated with Great Britain in the struggle against Ottoman rule in the Middle East during World War I. They claimed that the British had promised to assist in the establishment of a united Arab country spanning from the Persian Gulf to the Red Sea.

Increased pressure from the Arabs and their allies contributed to the British **White Papers** of May 1939, which terminated Great Britain's commitment to Zionism and, in effect, reversed the policy set forth by the Balfour Declaration twenty-two years earlier.

BAR GIORA. *See* HASHOMER.

BAR-ILAN (BERLIN), MEIR (1880–1949). Religious Zionist leader Meir Bar-Ilan was born Meir Berlin in Volozhin, Russia, and began his studies with his father, Rabbi Naphtali Zvi Judah Berlin ("Netziv"), who was a world-renowned rabbinic scholar. His father died when Meir was fourteen years old, and Meir then went on to study in the prominent *yeshivot* of Telshe, Brisk, and Novharudok. He was already taken with **Religious Zionism** in Novharudok, and his first public activity on its behalf was a lecture he gave to a local Zionist group. After that, Meir became increasingly dedicated to the propagation of religious nationalism. He was a delegate for the **Mizrachi** movement at the Seventh Zionist Congress in 1905 and was one of the minority who voted against the **Uganda Plan**. Shortly thereafter, he became one of the central leaders of the Mizrachi Council.

Bar-Ilan was appointed secretary of the world movement and when, in 1911, Mizrachi headquarters moved from Hamburg (Altona) to Berlin, he moved as well. Despite his staunch opposition to the adoption by the Tenth Zionist Congress of secular "cultural activity" by the **World Zionist Organization**, he refused to even consider Mizrachi's secession from the organization.

While in Berlin, he also founded and edited a Religious Zionist weekly, *Ha-Ivri* ("The Hebrew"). In 1913, Bar-Ilan was invited to the United States to help establish the American Mizrachi movement, and he came for a six-month speaking tour that was highly successful. In addition to his own powerful elocution skills, the fact that he was the son of a widely revered scholar gained Bar-Ilan and his ideas broad acceptance. His visit convinced him of America's future as a center for Jews, and he began to make plans for his own move there, which were realized in 1915. In the United States, Bar-Ilan reestablished the weekly *Ha-Ivri;* served as president of the American branch of Mizrachi; played active roles in a variety of Orthodox spheres, including the formation of the philanthropic organization Ezrat Torah; and in 1925 was named to the board of directors of the **Jewish National Fund**.

Aliya had long been a dream for Bar-Ilan and in 1926 he settled in Jerusalem, where he was appointed to head the World Mizrachi center.

Three years later, he was named to the Zionist Executive, and he served until 1931. Bar-Ilan was a consistent and uncompromising Zionist nationalist who adamantly opposed any partition of **Eretz Israel**. He believed that it would be a historical error and tragedy if the Zionist Organization voluntarily agreed to partition, and when in 1937 the **Peel Commission** proposed partition, he developed a comprehensive strategy of civil rebellion against the mandatory powers.

Bar-Ilan lived in Eretz Israel throughout the war years, and he actively participated in Zionist policy deliberations and in the preparations for the impending struggle for the State of Israel. He also traveled to the United States in 1943 to lobby congressmen and American Jewish leaders to take a more activist approach to rescuing Jews from the Holocaust. In 1944, Bar-Ilan's activity became drastically limited when he took ill, and he never fully recovered.

BASLE PROGRAM. Meeting in Basle, Switzerland, in August 1897, the First Zionist Congress adopted the principles that came to be known as the Basle Program. The program, drafted by **Max Nordau**, the Hungarian-born physician and Zionist author, defined the aim of Zionism as "to secure for the Jewish people in Palestine a publicly recognized, legally secured homeland." An earlier version of the wording, using the phrase "secured by international law," was rejected by the congress on grounds that it might be regarded by Turkey as an infringement upon its sovereignty in Palestine. The vaguer phrase "publicly recognized, legally secured" was adopted instead.

The remainder of the Basle Program specified some of the means for attaining a Jewish homeland in Palestine: promoting the settlement in Palestine of "Jewish agriculturists, artisans, and tradesmen"; organizing world Jewry on behalf of the Palestine project; strengthening "Jewish national sentiment and national consciousness"; and "securing the consent of the various governments" for the creation of a Jewish home in Palestine.

The Basle Program remained the guiding platform of the Zionist movement until after the establishment of the State of Israel, when the 23rd Zionist Congress, meeting in Jerusalem in August 1951, adopted the Jerusalem Program in its place.

BEGIN, MENACHEM (1913–1992). Leader of the **Irgun Zvai Leumi (IZL)** and later prime minister of Israel, Menachem Begin was born and raised in Brest-Litovsk. He received a traditional Jewish religious education and then graduated from the Warsaw University law school. He joined the **Revisionist Zionist** youth movement **Betar** in 1929, rising to become leader of the Polish Betar in 1938. Begin worked closely with Revisionist leader **Ze'ev Jabotinsky** during Jabotinsky's many visits to Eastern Europe during the 1930s.

Fleeing to Vilna in 1939 to escape the German occupation of Warsaw, Begin was arrested by the Soviets for his Zionist activity and sentenced to eight years of hard labor in Siberia. In late 1941, however, Polish citizens were amnestied, and Begin was set free. He joined the Russian-based Free Polish Army and accompanied it to Palestine. There he went underground and linked up with the Irgun Zvai Leumi.

When the Irgun reorganized in 1943 and began making preparations to end its cease-fire against the British, Begin was chosen as its new commander in chief. Under Begin's leadership, the Irgun launched its armed revolt against the British forces in Palestine in early 1944. To elude the British police, Begin grew a beard and disguised himself as "Israel Sassover," an Orthodox Jew. From his secluded Tel Aviv apartment, he personally directed the escalating Irgun military campaign of 1945–1947 that helped drive the British out of Palestine.

When the Irgun found itself the target of **Haganah** kidnappings in 1944–1945, the period known as the "Season," Begin insisted that the IZL not retaliate, a policy that was later widely credited with preventing a devastating Jewish civil war. Begin himself was nearly killed during the Haganah's shelling of the arms ship *Altalena* in 1948, but he again ordered his troops to refrain from a violent response.

After the establishment of Israel, Begin founded and led the nationalist Herut (Freedom) Party, which soon became the major opposition party. He joined the national unity government, as a minister without portfolio, on the eve of the 1967 Six-Day War but left the government in 1970 when it agreed to a U.S. proposal that would have involved surrender of territories that Israel won in 1967. Herut subsequently became the major component of the Likud bloc, which won the 1977 Israeli elections, and Begin became prime minister. He was re-elected in 1981. Among Begin's most significant actions as prime minister were the initiation of widespread Jewish settlement of Judea, Samaria, and Gaza; the signing of a peace treaty with Egypt (1979); the bombing of the Iraqi nuclear reactor (1981); and the war against the Palestine Liberation Organization in Lebanon (1982). After the death of his wife and because of his own failing health, Begin resigned from office in 1983.

BEN-GURION (GRUEN), DAVID (1886–1973). **Labor Zionist** leader and later prime minister of Israel, David Ben-Gurion was born David

Gruen in Plonsk, Poland. He was the sixth child in his family and received a traditional Jewish and secular education. His father was a Hebrew teacher and belonged to the **Hibbat Zion** movement.

In 1900 David founded the Ezra Sofer organization, which was devoted to speaking Hebrew and the spread of Hebrew culture among young people. From 1904 to 1906, he was a teacher in Warsaw. At age seventeen, he joined **Poalei Zion** and was soon an activist and recruiter for the movement.

In 1906, at age twenty, he immigrated to **Eretz Israel**, where he Hebraized his name to Ben-Gurion. Soon named to Poalei Zion's central committee, he was a delegate to the 11th Zionist Congress. Ben-Gurion studied law in Istanbul, Turkey, in 1912. In 1915 he was expelled from Palestine because of his Zionist activity and went to Egypt, where he met **Yosef Trumpeldor** and learned of the "Zion Mule Corps." Ben-Gurion regarded the project as ineffective and even dangerous. Later that year he went to the United States, where he helped found the Zionist pioneering movement Hehalutz. During his stay in New York, in 1917 Ben-Gurion met and married Paula Munweis, a nurse. After the **Balfour Declaration**, he volunteered for the British Army's Jewish Battalion and then returned to Eretz Israel, where he became increasingly active in Poalei Zion and participated in the founding conference of **Ahdut Ha'avoda**, where he and his colleagues mapped out a blueprint for the future development of Eretz Israel.

Ben-Gurion was one of the founders of the **Histadrut** labor union in 1920, and in 1921 he was elected its first secretary general, a position he held until 1935, when he was elected chairman of the **Jewish Agency**. His strong personality—which some have characterized as "domineering"—enabled Ben-Gurion to determine the character of the Histadrut and to render it the dominant socioeconomic institution in Israel for many decades. When he took charge of the Jewish Agency, he applied the same leadership skills there and made the Jewish Agency into the most significant modern Jewish political institution. Ben-Gurion also was a key player in the unification of the various wings of **Labor Zionism** into the Mapai party in 1930. Under his leadership, Mapai was the dominant political party in the *yishuv,* and later in Israel, until the 1970s.

As chairman of the People's Executive, a position to which he rose in March 1948, he proclaimed independence for the new State of Israel on May 14, 1948, and became the new nation's first prime minister and minister of defense. He rapidly molded the socio-political structure of the country with his emphasis on "statism" (*mamlakhtiut*), according to which all political functions that had previously been assigned to political parties were now the domain of the state. Despite his strong socialist roots, he cast a definite pro-Western character to Israel's foreign policy. On the issue of Zionism, Ben-Gurion bluntly declared that Zionism means *aliya,* immigration to Israel. One can be pro-Israel from abroad but to be a Zionist, he averred, one must actually be an Israeli.

In 1953 Ben-Gurion resigned and moved to Kibbutz Sde Boker in the Negev, ostensibly to set an example for Israel's youth and to emphasize the significance of the Negev. However, as a result of the Lavon Affair, Ben-Gurion returned to political leadership and continued as prime minister until 1963, when he resigned again, primarily because of growing opposition within his own party to his attempts at political reform, as well as opposition to his pro-German foreign policy.

His wife, Paula, died in 1968, and Ben-Gurion was never the same afterward. He died in 1973 and was buried in Sde Boker, which had established the Ben-Gurion Archives and Research Institute and has since become a major tourist attraction as well as a study center.

BEN-YEHUDA (PERELMAN), ELIEZER (1858–1922). Known as the father of the modern Hebrew language, Eliezer Ben-Yehuda was born Eliezer Perelman in Lushky, Lithuania. His father, who died when Eliezer was five years old, was affiliated with the Habad movement of Hasidism. The young orphan received a religiously traditional Jewish as well as gymnasia education. He was approximately thirteen years of age when he became acquainted and fascinated with Hebrew literature. It was not long before Eliezer began to display a growing interest in living in **Eretz Israel** and became convinced of the need for a national movement to restore the Jews to their land and their language. As a practical move, he went to Paris in 1878 to study medicine. While there, Ben-Yehuda wrote an article in 1879 in the Hebrew periodical *Hashahar,* in which he espoused his notion of a national spiritual center in Eretz Israel and developed the argument that Jewish national revival was part of the broader pattern of national awakening in Europe.

Ben-Yehuda was stricken with tuberculosis in 1878 and was forced to give up his medical studies. He then decided to realize his aspiration of living in Eretz Israel, especially since its climate was much more favorable to his condition. While he was in the hospital in Paris, Ben-Yehuda met a scholar from Eretz Israel who convinced him of the historic authenticity of the Sephardic pronunciation in Hebrew. Shortly afterward, he wrote a number of articles urging that Jewish schools in Eretz

Israel teach only in Hebrew and that they do so in the Sephardic pronunciation.

He and his wife, Deborah, settled in Eretz Israel in the fall of 1881 and commenced speaking only in Hebrew. Ben-Yehuda participated in the publication of *Hahavatzelet* and *Mevaseret Zion* and established his own publication, *Hazvi,* which began as a weekly and grew into a daily. In his writing as well as in his speaking, Ben-Yehuda joined with a number of other prominent Hebraists and educators in opposing the *halukah* system, that is, the system of organized charity from funds solicited in Diaspora communities abroad and distributed by a local religious charity institution.

In 1890 Ben-Yehuda and his colleagues founded the Hebrew Language Committee, with the task of developing modern Hebrew as the official language of the *yishuv* and setting its standards. The committee later developed into Israel's Academy of the Hebrew Language. His wife died in 1891, and he married her sister, Hemdah. She was even more antagonistic than he toward the Orthodox religious authorities in the *yishuv,* and he subsequently became even more outspokenly forceful in his opposition to the *halukah* system.

Ben-Yehuda supported the **Uganda Plan**, and wrote a number of articles and a pamphlet in favor of it, much to the consternation of a number of his colleagues who strongly opposed it. During World War I, the Turkish authorities imposed a strict censorship, which forced Ben-Yehuda to cease publishing. He left and moved to the United States, where he remained until after the war. Upon his return in 1919, Ben-Yehuda was stunned when the British high commissioner welcomed him with the traditional Hebrew greeting, *"Shalom 'Aleikhem."* He subsequently influenced the commissioner to accept Hebrew as one of the country's three official languages.

Ben-Yehuda began constructing a dictionary of modern Hebrew, a project that was as yet incomplete upon his death and was first published in its entirety in 1959. He is universally recognized as the "father of modern Hebrew," because he encouraged spoken Hebrew, set standards for the language, embarked on the dictionary, and wrote voluminously in Hebrew.

BEN-ZVI, IZHAK (1884–1963). **Labor Zionist** leader and future president of Israel, Izhak Ben-Zvi was born in Poltava, Ukraine. His father had deep attachments to **Eretz Israel** and traveled there when Izhak was a youngster, to investigate the possibilities of settling in the Land. Izhak received a traditional primary Jewish as well as secular education. He completed Russian gymnasium in 1905 and then went to the University of Kiev. He did not complete any studies there, however, because the university was shut down by a strike. Izhak's first visit to Eretz Israel was in 1904, when he stayed for two months. He was active, along with his friend **Ber Borochov**, in the founding of a Jewish self-defense organization and the socialist **Poalei Zion** party in 1906. In June of that year, Ben-Zvi escaped from the police in Poltava, who charged him with illegal Zionist activity, and went to Vilna, where he continued activity on behalf of Poalei Zion. The following year he settled in Eretz Israel and, shortly thereafter, Ben-Zvi served as a delegate to the Eighth Zionist Congress in the Hague on behalf of the Eretz Israel branch of Poalei Zion, which he had founded together with **David Ben-Gurion**. He was one of the founders of **Hashomer**, the *yishuv*'s first organized self-defense group in 1909, and the following year Ben-Zvi participated in founding the first Hebrew-language socialist periodical in the *yishuv*. In the fall of 1918, he married his longtime colleague Rahel Yanait.

Ben-Zvi was one of the founders of the **Histadrut** in 1920 and was appointed to its secretariat. He was also one of the founders of the **Ahdut Ha'avoda** party. He was chairman and in 1945 president of the *yishuv*'s **Va'ad Leumi**, the agency responsible for all social welfare matters.

With the establishment of the State of Israel, Ben-Zvi was elected to the Knesset in 1949. Following the death of **Chaim Weizmann**, Ben-Zvi was nominated Israel's second president, a position to which he was subsequently re-elected three times, serving from 1953–1963. He died early in his third term.

In addition to engaging in these political activities, Ben-Zvi was a scholar who specialized in the study of the history of Eretz Israel and the social history of Diaspora Jewish communities. Among his many writings is the highly regarded *The Exiled and the Redeemed,* which was published in numerous languages. One of Israel's most prestigious publishers of scholarly works in Jewish social history, Yad Izhak Ben-Zvi, is named for him.

BENEI BERIT. One of the earliest modern Zionist organizations, the Benei Berit ("Sons of the Covenant") was established by German Jews in 1882 to support the settlement of Russian, Romanian, and Moroccan Jews in Palestine. It provided financial support to early Zionist colonies in **Eretz Israel**, published the weekly newspaper *Der Kolonist,* and collaborated with the Russian Zionist group **Hibbat Zion**. In 1884 the Benei Berit merged with the German branch of the American Jewish organization **B'nai B'rith**.

BENEI MOSHE. A handful of Russian Zionist intellectuals close to Asher Ginzberg, better known by his pen name **Ahad Ha'am**, organized the semisecret Benei Moshe ("Sons of Moses") group in 1889. With their elaborate initiation rituals and code names, the Benei Moshe bore some resemblance to a masonic order. Aspiring to the austere lifestyle, passionate commitment, and moral exemplitude of the biblical patriarch Moses, the Benei Moshe imagined themselves as the future elite leadership of the Jewish people.

The Benei Moshe devoted themselves to Ginzberg's philosophy of **Cultural Zionism**, the idea that Zionism should focus on creating a small but influential Jewish cultural and intellectual center in Palestine, rather than developing the land or establishing a sovereign Jewish state. Ginzberg was the group's unquestioned leader, even going so far as to scrutinize and supervise aspects of his followers' personal lives. For their part, Ginzberg's devotees related to him as Hasidim regard their *rebbe,* venerating his every word and action.

In the course of the group's seven years of existence, the Benei Moshe published several Hebrew-language periodicals, helped create the Hebrew publishing houses Tushiya and Ahiasaf, aided in the establishment of the agricultural colony of Rehovot, and played an important role in the founding of Hebrew-oriented schools in Eastern Europe and Palestine.

A variety of problems gradually beset the Benei Moshe. The lack of a clear program or any specific actions for members to take sparked internal conflicts about both strategy and goals. A partially successful attempt by the Benei Moshe to take over the leadership of the **Hibbat Zion** organization caused resentment among some Hovevei Zion activists. By late 1896, Ginzberg had lost interest in the Benei Moshe and turned his attention to a new periodical, *Hashiloah,* leading to the dissolution of the Benei Moshe the following year.

BERGSON GROUPS. Followers of the **Revisionist Zionist** leader **Vladimir Ze'ev Jabotinksy,** some of them connected to the militant **Irgun Zvai Leumi** underground in Palestine, established the New York–based American Friends of a Jewish Palestine in 1939. Its purpose was to solicit funds and public support for the Irgun's efforts to bring European Jewish refugees to Palestine in defiance of British immigration restrictions.

The group received a considerable boost when Irgun emissary **Hillel Kook** arrived in New York from Jerusalem in June 1940. Adopting the name "Peter Bergson" to avoid embarrassing his uncle, the chief rabbi of Palestine, the charismatic Kook quickly assumed leadership of the group. He soon redirected its attention to the issue of creating a Jewish army to fight alongside the Allies against the Nazis and in 1941 launched a new organization, the Committee for a Jewish Army of Stateless and Palestinian Jews. Bergson utilized dramatic techniques such as full-page newspaper advertisements and protest rallies to focus public attention on the Jewish army issue. His efforts helped prod the Allies to eventually establish the Jewish Brigade, an all-Jewish military unit that was part of the British Army and saw action against the Nazis during the final weeks of the war.

When news of the Nazi genocide was verified in late 1942, Bergson set aside the Jewish army campaign and established a new organization, the Emergency Committee to Save the Jewish People of Europe. Although Bergson and his closest aides controlled the new committee just as they had directed the two previous groups, the Emergency Committee also attracted the support of a significant number of celebrities, prominent intellectuals, and members of Congress. News of Nazi atrocities generated sympathy for the committee's demand that the Allies take more vigorous action to aid Hitler's Jewish victims. Bergson's campaign for rescue measures included public rallies, newspaper advertisements, and a dramatic march to the White House by four hundred Orthodox rabbis just before Yom Kippur, 1943. The march led to the introduction of a congressional resolution on rescue that, in turn, helped persuade President Franklin D. Roosevelt to establish the War Refugee Board, a U.S. government agency devoted exclusively to helping refugees escape the Nazis.

Because of Bergson's penchant for creating new organizations, both his supporters and his detractors increasingly referred to them collectively as the "Bergson groups" or "Bergson committees." In late 1943, he established the American League for a Free Palestine, to rouse American public support for the Jewish armed revolt against the British Mandate authorities in Palestine. The British government, angered by the league's activities, repeatedly urged the U.S. government to restrict its fundraising activities. In mid-1944 Bergson created the Hebrew Committee of National Liberation, which claimed to serve as a government-in-exile for the Jewish rebels in Palestine and those European Jews seeking to reach the Holy Land.

Bergson's campaigns angered many leaders of established Jewish organizations. Part of the opposition stemmed from those leaders' antipathy toward the Irgun, with which Bergson was associated, but much of the hostility was due to fear that Bergson's successes were upstaging the mainstream Jewish leadership. Despite the efforts of his critics, Bergson helped reshape American Jewry's agenda during the Holocaust era, galvanized Jewish leaders to adopt a more activist approach, and played a role in bringing about modest changes in Allied policy, such as the creation of the Jewish Brigade and the War Refugee Board, which rescued tens of thousands of Jews from the Nazis during the final months of the war.

BERGSON, PETER. *See* KOOK, HILLEL.

BERIT HA'OLIM. *See* HABONIM.

BERMUDA CONFERENCE. In response to mounting public criticism of the Allies' failure to aid the Jews in Nazi-occupied Europe in late 1942 and early 1943, the American and British governments decided to co-sponsor a conference to discuss the refugee problem. Originally slated to be held in Ottawa, Canada, the conference site was changed to the island of Bermuda, where wartime regulations would restrict access by the media and potential critics. The U.S. delegation to the conference was led by Princeton University president Harold Dodds and included two congressmen known for their support of the Roosevelt administration's policies on refugee matters, Senator Scott Lucas (Democrat of Illinois) and Representative Sol Bloom (Democrat of New York), chairman of the House Foreign Affairs Committee.

The conference opened on April 19, 1943, and lasted twelve days. Both the U.S. and British delegations operated under instructions from their respective governments to exclude the possibility that either of their countries would take in additional refugees. Rejecting pleas by Jewish and Zionist organizations, the British insisted that Palestine be excluded from consideration as a refuge. The delegates focused on locating neutral European countries or other sites to serve as temporary havens for those refugees who might escape Hitler. The participants' final report to their governments recommended that refugees be settled in the Cyrenaica region of Libya.

At the conclusion of the Bermuda conference, the delegates issued a brief statement explaining that the details of the proceedings would remain confidential. The secrecy shrouding the gathering, and the apparent lack of any concrete results from the conference, galvanized congressional and Jewish criticism of Allied policy toward European Jewry.

BETAR. The international youth movement of **Revisionist Zionism**, Betar was founded in Riga, Latvia, in 1923 by the Zionist leader **Ze'ev Jabotinsky**. Betar is an acronym for Brit Al Shem Yosef Trumpeldor, or the "Covenant in Memory of **Yosef Trumpeldor**," referring to the legendary Zionist pioneer who was killed while defending the Tel Hai outpost from Arab attackers in 1920. Betar advocated a Jewish state on both sides of the Jordan River, armed self-defense for Jews both in Palestine and abroad, and national arbitration instead of strikes to settle labor disputes in **Eretz Israel**.

Expecting military force to be crucial to the establishment and survival of a Jewish state, Betar focused on paramilitary training and preparedness. In the 1930s, Betar graduates helped create and lead two of Palestine's Jewish underground forces, the **Irgun Zvai Leumi** and the **Lohamei Herut Israel** (the Stern Group). Betar ran Jewish naval training bases in Italy and Latvia, and aviation training schools in Paris, Lod (central Palestine), Johannesburg, and New York.

At its peak, on the eve of World War II, Betar had almost 100,000 members in 26 countries. Its appeal was especially strong in Poland, where the Betar themes of Jewish nationalist pride and *aliya* as the answer to inevitable Diaspora anti-Semitism resonated in a Jewish community suffering from poverty and anti-Jewish discrimination. Betar played an active role in prewar efforts to smuggle European Jews into Palestine in defiance of British immigration restrictions. During the war, Betar members figured prominently in armed resistance against the Nazis in a number of ghettoes in Europe, including the Warsaw Ghetto uprising. The majority of Betar members in Europe were killed in the Holocaust.

After the war, Betar activities were revived, although on a much smaller scale, in a number of Western countries. Betar today is primarily an educational movement, with an emphasis on encouraging its members to immigrate to Israel.

BIALIK, HAYIM NAHMAN (1873–1934). Zionist author and poet Hayim Bialik was born in Radi, a Ukrainian village, to a traditional Jewish family. His father died when Hayim was seven years old, and the child was sent to Zhitomir to be raised by his rigid grandfather and to study at a yeshiva there. Several years after his bar mitzvah, Bialik went to study at the famous yeshiva in Volozhin, Lithuania, but there he became attracted to the *Haskala,* the Jewish Enlightenment movement. He joined the **Hovevei Zion** group and began to write Hebrew poetry. Bialik gradually drifted away from the world of the yeshiva, finding it too stifling, and at age eighteen went to Odessa. There he joined Jewish literary circles, began to achieve recognition as a Hebrew poet and prose writer, and first met **Ahad Ha'am**, who had a major impact on his Zionism.

Initially, Bialik did not make his livelihood from writing. For four years, he was a lumber salesman and bookkeeper in his father-in-law's business in Zhitomir. He then returned to Odessa, where he taught, published and translated, and was literary editor of the weekly *Hashiloah*. Bialik wrote profusely and continuously grew in stature. He took an active role in the Zionist movement; participated in the 8th, 11th, 12th, and 17th **Zionist Congresses**; and became the inspiring national poet of Zionism throughout Eastern Europe and in **Eretz Israel**.

In 1921 Bialik moved to Berlin. During his three years there, he established the Dvir publishing house. Bialik went on *aliya* and settled in Tel Aviv in 1924, where he soon became a literary legend. He established the Hebrew Writers Union, was named its president in 1927, reestablished the Dvir publishing house in Tel Aviv, and participated in the establishment of the Hebrew University. Bialik died in Vienna, where he had gone for medical treatment. His home in Tel Aviv became the Bialik Museum. More than half a century after his death, Bialik retains the title as modern Jewry's "national poet."

BILTMORE PROGRAM. Shaken by reports of Nazi massacres of Jews in Eastern Europe and prodded by **David Ben-Gurion** to adopt a more activist approach to Zionist concerns, the member-organizations of the **Emergency Committee for Zionist Affairs** convened an "Extraordinary Conference of American Zionists" at the Biltmore Hotel in New York City in May 1942. The six hundred delegates adopted resolutions denouncing the 1939 British **White Paper** as "cruel and indefensible"; urging "that Palestine be established as a Jewish Commonwealth"; and endorsing the creation of "a Jewish military force fighting under its own flag" alongside the Allies.

Delegates from **Hadassah** and **Hashomer Hatzair** urged the Biltmore conferees to take a greater interest in the issue of Arab–Jewish relations, but the resolution that was adopted echoed the traditional position of the Zionist movement, expressing a general "readiness and desire" by Zionists for "full cooperation with their Arab neighbors."

At the time, many of the Biltmore attendees as well as commentators in the Jewish press saw little that was new or significant in the conference's resolutions. Many historians, however, regard Biltmore as a turning point in American Zionist affairs. It was the first national Zionist gathering in the United States since Pearl Harbor and represented a break from the cautious attitude that had enveloped American Zionists during the first months following the United States' entry into the war. The wording of the Biltmore resolutions also constituted a clear triumph of Ben-Gurion's activist line over the more conservative approach of **Chaim Weizmann** and his followers.

In the months after the conference, the Biltmore resolutions became a sort of touchstone of Zionist commitment, with each of the major American Zionist organizations specifically pledging themselves to promote the Biltmore program.

BILU. Russian Jewish students in Kharkov organized the Bilu movement in the wake of the 1881 pogroms. Previously committed to the idea of Jewish integration into a reformed Russia, the students were disillusioned both by the government's role in the pogroms and the Russian revolutionaries' justification of the anti-Jewish violence. The name "Bilu" was an acronym for the biblical verse "O House of Jacob, come, let us go . . ." (Isaiah 2:5), symbolizing the group's commitment to personally emigrate to Palestine.

Bilu chapters were established in more than twenty Russian cities, with as many as five hundred members, making it the first nationwide Russian Zionist movement. But Turkey's April 1882 announcement of new restrictions on immigration to Palestine dealt Bilu a serious setback. An attempt by the British statesman Laurence Oliphant to win a reversal of the Turkish decree failed, crushing Bilu's hopes and leading to the dissolution of most of the movement.

Despite these developments, a group of fourteen Bilu members traveled to Palestine in the summer of 1882. No preparatory work or acquisition of land for them had been undertaken prior to their arrival. They initially worked at the Mikveh Israel Agricultural School (southeast of the area that was to become Tel Aviv), and there organized the first workers' cooperative in modern Eretz Israel.

Two years later, the Bilu pioneers, together with a handful of additional Biluim who came from Russia after them, founded the village of Gedera, south of Jaffa. Despite severe conditions there, the colonists persisted and the settlement eventually prospered. Because of their determination in the face of adversity and their commitment to settle the land despite their complete unfamiliarity with local conditions, the Biluim served as a source of inspiration for subsequent groups of Zionist pioneers. Indeed, the **First Aliya** is often identified as the Bilu Aliya, even though only a small portion of the Eastern European immigrants who arrived during that period were connected to the Bilu movement.

BINYAN HA'ARETZ. Three small, short-lived European Zionist groups, independent of each other, operated under the name Binyan Ha'aretz

("Building the Land") during the interwar years. One was active in Austria in the mid-1930s, a second in Czechoslovakia in the early 1920s. The most prominent of the three, established in Germany in 1919, stirred controversy by opposing the use of socialist methods in Palestine settlement and emphasizing the value of private initiative instead. The German Binyan Ha'aretz fared poorly at the 1921 Zionist convention in Hanover and disbanded shortly afterward.

BLACKSTONE, WILLIAM E. (1841–1935). A pioneer of modern **Christian Zionism**, William Blackstone was born in Adams, New York. Blackstone was raised in a Methodist church and was exposed to Evangelicalism early on. He was a successful Chicago businessman who had become a disciple of John Nelson Darby, the London-born major spiritual leader of the millenarian Plymouth Brothers group, and he was a driving force in the founding of the Chicago Hebrew Mission, which later became the American Messianic Fellowship, a movement devoted to missionary work among Jews. In 1890 Blackstone organized the first conference between Jews and Christians in Chicago.

Blackstone's book *Jesus Is Coming* (1887) became a best-seller and was translated into dozens of languages, including Hebrew. It contended that the return of Jesus would be preceded by the return of the Jews to Zion. Blackstone visited Palestine in 1888–1889, and in March 1891 he presented President Benjamin Harrison and Secretary of State James G. Blaine with a petition, signed by 413 Jewish and Christian leaders, calling for an international conference on the Jews and Palestine and for the return of Palestine back to the Jews. The petition was ignored by the political authorities, and in 1916 Blackstone sent a second pro-Zionist petition to President Wilson. It has been suggested that President Woodrow Wilson's favorable disposition to the **Balfour Declaration** may have been influenced by Blackstone's petition.

B'NAI B'RITH (Children of the Covenant). Established as a Jewish social service organization in the United States in 1843, B'nai B'rith was officially non-Zionist but took a sympathetic interest in the welfare of Palestine Jewry, beginning with the funds it raised for victims of the 1865 cholera epidemic in **Eretz Israel**. B'nai B'rith lodges were organized in Jerusalem in 1888 and in Jaffa in 1889. The Jerusalem branch helped establish the agricultural settlement of Motza. During the 1930s, funds raised by B'nai B'rith purchased the Galilee land on which Moshav Moledet-B'nai B'rith, a haven for refugees from Nazism, was established.

B'nai B'rith also helped sponsor the establishment of Moshav Ramat Zvi in 1941.

The ascension of Henry Monsky, a Zionist, to the presidency of B'nai B'rith in 1938 marked the beginning of the organization's shift to a more openly pro-Zionist position. Backed by a constituency deeply shaken by news of the Nazi mass murders, Monsky initiated the convening of the 1943 **American Jewish Conference**, at which B'nai B'rith joined all other major Jewish groups—except the **American Jewish Committee**—in endorsing the establishment of Palestine as a Jewish Commonwealth. B'nai B'rith actively lobbied the Truman administration and the United Nations to support Jewish statehood in 1947–1948.

After the creation of Israel, B'nai B'rith intensified its Israel-related programming and fundraising for the Jewish state, including the sale of Israel bonds, the planting of forests, the provision of scholarships for disadvantaged Israeli students, and the creation of a wide range of medical and charitable institutions throughout Israel. B'nai B'rith's university campus organization, Hillel, maintains branches at Israeli universities, and the Israeli youth movement Noar le'Noar is part of the B'nai B'rith Youth Organization. The Anti-Defamation League, an arm of B'nai B'rith until 1993, has played a prominent role in pro-Israel information campaigns in the United States.

B'NAI ZION. One of the earliest American Zionist organizations, B'nai Zion, also known as the Order of the Sons of Zion, was established in New York in 1908. B'nai Zion, a fraternal society, engaged in educational and fundraising activities for Palestine and took part in the creation of the Provisional Executive Committee for General Zionist Affairs (1914), the **American Jewish Congress** (1918), and the **Keren Hayesod** (1921). By the 1920s, much of its activity revolved around its Judea Insurance Company Ltd., the first Jewish insurance company in modern Palestine. A *moshav* named after B'nai Zion, and partly financed by it, was established in the Sharon Plain region in 1947.

Today B'nai Zion engages in pro-Israel educational and cultural activities, assists medical institutions and other humanitarian projects in Israel, and distributes awards for excellence in Hebrew to American high school and college students.

BNEI AKIVA. The youth wing of the **Religious Zionist** movement **Mizrachi**, Bnei Akiva ("Children of Akiva") was founded in Palestine in 1922. Although it began as an educational movement, Bnei Akiva shifted its focus to agricultural pioneering, within the framework of a religious lifestyle, in response to the Palestinian Arab violence of 1936–1939. Bnei Akiva members established several of the earliest religious kibbutzim, including Ein Tzurim, in the Hebron hills (1946); Birya, in the Upper Galilee (1946); and Sa'ad, in the Negev (1947). Bnei Akiva graduates played a major role in the development of additional religious kibbutzim and were also prominent in the Israeli Army's Nahal program, which combined military service with the development of new agricultural outposts in border regions.

Bnei Akiva has also organized a network of several dozen Religious Zionist high schools throughout Israel. Some of its graduates are sent abroad as emissaries to work with Bnei Akiva chapters in other countries. An international Bnei Akiva conference in Israel in 1954 brought Bnei Akiva and like-minded movements, such as **Bachad** in Europe and **Hashomer Hadati** in the United States, into a single multifaceted organization. Today there are Bnei Akiva branches in more than thirty countries, with a combined membership of over 50,000.

BOARD OF DEPUTIES OF BRITISH JEWS. Since its inception in 1760, the Board of Deputies of British Jews has served as the central defense organization of British Jewry. Its membership includes all major British synagogues, philanthropic agencies, and Zionist organizations. In 1878 the board joined with the Anglo-Jewish Association to establish the Conjoint Foreign Committee as the voice of British Jewry on foreign affairs.

With **Sir Moses Montefiore**, the noted financier of Palestine development activity, as its president, the board aided philanthropic projects in the Holy Land during the late 1800s, although its leadership was unsympathetic to the goals of **Political Zionism**. In May 1917, during the British-Zionist negotiations that would eventually produce the **Balfour Declaration**, the leaders of the Conjoint signed a letter to the *London Times* condemning Zionism for "stamping the Jews as strangers in their native lands, and undermining their hard-won position as citizens and nationals of those lands." The letter played a role in persuading the British cabinet to water down some of the stronger pro-Zionist language that had appeared in early drafts of the Balfour Declaration.

At the time, the British-Jewish community was in the throes of a power struggle between an elite, composed of wealthy, socially prominent anti-Zionists, and a grass roots that included growing numbers of pro-Zionist Eastern European immigrants. The Conjoint letter was the spark that ignited a full-scale confrontation, resulting in the dissolution of the Conjoint and the replacement of the board's president with a local Zionist leader.

The board represented a wide spectrum of communal opinions and consequently did not always take as forthright a stand as some activists wanted. During the 1930s, the board focused on aiding Jewish refugee immigrants to Great Britain and combating local anti-Semitism. It also cooperated with the **Jewish Agency** and opposed British restrictions on Jewish immigration into Palestine. By 1943, the Zionists within the board had sufficient numbers to bring about the board's formal dissolution of its partnership with the Anglo-Jewish Association because the latter was non-Zionist. In 1944, with the British Zionist leader Selig Brodetsky as its president, the board endorsed the goal of Jewish statehood in Palestine.

BOROCHOV, BER (DOV) (1881–1917). The ideologist of Marxist Zionism, Ber Borochov, was born in the Ukraine. He had a formal high school education and subsequently was self-educated. As a young adult, Borochov was attracted to the Zionist Socialist Workers Union. He wrote numerous essays in which he developed a synthesis of class and nation and argued that for Jews, nationalism was the most viable institution for conducting the class struggle. Once a Jewish society was reestablished, Jews would control their own economic infrastructure, Jews would be integrated into the revolutionary process, and the Jewish economic structure would be reconstituted as a base for the class struggle of the Jewish proletariat. Zionism, Borochov asserted, would help create "the new territory," **Eretz Israel**, and pioneer a new migration pattern among Jews that would culminate in the "stychic," or "elemental," migration of the Jewish masses to Eretz Israel, which is a precondition for Jewish national and economic liberation.

Borochov opposed **Theodor Herzl** on the **Uganda Plan** and, at the Seventh **Zionist Congress** in 1905, he headed a faction of Poalei Zion delegates who opposed the plan. Several years later, Borochov played a central role in the secession of the Russian Poalei Zion, which had moved much further left than the congress and the **World Zionist Organization**. He left Russia in 1907, and from then until the beginning of World War I, he was a publicist for the World Union of Poalei Zion in Western and Central Europe. Borochov came to the United States in 1914, where he continued his work as publicist for Poalei Zion and also did publicity work for the **American Jewish Congress**. Borochov was in Kiev on behalf of Poalei Zion when he contracted a fatal bout of pneumonia.

Buried in Russia, he was reinterred in the cemetery of Kibbutz Kinneret in 1963, next to other founders of **Socialist Zionism**.

BRANDEIS, LOUIS D. (1856–1941). Supreme Court justice and American Zionist leader Louis D. Brandeis was born to an acculturated Jewish family in Louisville, Kentucky. He graduated from Harvard Law School and established a practice in Boston, where he became known as "the people's attorney" for his defense of consumers and small businesses and his outspoken advocacy of social reform causes.

Brandeis's first significant contact with Jewish matters came at age fifty-six, when he arbitrated the 1911 garment industry strike in New York City. Both sides in the dispute were Eastern European Jewish immigrants, and Brandeis later reported that he was profoundly impressed by the ethical standards and idealism of strikers and bosses alike.

Contacts with former **Theodor Herzl** aide Jacob De Haas and *yishuv* emissary **Aaron Aaronsohn** in 1912–1913 aroused Brandeis's interest in the Zionist cause. American Zionist activists sought to recruit Brandeis as the leader of their movement, but he hesitated, uncomfortable over possible conflicts between Zionist ideology and loyal Americanism. The social philosopher **Horace Kallen** helped Brandeis resolve the conflict with his contention that ethnic groups retaining their differences—what he called cultural pluralism—would in the end strengthen the overall fabric of American society. From his discussions with Kallen, Brandeis came to believe that "to be good Americans we must be better Jews, and to be better Jews we must become Zionists." Convinced that there was no contradiction between Zionism and Americanism, Brandeis accepted the chairmanship of the **Provisional Executive Committee for General Zionist Affairs** in 1914.

Brandeis's leadership reaped significant political and financial benefits for the American Zionist movement. His contacts with the Woodrow Wilson administration helped ensure U.S. support for the **Balfour Declaration** and the British Mandate over Palestine. His personal prestige, especially after he became the first Jew to be appointed to the United States Supreme Court in 1916, significantly increased the popularity of Zionism in the American Jewish community. At the same time, his insistence that the organization operate at maximum efficiency and in accordance with strict business principles helped the American Zionist movement grow quickly. Boosted by the Balfour Declaration and the British capture of Palestine, the **Zionist Organization of America (ZOA)** had more than 175,000 members by 1919, up from just 12,000 five years earlier.

In 1920, a rift developed between Brandeis and **Chaim Weizmann** over the future direction of the Zionist movement. Brandeis believed that with the Palestine Mandate in Great Britain's hands, the time had come to cease political and educational activities and concentrate on practical development projects in Palestine, preferably with the assistance of wealthy **Diaspora** non-Zionists. Weizmann rejected Brandeis's approach and set up the **Keren Hayesod** as the fundraising arm of the **World Zionist Organization**, intending to attract Diaspora donations whose disbursement he and his colleagues would control. The struggle between Brandeis and Weizmann reached its climax at the 1921 ZOA convention, where Weizmann loyalists outnumbered Brandeis and his followers, resulting in the resignation of the latter.

Brandeis never returned to a formal leadership position in the movement, but he remained active in a variety of Palestine investment projects, including the Palestine Cooperative Company (later the Palestine Economic Corporation) and the Palestine Endowment Fund. During the 1930s, Brandeis repeatedly tried, without success, to persuade President Franklin D. Roosevelt to press the British on Palestine. Long after Brandeis had left the helm of the movement, American Zionist leaders regularly sought his counsel on policy matters.

BREIRA. American Jewish critics of Israel established the organization Breira (Hebrew for "Choice" or "Alternative") in 1974. The name was intended as a rebuke to the popular Israeli saying "Ein breira," meaning that in the face of Arab hostility, Israel had no alternative but to remain militarily powerful. Breira's ranks consisted primarily of former 1960s Jewish radicals and liberal Reform and Conservative rabbis. They called for an Israeli withdrawal to the pre-1967 borders and the creation of a Palestinian Arab state in the vacated territories, with Jerusalem to be shared by Israel and the new state. They also criticized what they perceived as the centrality of Israel in American Jewish life.

Public Jewish criticism of Israeli policy was rare in the mid-1970s, and Breira's activities therefore caused something of a sensation in the American Jewish community. Meetings between Breira activists and officials of the Palestine Liberation Organization likewise stirred up controversy. Spirited debates over the propriety of Breira's actions filled much of the Jewish press during 1977–1978. Breira's credibility was harmed by disclosures that some of its founders had previously been involved in groups or activities that were unfriendly to Israel. Stung by the negative publicity and the resignations of a number of its members, Breira disbanded in 1978. Many of its most active members subsequently joined similar-minded successor organizations such as **New Jewish Agenda** and the American branch of **Peace Now**.

BRENNER, YOSEF HAYIM (1881–1921). **Socialist Zionist** author and activist Yosef Brenner was born in the Ukraine in 1881, to a traditional Jewish family. He grew to be one of the most forceful advocates of a thoroughly secular Hebrew identity. After studying at a yeshiva, Brenner went to Gomel, where he became active in the Jewish labor movement. He was also influenced by the works of Lev Tolstoy and Fyodor Dostoyevsky, and began to write. Brenner moved to Bialystok and Warsaw at the turn of the century, where he earned his livelihood by teaching Hebrew. His first book, consisting of short stories, was published in 1901 and shortly thereafter he was drafted into the army. He managed to get out of the country, settling in London where he worked in a printing firm. Brenner also joined and became active in the new **Poalei Zion** movement. He published a Hebrew monthly for a brief period, and in 1909 he settled in **Eretz Israel**, where he contributed to a number of periodicals and became one of the most prominent intellectuals of the **Second Aliya**.

Brenner vehemently disparaged the **Diaspora**, which he portrayed in pessimistic and, at times, vicious terms. He averred that the rabbinate had a stranglehold on Jewish life there, which prevented the emergence of Jewish genius and creativity. Toward the end of 1920, Brenner joined the Gedud Ha'avoda and worked on road construction in Galilee. He also participated in the founding of the **Histadrut** labor union.

Although Brenner wrote eloquently of the need for "brotherhood" between Arab and Jewish workers in Palestine, he was murdered by Palestinian Arabs during the May 1921 riots in Jaffa. One of Israel's largest kibbutzim, Givat Brenner, near Rehovot, is named for him.

BRICHA. *Bricha,* the Hebrew term for "escape," is used to refer to both the mass migration of Holocaust survivors from Eastern Europe to Southern and Western Europe, during the late 1940s, in preparation for their settlement in Palestine, and the movement that organized that migration.

The Bricha phenomenon began in the final months of World War II, when Zionists active in the anti-Nazi partisan movement smuggled large numbers of Jews out of Soviet territory into the relative safety of Romania and then southward to Italy. By autumn of 1945, more than 20,000 such refugees had been brought to the overflowing Bricha centers in Italy, often with the aid of veterans of the **Jewish Brigade**. With the refugee facilities in Italy filled, Bricha directed tens of thousands of survivors to the Allies' **Displaced Persons (DP)** camps in occupied Germany. Then, in the wake of the July 1946 pogrom in Kielce, Poland, Bricha activists organized the emigration of over 70,000 Polish Jews.

The presence of hundreds of thousands of Holocaust survivors in the DP camps, clamoring for permission to settle in Palestine, was an important factor in galvanizing international pressure on Great Britain to withdraw from Palestine.

BRIT IVRIT OLAMIT. The Brit Ivrit Olamit, or World Association for Hebrew Language and Culture, was established in Berlin in 1931 as the international umbrella organization for groups involved in the promotion of Hebrew. Chapters of Brit Ivrit Olamit in some twenty-one countries engage in a variety of Hebrew language activities, including song and dance clubs, Hebrew literature study groups, and the production of Hebrew-language radio programs.

BRITH SHALOM. A small group of liberal Zionist intellectuals in Palestine, led by **Arthur Ruppin**, chief of the settlement division of the **World Zionist Organization**, established Brith Shalom (literally, "Covenant of Peace") in 1925, to advocate a more conciliatory Zionist attitude toward the Palestinian Arabs. The group's platform called for repudiation of the **Balfour Declaration** and establishment of a binational Arab-Jewish state in Palestine, in which Jews would be a minority. Many of the Brith Shalom activists were proponents of **Ahad Ha'am**'s idea of Palestine as a cultural center for Judaism, and some had previously been part of Ha'am's **Benei Moshe** group in Russia. The philosopher Martin Buber was Brith Shalom's spiritual mentor.

Brith Shalom succeeded in provoking a spirited public debate about Arab–Jewish relations and enjoyed some private sympathy from **World Zionist Organization** president **Chaim Weizmann**, but its efforts to influence official Zionist policy were a failure. The intense opposition it encountered from Zionist groups gradually prompted a number of Brith Shalom's members to resign. The inability of Brith Shalom to find even one Palestinian Arab group that would cooperate with it discredited Brith Shalom's claim that an Arab-Jewish peace accord was possible. Brith Shalom disbanded in 1933, although some of its members continued to undertake similar political activities in subsequent years and served as mediators in unsuccessful contacts between Zionist and Palestinian Arab leaders in the late 1930s.

BUND. *See* DIASPORA NATIONALISM.

-C-

CANAANITE MOVEMENT. During the 1930s and 1940s, a small group of Jewish intellectuals, mostly in Palestine, began advocating that the *yishuv* reject Jewish traditions and model a new culture linked to the ancient people of Canaan. Supporters of this idea were popularly referred to as "Canaanites," although they themselves did not formally adopt that designation. In their view, the Jewish residents of **Eretz Israel** constitute a nation separate from world Jewry. Instead of a Jewish state in Palestine, they proposed the establishment of a broader Land of Kedem that would include both Palestine and all neighboring areas in which Hebrew dialects were spoken in ancient times, encompassing modern-day Syria, Lebanon, and Jordan. Both Jews and Arabs would shed their particularistic religions and cultures and instead adopt the "original" Hebrew culture that they supposedly shared long ago.

The poet and journalist Yonatan Ratosh (1909–1981) was the movement's most prominent spokesman as well as editor of its journal, *Alef.* The Canaanites also published the periodicals *Bama-avak* ("In the Struggle") and *Eretz Israel Hatze'ira* ("The Young Land of Israel").

A version of the Canaanite program was promoted in the United States during the mid-1940s by the Hebrew Committee of National Liberation (also known as the **Bergson Group**). It argued that the term *Jew* should be applied only to Jews intending to remain in the **Diaspora**, whereas Jews residing in Palestine and European Jews planning to immigrate there should be considered members of a separate and distinct "Hebrew" nation. The proposal was too radical a departure from traditional concepts of Jewish identity to attract any substantial number of American Jewish supporters.

During the 1950s, Canaanite sympathizers in Israel established the Semitic Action Party. It urged Israel to formally sever ties with Diaspora Jewry and integrate itself into the Middle Eastern cultural and political milieu. Uri Avnery, editor (as of 1950) of the magazine *Ha'olam Hazeh* ("This World"), was a leading proponent of the new movement. Semitic Action never succeeded in garnering the sympathy of more than a tiny fraction of the Israeli public and ceased to exist by the late 1960s, although Avnery himself was elected to the Knesset in 1965 and continued to promote a Canaanite-oriented agenda in his journalistic and political activities.

CENTRAL CONFERENCE OF AMERICAN RABBIS. *See* COLUMBUS PLATFORM; PITTSBURGH PLATFORM.

CHRISTIAN ZIONISM. Over the centuries there have been various manifestations of attempts by Christians to restore Jewish sovereignty in the Holy Land, rooted in the belief that the return of Jews to the Holy Land and the restoration of Zion under Jewish sovereignty are biblically designated preconditions to the Second Coming of Jesus. As early as the latter half of the seventeenth century, the Danish pietist Holeger Paulli (1644–1714) tried to recruit various European rulers in his effort to establish a Jewish monarchy there. He published numerous books and letters that he sent to the French and English kings, calling on them to help the Jews return to Zion and regain their sovereignty. Christian Zionism became more prevalent during the nineteenth century with the spread of Christian millenarianism, although most millenarians were neither pro-Zionist nor favorably disposed to Jews. To the extent that they were concerned with Jews, it was in their efforts to convert them to Christianity.

One of the earliest American proponents of active Christian Zionism was the Chicago businessman **William E. Blackstone** (1841–1935), who was an evangelist and Dispensationalist—that is, a follower of an extreme form of millenarianism that has a very vivid religious conception of the ultimate fate of the Jews and their role in the "End of Days." Blackstone staunchly supported the return of the Jews to Zion and organized groups of Christians and Jews to further that cause.

One especially colorful individual was Warder Cresson, whose Christian Zionism led him to Judaism. Born to a well-known Quaker family in 1798, he was a spiritual searcher who left Quakerism and became a Shaker, then a Mormon, and then, alternately, a member of various other evangelical denominations. In 1840, he began an association with Rev. Isaac Leeser, one of the most prominent leaders of American Judaism at the time, and during the next four years Cresson developed a special interest in Jerusalem. In 1844 he succeeded in getting himself appointed as the first American consul to Jerusalem. Although he arrived in Jerusalem as a practicing Christian, Cresson was increasingly attracted to Judaism, and in March 1848 he became a devout convert to Judaism, with the name Michael Boaz Israel. He died in 1860 and was buried on Mount Olives with honors typically reserved for great rabbis.

Since the Six-Day War of June 1967, a number of prominent Christian fundamentalists have been strongly supportive of Israel and have favored Likud policies over those of the Labor Party.

COLUMBUS PLATFORM. The Central Conference of American Rabbis (CCAR), the rabbinical association of Reform Judaism, meeting in Columbus, Ohio, in 1937, adopted a resolution on Palestine far more sympathetic than any previous pronouncement by the Reform movement on the subject. The Columbus statement declared that it was "the obligation of all Jewry to aid in [the] upbuilding [of Palestine] as a Jewish homeland by endeavoring to make it not only a haven of refuge for the oppressed but also a center of Jewish cultural and spiritual life." The Columbus Platform, as it came to be known, marked the culmination of a gradual shift away from anti-Zionism that had been underway in the Reform movement for more than a decade.

The American Reform movement's first official position on Zionism, the **Pittsburgh Platform** of 1885, unequivocally rejected the concept of Zionism as anathema to the Reform ideals of universalism and Jewish integration among the nations of the world. During the early 1900s, a small but vocal and growing minority of Zionist sympathizers within the Reform rabbinate, most prominently **Stephen Wise** and **Abba Hillel Silver**, began influencing the movement away from the staunch anti-Zionism of the Pittsburgh Platform. Later, developments abroad played a significant role in reshaping Reform attitudes toward Palestine, including the international approval for Zionism expressed in the **Balfour Declaration**; the eruption of Palestinian Arab violence in the 1920s; and the rise of Nazism and persecution of European Jews in the 1930s.

The 1920 convention of the CCAR adopted a resolution "rejoicing" at the League of Nations decision to grant the Palestine mandate to Great Britain and asserting that it was "the duty of all Jews to contribute to the reconstruction of Palestine," while continuing to eschew Jewish nationalism per se. Two years later, the CCAR reached a formal agreement with the Palestine Development Council to promote joint projects for developing **Eretz Israel**. In 1928 the CCAR passed a resolution praising the **Jewish Agency** for Palestine, and in 1930 it voted to include the Zionist anthem "**Hatikvah**" in the Reform movement's hymnal. In early 1935, 241 Reform rabbis—out of 401 CCAR members—signed a petition praising the accomplishments of **Labor Zionism** in Palestine. The 1935 CCAR convention took "no official stand on the subject of Zionism," thus officially acknowledging the movement's shift from anti-Zionism to non-Zionism. It also pledged to "cooperate in the upbuilding of Palestine." In the final pre-Columbus indication of Reform Judaism's changing view of Zionism, in early 1937 the Union of American Hebrew Congregations, the national association of Reform synagogues, adopted a resolution urging "all Jews, irrespective of ideological differences, to unite in the activities leading to the establishment of a Jewish homeland in Palestine." The Columbus Platform followed naturally.

CONFERENCE OF PRESIDENTS OF MAJOR AMERICAN JEW-ISH ORGANIZATIONS. Responding to complaints by Secretary of State John Foster Dulles about the growing number of Jewish representatives approaching him, American Jewish leaders established the Conference of Presidents of Major American Jewish Organizations in 1955 to serve as American Jewry's primary spokesman on foreign affairs.

From its founding membership of seventeen organizations, the conference has gradually expanded to its present constituency of fifty-five groups, including those from all points on the religious and political spectrums. Conference of Presidents delegations frequently visit Israel and Washington, D.C., to confer with government officials and convey their views on current issues involving Israel and Jewish communities around the world.

The chairman of the conference serves a maximum of two one-year terms. The chairman is chosen by a nominating committee, consisting of former conference chairmen and current organizational leaders, who are appointed to the nominating committee by the conference's executive vice chairman. The conference's policy positions are decided not by direct vote, but rather by the chairman and executive vice chairman, who develop and articulate what they consider to be the consensus view among the member-organizations.

CULTURAL ZIONISM. Although its roots may be found in the thought of pre-Herzl Zionists such as **Moses Hess** and Peretz Smolenskin, Cultural Zionism, also sometimes referred to as Spiritual Zionism, is most closely associated with the thought of **Ahad Ha'am** (Asher Zvi Ginzberg), a prominent Russian Jewish writer (1856–1927). A sharp critic of **Theodor Herzl**'s Practical Zionism and the notion that a state would resolve the problems of the Jews, Ahad Ha'am looked to Zionism as the means for the realization of a Jewish cultural renaissance. His goal was not a nation state, like other nation states, but rather a Jewish national cultural (spiritual) center for Jews in **Diaspora** communities around the world, which would serve to revive Jewish creativity and national consciousness. Cultural Zionism typically placed emphasis on educational activity among Jews, as well as on uncontroversial settlement programs in **Eretz Israel**. Much of the contemporary debate between the Zionist left and the Zionist right is rooted in the historic debate between Cultural Zionism and Political Zionism.

CYPRUS PLAN. In late 1897, Davis Trietsch, a German-born writer and statistician who served as a delegate to that year's First **Zionist Congress,**

began promoting the idea of settling Jews in the British colony of Cyprus. Trietsch envisioned the settling of Cyprus as part of a Greater Palestine scheme that would encompass Palestine, Cyprus, and El 'Arīsh. Trietsch established contacts with the Cypriot authorities, visited the island to survey settlement possibilities, and even arranged for an initial group of thirteen Jewish workers from Galicia to take up residence on Cyprus in 1899.

Theodor Herzl at first displayed little enthusiasm for the Cyprus proposal, but he reconsidered after pogroms in Galicia in the summer of 1898 and after encountering obstacles in his attempts to win Turkish consent to settle Palestine. Herzl began to imagine Cyprus as a temporary shelter for European Jewish refugees, which would serve as a prelude to the colonization of **Eretz Israel**. In 1902 Herzl raised the Cyprus idea with British colonial secretary Joseph Chamberlain, only to have it rejected on the grounds that the island's inhabitants would object. The following year, Trietsch, on his own, raised the Cyprus plan with British officials, but his entreaties came to naught. Both the British and the Zionist leadership increasingly focused their attention on the possibility of settling Jews in East Africa instead, and the Cyprus scheme was soon forgotten.

-D-

DE HAAN, JACOB ISRAEL (1881–1924). *Haredi* anti-Zionist polemicist Jacob de Haan was born in Smilde, Netherlands. De Haan gained a reputation as a poet and journalist with socialist and anarchist tendencies. Controversy over his personal lifestyle resulted in his expulsion from the Dutch Socialist Party. In 1907 he married a Christian physician who encouraged him into the study and profession of law, but his poetic talents won out and he abandoned law and published several collections of poetry in Dutch.

He became a *ba'al teshuvah,* a newly Orthodox Jew, just prior to World War I and, at first, joined **Mizrachi**, the movement of **Religious Zionism**. He left his wife and family and in 1918 went to Jerusalem, where he was a journalist for several European newspapers. There he identified with the ultra-Orthodox (*haredi*) camp headed by Rabbi Joseph Hayim Sonnenfeld, the rabbi of the anti-Zionist sectarian Ashkenazi community in Jerusalem. He wrote numerous anti-Zionist articles for the European press and engaged in a number of political activities that were deemed subversive by the Zionist authorities and much of the *yishuv*. **Haganah** authorities allegedly ordered his assassination, which was carried out by two Haganah soldiers on June 30, 1924, as he was leaving the synagogue of Jerusalem's Shaarei Zedek Hospital. The assassination gave rise to a bitter dispute, with numerous secularists condemning it as unconscionable.

DEMOCRATIC FACTION. The first distinct ideological faction within the World Zionist movement, the Democratic Faction was organized in 1901 by Zionist students and intellectuals living in Germany and Switzerland. A number of future Zionist leaders, including **Chaim Weizmann** and **Leon Motzkin**, were among its founders. Some of them were also involved in **Ahad Ha'am**'s **Benei Moshe** society.

In December 1901, on the eve of the Fifth **World Zionist Congress**, the Democratic Faction activists met to formalize their agenda. Their use of the term *democratic* in their name was meant as a slap at Zionist leader **Theodor Herzl**, who, they argued, ruled the Zionist movement in an autocratic fashion, without sufficiently consulting the movement's committees or leading activists. Challenging Herzl's emphasis on political negotiations, the Democratic Faction called for devoting more resources to actual settlement activity in Palestine. The faction also urged the involvement of the Zionist movement in the shaping of a secular Zionist culture, a position staunchly opposed by **Religious Zionists**. Indeed, the faction's lobbying on this point in 1901–1902 helped galvanize the establishment of the **Mizrachi** party by religious members of the **World Zionist Organization**. After a stormy debate, the Zionist Congress agreed to the Democratic Faction's demand for a scientific study of settlement conditions in Palestine, as well as to its call for greater personal involvement in Zionist activity by members of the movement. However, the congress skirted the "culture" controversy, by endorsing the movement's involvement in "cultural" and "educational" activities without defining either term. The following year, a national conference of Russian Zionists, meeting in Minsk, adopted the Democratic Faction's proposal to resolve the cultural controversy by recognizing the secular and religious approaches to Zionist culture as two separate but equal methods. Having substantially accomplished its major aims, the Democratic Faction dissolved soon after the Minsk conference.

DIASPORA. *Diaspora* is a Greek word that means "scattered" or "dispersion." Since the exile of the Jews from **Eretz Israel** by the Babylonian king Nebuchadnezzar in 586 B.C.E., the term *Diaspora* has referred to

Jewish life outside of Eretz Israel, the "Exile." In Hebrew, it is referred to as *Galut*. In traditional Judaism, as well as in modern Zionism, the term has a strong normative connotation that views the dispersion as abnormal. *See also* NEGATION OF THE DIASPORA.

DIASPORA NATIONALISM. A philosophy of Jewish national existence that developed in the late nineteenth century, **Diaspora** nationalism had a profound impact on Zionist, as well as on non-Zionist and anti-Zionist movements. Its underlying thesis, regardless of its specific form, is that Jews around the world are a collective entity, bound by a common history and culture, and that the Jewish people must create the social and cultural conditions that would enable them to retain their Jewish identity while living as minorities in non-Jewish societies.

The two most prominent proponents of Diaspora nationalism, although they had strong disagreements between themselves, were Chaim Zhitlowsky (1865–1943) and Simon Dubnow (1860–1941). Zhitlowsky was a socialist and a Yiddishist who aspired for Jews to become a nation as all others, which included autonomy in the social, political, and economic realms. Dubnow was a prominent Jewish historian who saw the unique communal character of the Jewish people as the key to their survival in the Diaspora throughout the centuries. Since the Middle Ages, the Jews have become an autonomous nationality within larger nation-states, and Dubnow posited this Jewish situation as a model for others in Europe. He looked to the development of a Russian-Polish center of Jewish life and a culture that would not only rival but surpass such previous centers as those of Palestine, Babylon, and Spain. Dubnow was a secularist who also viewed the Jewish religion as a mark of Jewish cultural creativity and genius. In the new conditions of the Russian-Polish center, however, he looked forward to the end of the religious character of the community. As was Zhitlowsky, Dubnow was a Yiddishist, and he looked to Yiddish as the language of the newly developing Jewish culture.

Among the anti-Zionist movements, the most prominent form of Diaspora nationalism was that of the Bund. It was founded near Vilna in October 1897 by a small group of Marxist social democrats dedicated to the economic and political liberation of the Jewish working masses, as well as to universal social and economic justice. The Bund asserted that the survival and development of Jewish life was dependent upon Jews joining the struggle for social change and social justice in their respective countries. The organization was staunchly opposed to Zionism and the notion of a collective Jewish national identity, as well as to the Zionist emphasis on Hebrew as the Jewish national language. The home of the Jews, to the Bund, was the Jewish Diaspora, and it promoted the value of Yiddish. It developed a secular Jewish nationalism with an emphasis on the cultural autonomy of Jewish life in Eastern Europe.

Among Zionists, Diaspora nationalism figured prominently in the ideology of **Poalei Zion**. As a movement whose ideology was a combination of Zionism and socialism, it emphasized the inseparable connection between the construction of a Jewish state in Palestine and the political and social struggles of the Jewish masses around the world. It valued the pluralistic character of Jewish culture and promoted its development in Yiddish and other languages as well as in Hebrew.

DISPLACED PERSONS (DPs). When the European phase of World War II ended in the spring of 1945, the Allied occupation forces found themselves dealing with millions of refugees—people who had fled the advancing Nazi armies, former inmates of labor camps, Jewish survivors of the death camps, and others. They were given temporary shelter in a series of Displaced Persons Assembly Camps, better known as DP camps, that were established throughout the Allied zones.

Most of the Jewish DPs were housed in camps in the American and British zones in Italy, Germany, and Austria. Some of them, primarily Hungarian and Czech Jews, stayed in the camps only briefly and opted to be repatriated. But in the summer of 1945, some 65,000 of the Jewish DPs, mostly Polish Jews, still remained, refusing to return to their home towns because of the intensity of anti-Semitism there. Many set their sights on Palestine, but tight British immigration restrictions kept **Eretz Israel** off limits for most.

Alarmed by overcrowding and deteriorating health conditions in the camps, in June 1945 the Truman administration dispatched an investigatory committee, headed by former U.S. Immigration commissioner Earl Harrison, to survey conditions in the camps. In his report, Harrison criticized the administration of the camps as inefficient and insensitive; urged approval of the Jewish DPs' demand to be housed separately from non-Jewish Eastern European DPs, many of whom were anti-Semitic; and expressed sympathy for the Jewish DPs' demand for permission to enter Palestine. The report led to a presidential directive to improve conditions in the camps and galvanized President Harry S. Truman to put more pressure on the British to increase Jewish immigration to Palestine.

The number of Jewish DPs rose steadily in late 1945, as thousands who had gone back to their home towns encountered local anti-Semitism and opted to return to the camps. In addition, rising anti-Semitism in Poland provoked a steady stream of Polish Jews to seek shelter in the DP camps, especially after pogroms in the Polish city of Kielce in the summer of 1946. By early 1947, there were well over 200,000 Jewish DPs in the Allied camps.

Many DPs were among the approximately 70,000 Holocaust survivors who were smuggled into Palestine during 1945–1948, mostly by the **Haganah**. The passengers who filled the *Exodus* and other ships that were intercepted by the British while trying to reach Palestine also came from the ranks of the DPs. More than 50,000 of the would-be immigrants were held in detention camps in Cyprus after being captured at sea. Following the establishment of Israel, the Cyprus detainees, as well as the DPs still in Europe, were finally able to enter Eretz Israel.

DROR. Russian Zionist activists organized the group that would later become known as Dror ("Freedom") in Kiev in 1909. It advocated focusing on educational efforts to unite **Diaspora** Jewry on behalf of Zionism, rather than exclusively emphasizing actual settlement activity in Palestine. In 1917, the group broke off from the mainstream **World Zionist Organization** and adopted the name Dror. In the turmoil of the Russian Revolution and subsequent civil war (1917–1921), many of its founders fled the country, some to Palestine with the settlers of the **Third Aliya**. The others regrouped in Poland, where they became affiliated with the **Hehalutz** organization. They later formed the nucleus of its youth movement, Hehalutz Hatzair, and settled in Palestine. In 1981, Dror officially merged with the Ihud-Habonim Labor Zionists to become Habonim-Dror, the youth movement of the United Kibbutz Movement.

-E-

ELDAD, ISRAEL (1910–1998). One of the leaders of the Palestine Jewish underground group **Lohamei Herut Israel (Lehi)**, Israel Eldad was born Israel Scheib in Galicia in 1910. He studied at the Lodz Hebrew High School, the Vienna Rabbinical Seminary, and the University of Vienna. Scheib became active in the **Revisionist Zionist** youth movement **Betar** and rose to its leadership ranks before settling in Palestine in April 1941. There he Hebraized his name to Eldad and joined Lehi. An accomplished writer and political philosopher, Eldad was soon named editor of the Lehi publications *Hazit* and *Hama'as*. Eldad, **Yitzhak Shamir**, and Natan Yellin-Friedman comprised the ruling triumvirate of

Lehi when it was reorganized after the death of its founder, **Avraham Stern**. Eldad's primary role was as Lehi's ideological guide.

Eldad suffered a serious back injury while attempting to avoid arrest by the British police in 1944. Throughout the next year and a half, Eldad continued his leadership role in Lehi from his prison cell, via messages smuggled back and forth by his comrades. Brought by the prison authorities to a Jerusalem hospital to have his body cast removed in May 1946, Eldad escaped and remained free for the remainder of the British Mandate period.

After the establishment of Israel, Eldad organized a nationalist opposition group called Hazit Hamoledet, which was outlawed by the Israeli government following the assassination of United Nations mediator Count Folke Bernadotte. Eldad subsequently served as editor of a militant nationalist journal, *Sullam* ("Ladder"); authored several books expounding his philosophy of maximalist Zionism; edited a series called *Chronicles* that portrayed ancient Jewish historical events in a modern newspaper format; and taught humanities at the Haifa Technion.

EMERGENCY COMMITTEE FOR ZIONIST AFFAIRS. *See* AMERICAN ZIONIST EMERGENCY COUNCIL.

EMUNAH. (Hebrew for "Faith") Founded in 1977 as the **Mizrachi** Women's Organization, Emunah's 130,000 members, in 23 countries, provide financial support to an array of Israeli charitable institutions. In addition to Religious-Zionist schools, recipients of Emunah aid include some 200 Israeli day-care centers, children's residential homes, vocational schools for the underprivileged, and senior-citizen centers. Emunah is also involved in programs to facilitate the absorption of new immigrants from Ethiopia and the former Soviet Union.

Emunah's New York headquarters publishes *Emunah Magazine* and a newsletter, *Lest We Forget. See also* RELIGIOUS ZIONISM.

ERETZ ISRAEL. Eretz Israel is the Hebrew phrase for "Land of Israel." The name is biblical in origin, where it refers, variously, to parts of the region that were under Jewish sovereignty at different times. Since the dispersion in 70 C.E., it has been used to designate Zion and "the Promised Land." It was also the Hebrew name for Palestine under the British Mandate.

ÉVIAN CONFERENCE. In March 1938, U.S. president Franklin D. Roosevelt invited thirty-two countries to send representatives to an international conference on the European refugee problem, to be held in

July in the French resort town of Évian-les-Bains. The U.S. initiative came in response to the wave of anti-Jewish persecution in Austria following the German occupation of that country. Roosevelt's action was also intended to head off growing criticism in the media and in Congress of the administration's failure to alleviate the refugee crisis. Myron Taylor, the recently retired chairman of United States Steel, was chosen to head the U.S. delegation to Évian.

Thirty-one of the thirty-two invited nations agreed to attend (Italy was the exception). American officials assured the attendees that none would be expected to alter their existing immigration restrictions and that the financial backing for refugee resettlement would continue to be borne by private organizations, not governments.

Some forty private organizations also attended, including representatives of twenty-one different Jewish groups. The effectiveness of the Jewish delegations was hampered by a deep division between Zionist organizations that wanted to focus on Palestine as the solution to the refugee problem and non- and anti-Zionists who preferred to explore other options.

At the conference, the various representatives reiterated their countries' refusal to absorb additional refugees, citing local unemployment or the potential for ethnic unrest in the event of an influx of foreigners. The British representatives refused to discuss the possibility of allowing increased Jewish immigration to Palestine, and a request by Zionist leader **Chaim Weizmann** to address the conference was rejected. The conference's only concrete action was to establish an Intergovernmental Committee on Refugees (ICR), which it hoped would negotiate with Germany and potential countries of refuge to organize an orderly exodus of Jews from German territory. Underfunded and operating with only limited authority, the ICR did not live up to the high expectations that accompanied its creation.

EXODUS. The *Exodus* was the most famous of the sixty-four refugee ships that Zionist activists sought to bring to Palestine, in defiance of the British authorities, during the 1940s. Originally known as the *President Warfield,* the ship had seen action in the Normandy invasion and served as a troop ferry during the final months of World War II. Auctioned for scrap at the end of the war, it was purchased by agents of the **Haganah** and repaired in the Baltimore harbor in late 1946 and early 1947. In July 1947, the *President Warfield,* manned by a crew that included numerous American volunteers, took aboard more than 4,500 Holocaust survivors at a rendezvous point on the coast of France.

As the ship, now renamed the S.S. *Exodus,* sailed across the Mediterranean, it was trailed by a British warship and became the subject of international media attention. When the *Exodus* approached Palestine on July 18, it was intercepted by the British navy. Truncheon-wielding British soldiers charged aboard the *Exodus* and beat many of the passengers and crew, including American crewmate Bill Bernstein, who died of his injuries. More than 20,000 New Yorkers filled Madison Square Garden several weeks later for a memorial ceremony in Bernstein's honor.

International controversy over the *Exodus* intensified when the British, instead of deporting the refugees to nearby Cyprus as they had done in previous such cases, shipped them back to France. When the three shiploads of refugees reached Port de Bouc, however, all but a handful of the passengers refused to disembark, and the French authorities declined to compel them to do so. The ships remained there for more than three weeks, focusing embarrassing attention on Great Britain's harsh policy toward Jewish immigrants. On August 22, the British ordered the refugees sent to the British Zone of occupied Germany. Upon arrival at Hamburg, many of the *Exodus* passengers staged a sit-down strike and had to be dragged ashore by British troops. Others physically resisted disembarking and fought a two-hour pitched battle with the British soldiers. Media coverage of the struggle further galvanized international criticism of Great Britain's policies.

The passengers of the *Exodus* finally reached the Holy Land in late 1948, following the establishment of the State of Israel. *See also* ALIYA BET.

EZRA. Religious Zionist students established the Ezra movement in Germany in 1919. It held educational functions and summer camps, eventually creating its own Zionist training farm. Some Ezra members joined the **Mizrachi**-affiliated Bachad settlements in Palestine in the early 1930s. Others fled Germany after the rise of Nazism and joined Poalei Agudat Israel, the pro-Zionist splinter group of the *haredi* (ultra-Orthodox) **Agudat Israel** movement. In 1948, Ezra formally became part of Poalei Agudat Israel.

-F-

FAISAL-WEIZMANN AGREEMENT. Hoping to preempt Arab opposition to Jewish colonization of Palestine, Zionist leader **Chaim**

Weizmann initiated talks with the Emir Faisal, one of the most prominent Arab leaders of the day, in June 1918. Additional discussions between Faisal and Zionist leaders were held during the Paris Peace Conference of 1918–1919, and on January 3, 1919, Faisal and Weizmann
signed a formal accord.

The agreement called for "the closest possible collaboration in the development of the Arab State and Palestine" (Preamble); endorsed the
Balfour Declaration (Art. III); and specified that "all necessary measures shall be taken to encourage and stimulate immigration of Jews into
Palestine," while at the same time promising that "the Arab peasant and
tenant farmers shall be protected in their rights, and shall be assisted in
forwarding their economic development" (Art. IV). In a handwritten
addendum in Arabic, Faisal emphasized that his participation in the
agreement was conditional upon "the Arabs obtaining their independence" from Great Britain.

Zionist leaders hailed the accord, believing it would defuse Arab opposition to Zionism and reassure British officials who were concerned
about Arab reaction to Great Britain's support for a Jewish homeland.
But the Zionist leaders' joy was short-lived. From media interviews given
by Faisal in the aftermath of the agreement, it seems he regarded the accord as a means to pave the way for British acquiescence in the creation
of a vast Arab kingdom, of which Faisal would be the leader, which
would include only a Jewish province, not an independent Jewish state.
He expected world Jewry to finance the Jewish province and perhaps
provide financial assistance to the Arab kingdom as well. In an interview
with the French newspaper *Le Matin* on March 1, 1919, Faisal said he
had agreed to Jewish immigration into Palestine but would never accept
the establishment of a sovereign Jewish state there. In response to Jewish protests over that statement, Faisal telegrammed American Zionist
leaders that "We Arabs . . . look with the deepest sympathy on the Zionist movement." But he skirted the issue of Jewish statehood, remark-
ing only that "there is room in Syria [Arabs widely regarded Palestine
as southern Syria] for us both." Testifying in July 1919 before the **King-
Crane Commission**, a U.S. government body surveying conditions in
the Middle East, Faisal reiterated that he would assent to "a certain
amount of [Jewish] immigration" but that he opposed "the wider Zionist aspirations."

Faisal, who subsequently became leader of Syria and was later
crowned king of Iraq, never took any steps to implement the agreement
with Weizmann. At the 1929 hearings of the **Shaw Commission**, a Brit-

ish inquiry into that year's Palestinian Arab riots, the issue of the Faisal-Weizmann agreement was raised. Members of the Arab delegation to the Shaw hearings wrote to Faisal for confirmation that he had signed such an accord, to which the king's spokesman replied that Faisal had no recollection of the agreement.

FARBAND-LABOR ZIONIST ORDER. American Labor Zionists established the Farband-Labor Zionist Order, a New York–based fraternal aid society, in 1910. It provided its members with life insurance as well as a variety of Zionist cultural and educational activities. Its insurance program, which began with several hundred subscribers, grew to over 35,000 by 1979, when it withdrew from the insurance field. The Farband's Zionist activities, in conjunction with the main U.S. Labor Zionist group, **Poalei Zion**, included after-school education programs, summer camps, and fundraising for the **Histadrut** labor union. In 1975, the Farband merged with the **Labor Zionists/Poalei Zion** and American **Habonim** to become the Labor Zionist Alliance.

FEDERATION OF AMERICAN ZIONISTS. *See* ZIONIST ORGANIZATION OF AMERICA.

-G-

GALUT. *Galut* is a Hebrew term meaning "exile," or "dispersion," and refers to the Diaspora. Traditional Judaism emphasized a powerful negation of *Galut,* and this was a major theme in Jewish philosophy. *Galut* is to Zion what night is to day. *See also* ALIYA-YERIDA.

GENERAL ZIONISTS. After the emergence in the early 1900s of the first distinct political factions within the Zionist movement, **Mizrachi** (the Religious Zionists) and **Poalei Zion** (the Socialist Zionists), the majority of Zionists, who were not affiliated with either of those factions, came to be known as General Zionists. While loyal to the **Basle Program** and the broad principles of Zionism, the General Zionists lacked a specific ideology or platform until 1931, when an international conference of General Zionists was held, on the eve of the 17th **World Zionist Congress**. The conference produced a new, formal party, the World Union of General Zionists, and elected Galician Zionist leader Dr. Isaac Schwarzbart as its first president.

By 1935, two distinct factions had emerged within the World Union of General Zionists. The "General Zionists A," as they called themselves, sympathized with **Labor Zionism**'s economic positions and favored **Chaim Weizmann**'s cautious approach to relations with the British authorities. The "General Zionists B" were critical of socialist economic practices and preferred more forthright opposition to Great Britain's Palestine policy. The growing tensions within the General Zionist movement contributed to its steadily waning fortunes in Zionist elections during the 1930s.

At the 1946 World Zionist Congress, the General Zionists sought to inject new life into their movement, reorganizing themselves as the World Confederation of General Zionists and choosing the longtime American Zionist leader Dr. Israel Goldstein as their new president. The success of the **Zionist Organization of America (ZOA)** during the mid- and late 1940s, under the leadership of **Abba Hillel Silver**, was also a boon for the General Zionists, since Silver and his colleagues identified with General Zionism. At the 1946 Zionist Congress, a Silver-led ZOA delegation joined forces with General Zionist delegates from Palestine and **David Ben-Gurion**'s Mapai faction to defeat Weizmann's call for a more compromising approach to the British.

After the establishment of the State of Israel, the divisions within the General Zionist movement widened. The General Zionists A competed in the 1949 Knesset election as the Progressive Party, won five seats, and became part of the Labor-led governing coalition, while the "B" faction, running as the General Zionists, won seven and chose to remain in the opposition. The majority in the ZOA sympathized with the "B" faction and in 1950 issued a public statement expressing their support for it. That set off a long-running feud within the ZOA that in 1957 culminated in a minority faction breaking away from the ZOA and establishing the **American Jewish League for Israel** under the leadership of **Louis Lipsky**.

A first major step toward rapprochement between the General Zionists and the Progressives in Israel was taken in the early 1950s, when the General Zionists established their own faction within the **Histadrut**, thereby casting aside their previous policy of rejecting all cooperation with the socialist trade union. Reconciliation talks between the Progressives and the General Zionists in 1960–1961 concluded with their merger into the unified Liberal Party, which won seventeen seats in the 1961 Knesset elections. The rival **Diaspora** factions of the Progressives and the General Zionists, however, refused to unite.

By 1965, the Liberal Party had split in two, this time over a proposal to run for the Knesset jointly with **Menachem Begin**'s Herut Party. The majority supported the proposal, and the Liberals and Herut competed as the Gahal bloc. The minority, mostly those who had been affiliated with the Progressive Party, seceded from the Liberal Party and established their own Independent Liberal Party, which won five seats in the 1965 elections. After capturing four seats in the subsequent elections of 1969 and 1973, the Independent Liberals won just one seat in the 1977 vote and faded from the political map soon afterward. The Liberal Party, for its part, remained with Herut in the Gahal bloc and eventually disbanded as a separate party, fully merging into Gahal's successor, the Likud. *See also* ALIYA HADASHA.

GOLDMANN, NAHUM (1894–1982). Zionist diplomat Nahum Goldmann was born in Vishnevo, Lithuania, and raised in Frankfurt, Germany. Goldmann's parents were highly identified with Jewish activities, and he developed intense Zionist affinities as a youth. He studied law and philosophy at the University of Heidelberg from 1912 to 1914 and again in 1919–1920, when he received his doctorate in law. He visited Palestine in 1913. During World War I, Goldmann worked in the Jewish division of the German Foreign Ministry, and he attempted to gain Germany's support for the establishment of a Jewish state in Palestine.

During the 1920s, Goldmann co-founded a Zionist periodical in Heidelberg and participated in establishing a German-Jewish encyclopedia, which was never completed because of the Nazi rise to power. Many years later, in 1972, he saw his project realized when he played a pivotal role in the publication of the *Encyclopedia Judaica,* on whose board he served as honorary president.

Goldmann participated in many Zionist activities, including attendance at the 13th **Zionist Congress** and all subsequent congresses. He initially opposed **Chaim Weizmann**'s proposal to expand the **Jewish Agency** but ultimately accepted the majority decision. He was a supporter of the partition of Palestine, arguing that sovereignty was primary for a viable Jewish state. He helped develop the **Biltmore Program** in 1942.

Goldmann fled Germany in 1935 and, after a brief stay in Honduras, went to New York, where he represented the Jewish Agency. He was also very active in **Diaspora** Jewish communal affairs. In contrast to many Zionists who negated the Diaspora, he believed in the necessity of strengthening Diaspora communities, and in 1936 he helped organize the **World Jewish Congress**, serving as its first chairman. In 1949 he was named acting president and in 1953 its president, a position that he held for the remainder of his life.

With the approval of the Israeli government, Goldmann played a central role in negotiating German reparations to Holocaust survivors in 1951, a move that was bitterly opposed by **Menachem Begin** and the Herut Party. He helped establish and, from 1954–1959, served as chairman of the **Conference of Presidents of Major American Jewish Organizations**, and he founded the Memorial Foundation for Jewish Culture in 1964. Goldmann's involvement with the campaign on behalf of Soviet Jewry was a source of some controversy; his preference for "quiet diplomacy" was opposed by more activist elements in the American Jewish community.

Goldmann became a citizen of Israel in 1962 but did not actually move there. Rather, he lived in Switzerland and made frequent trips to Israel. Goldmann's increasing criticism of Israeli foreign policy, Israeli attitudes toward the Diaspora, and what he viewed as Israel's militarism put him at odds with the Israeli government and many Diaspora Jewish leaders. He was the center of a bitter controversy in 1970, when rumors spread of a possible meeting between himself and Egyptian leader Gamal Abdul Nasser. The Israeli government strongly disapproved of the meeting, and it never took place.

GORDON, AHARON DAVID (1856–1922). Zionist philosopher A. D. Gordon was born in Podolia, Russia, in 1856 to an Orthodox family. As a young man, he managed a farm but later left farming and became a clerk. Although a member of **Hovevei Zion**, it was not until he was forty-seven years of age that Gordon decided to go on *aliya*.

In **Eretz Israel**, he returned to the farming life, working in various agricultural settlements and finally joining Kibbutz Degania in the Galilee. He developed the notion of "the religion of labor," according to which the physical working of the land is the ultimate religious value; it is a religious experience resulting in the redemption both of the individual directly involved and also of the Jewish people. His thought as well as his own personal example became a model for the **Labor Zionist** movement.

GORDONIA. A Zionist youth movement established in Galicia in 1923, Gordonia was based on the ideology of the Zionist philosopher **Aharon David Gordon**. His mystical "religion of labor," rooted partly in Russian populism, regarded working the soil of Palestine as the means for the individual Jew to experience his or her cosmic purpose.

Gordonia members idolized the communal-agricultural lifestyle and the movement educated its members to personally settle in kibbutzim, particularly those affiliated with its Hever Hakevutzot-Igud Gordonia (created in 1933). The arrival of European Gordonia activists in Palestine in the 1930s provided an important boost of morale and manpower for Degania and other kibbutzim that had been stagnating.

In 1945 Gordonia joined with a faction of a like-minded kibbutz-oriented group, Hamahanot Ha'olim, to establish Hatenua Hameuhedet. That, in turn, merged in 1959 with another **Socialist Zionist** youth movement, Hanoar Ha'oved, to form the official youth wing of the **Histadrut**, Hanoar Haleumi Ha'oved Vehalomed. Overseas branches of Gordonia eventually became part of **Habonim**, the Labor Zionist youth movement. *See also* SOCIALIST ZIONISM.

GREATER ACTIONS COMMITTEE. *See* ZIONIST GENERAL COUNCIL.

GREENBERG, HAYIM (1889–1953). American **Labor Zionist** leader Hayim Greenberg was born in Dodoreshti, Bessarabia. He was self-educated in both Hebrew and Russian. Greenberg acquired extensive knowledge of both languages and wrote prolifically on political subjects. He was also a dynamic orator in Yiddish, Hebrew, and Russian, and this became the source of his livelihood as a young man. Greenberg joined the Zionist movement as a teen and in 1906 was a delegate to a conference of Russian Zionists. In 1917 he was one of the leaders of Tarbut, an organization devoted to promoting Hebrew culture, and he edited a Hebrew literary magazine. He taught Jewish literature briefly at the University of Kharkov. Greenberg's Zionist activity led to his arrest by the Bolshevik authorities on a number of occasions, and in 1921 he went to Kishinev and then Berlin, where he was an editor of *Haolam* ("The World"), the Hebrew weekly of the Zionist Organization, and also became one of the leaders of **Hapoel Hatzair**.

Greenberg went to the United States in 1924 on behalf of Tarbut and became editor of the Labor Zionist's Yiddish-language periodical. In 1934, he became editor of the Labor Zionist monthly, *The Jewish Frontier,* as well as a permanent member of the Central Committee of the Labor Zionist Organization of America. Greenberg played a central role in the merger of Zeirei Zion and Poalei Zion. As the most prominent leader of U.S. Labor Zionism, he represented the movement in the **American Zionist Emergency Council** and played an active role in its deliberations during World War II. In his writings as well as in his political activity, he sought a synthesis between Zionism, socialism, and universalism. Greenberg subsequently became even more widely known for his essay "Bankrupt," published in *Der Yiddisher Kempfer* in 1943, which sharply criticized the American Jewish leadership's failure to actively protest the Allies' apathetic response to the Holocaust.

Greenberg was elected to the **Jewish Agency** Executive at the 22nd **Zionist Congress** in 1946 and was appointed to direct the Department of Education and Culture, a position he held for the remainder of his lifetime. During his tenure, he helped gain the support of a number of South American delegations to the United Nations for the establishment of the State of Israel, and he emphasized and encouraged the spread of Hebrew language and literature as well as strong Israel–Diaspora relations.

GRUENBAUM, YITZHAK (1879–1970). General Zionist leader Yitzhak Gruenbaum was born in Warsaw and raised in Plonsk, Poland. Gruenbaum was active in the Zionist movement as a youth. After completing high school, during which time he joined the movement, he began studying medicine, but in 1904 he switched to law. He became a Zionist activist and publicist at that time, writing in Hebrew and Yiddish periodicals. Gruenbaum was a delegate to the Seventh **Zionist Congress** in 1905 and to each subsequent Zionist Congress during his lifetime. He edited a number of newspapers, including the Hebrew-language *Hazefirah.* He was the spokesman for much of Polish Jewry between the two world wars.

Gruenbaum was the leader of the **Radical Zionists,** known in Poland as Al Hamishmar, and opposed the creation and then the expansion of the **Jewish Agency**. He was also a staunch advocate of the secularization of Jewish life and was active in Tarbut, the organization devoted to promoting Hebrew culture in Poland. Gruenbaum organized the "national minorities bloc" in the Polish elections of 1922, which resulted in the national minorities, including Jews, gaining considerable representation.

Gruenbaum moved to Paris in 1932 and in 1933 was elected to the Jewish Agency Executive at the Zionist Congress, after which he went on *aliya.* He subsequently held a number of major administrative positions in the Jewish Agency, including head of the Aliya Department from 1933 to 1935, head of the Absorption and Labor Departments from 1935 to 1948, one of the heads of the Organization Department from 1935 to 1946, treasurer of the Jewish Agency from 1949 to 1950, and attorney general, a position designed to ensure the honesty of the Jewish Agency's employees and administrators, from 1950 to 1951. As chairman of the Jewish Agency's Rescue Committee during the Holocaust years,

Gruenbaum was a leading proponent of pressuring the Allies to bomb Auschwitz and other death camps, and he helped persuade the agency's leaders in London, **Chaim Weizmann** and **Moshe Sharett**, to lobby the British government to bomb the camps. He was among the leaders of the Jewish Agency who were arrested by the British in 1946. From 1935 to 1948 he was also head of Mosad Bialik, a major publisher.

During the period of establishment of the State of Israel, Gruenbaum was a member of the People's Administration, in charge of internal affairs; was one of those who signed the Declaration of Independence; and served as minister of the interior in the Provisional Government in 1948–1949. In the latter capacity, he organized and administered the first elections to the Knesset. Ironically, he ran on his own, on the "Yitzhak Gruenbaum List," but did not gain sufficient votes to win even one seat. Although he retired from politics after that defeat, he remained active in Zionist activity, especially as a journalist and thinker. Gruenbaum became a forceful spokesman for the more extreme left faction of **Socialist Zionism**, which won him impassioned opponents as well as admirers.

GUSH EMUNIM. Gush Emunim, or the "Bloc of the Faithful," is the movement for the Jewish settlement under Israeli sovereignty of Judea and Samaria/the West Bank, which traditionally were important parts of **Eretz Israel**. The origins of Gush Emunim can be traced to the mystical Religious Zionist teachings of Rabbi Zvi Yehuda Kook. Even before the Six-Day War of 1967, Kook, the son and sole male heir of the first chief rabbi in Eretz Israel, interpreted the founding of Israel in messianic terms and emphasized the inherent holiness and wholeness of Eretz Israel. Following that war, Kook and his followers proclaimed that halakhah, Jewish religious law, prohibits Israel's relinquishing any of the newly captured territory because it is all part of Eretz Israel. After the Yom Kippur War of October 1973, fearing that Israel might cede parts of the territories, a group of Kook's followers established Gush Emunim in 1974, initially as a pressure group within the National Religious Party and then as an autonomous settlement movement.

From its inception until 1977, Gush Emunim was a movement that frequently utilized characteristic techniques of nonviolent protest and demonstration in its violation of government orders and its creation of illegal settlements. The movement's efforts had the overt support of a large segment of the secular Israeli population and also the covert support of some key government and military personnel, and many of the settlements finally received government approval.

The years 1977–1982 were a period of sharp conflicting tensions for the movement. On the one hand, with the victory of **Menachem Begin** and his Likud party in 1977, Gush Emunim had the blessings of the prime minister and the ruling party, and Begin used the movement to further his own settlement objectives. On the other hand, that very same Begin signed the Camp David peace accords with Anwar Sadat and promised to cede all of the Sinai peninsula, including the Israeli settlements there. Many Gush Emunim activists participated in the protest movement to prevent the withdrawal from the Sinai. That effort was a turning point, and with its failure, coupled with strong government support of the settlement of Judea and Samaria/the West Bank, Gush Emunim underwent a process of what sociologists, following Max Weber, refer to as "the routinization of charisma." Gush Emunim was transformed from a predominantly ideological movement to a much more institutionalized, traditional settlement movement. One manifestation of this process was in the fact that until 1984, there was no official leadership of the movement, and the widely recognized unofficial leader was the ideologue Rabbi Moshe Levinger, disciple of Zvi Yehuda Kook and founder of Kiryat Arba and the reestablished Jewish community in Hebron. In 1984, however, the movement decided to officially appoint an executive secretary and spokesperson, and the occupant of that position is widely perceived as the formal head of the organization.

Just as the overt ideological leadership was receding, the movement was cast into ideological turmoil and split over the arrest, in 1984, and the subsequent conviction of the Jewish terrorist underground. Some within the movement justified the activities of the underground as necessary because the government had not been sufficiently forceful in protecting Jewish lives and rights in the territories, whereas others denounced the underground's actions as beyond the limits of legitimate protest.

Despite its institutionalization, Gush Emunim remains a movement rather than an organization, and there are no official members. It has varying degrees of support among the Jewish population of Israel, ranging from the staunch opposition of supporters of the **Peace Now** movement to the strong support of the majority of Jewish residents in the territories. There is also a range of positions and views among those who consider themselves affiliates, and these are frequently reflected in the movement's monthly magazine, *Nekudah* ("Point").

The impact of the movement goes far beyond its size. Its ideology, through which it portrays itself as one of the very few true contemporary manifestations of classical Zionism-in-operation, and its actions during the critical decade of 1974–1984, have created "facts" and are seen by many as playing a determining role in Israeli domestic and foreign policy as well as in broader international politics. The aspirations of Gush Emunim were widely respected by the Jewish public, especially as long as Arab intransigence made the return of the territories a far-off theoretical possibility.

When peace agreements with Egypt (1977) and the Palestine Liberation Organization (1993) put the return of the administered territories onto the actual political agenda, Gush Emunim found itself in active opposition to the policies of the Israeli government.

In addition, after the Camp David accords, there were some nationalist rabbis who suggested that religious soldiers in the Israel Defense Forces should refuse, on religious grounds, to comply with military orders to evacuate land in the territories. This evoked a strong backlash that further tarnished the image of Gush Emunim, despite the fact that the movement itself never sanctioned such a rabbinic decree.

-H-

HA'AM, AHAD (Pen name of Asher Ginzberg) (1856–1927). Zionist philosopher Asher Ginzberg, later known as Ahad Ha'am, was born in Skvira in the Ukraine, to a wealthy Hasidic merchant. He acquired higher Jewish learning from a private tutor. Exposed to the secular literature of the *Haskala,* the Jewish Enlightenment, Ha'am abandoned his religious lifestyle while remaining deeply committed to the Jewish people and Jewish culture. He settled in Odessa in 1884 and there was attracted to **Hibbat Zion**. He joined the movement, which was led by **Leo Pinsker**, but then wrote an essay highly critical of its settlement activities and advocated, instead, educational activities aimed at the cultural revival of the Jewish people. Ha'am founded the secret order of **Bnei Moshe**, an elitist group that sought to revive the Hebrew language and Jewish culture, and for which Ha'am wrote numerous essays on these subjects.

After visiting **Eretz Israel** in 1891, and again in 1893, Ha'am was highly critical of the Zionist movement's emphasis on land purchase and cultivation, arguing instead for cultural work as the priority. Following the First **Zionist Congress**, he criticized **Theodor Herzl**—regarding him as basically alienated from Jewish life—and Political Zionism, which he viewed as self-defeating. Ha'am warned that its inevitable failure would be deeply disillusioning. Instead, he advocated Eretz Israel as a spiritual or cultural center in which a new national Jewish identity rooted in Jewish values would be created and which would thereby serve to strengthen Jewish life in the **Diaspora**.

After the Sixth Zionist Congress, Ha'am strongly denounced the **Uganda Plan** as further evidence of Political Zionism's detachment from Jewish values. He moved to London in 1907, where he earned his livelihood as the agent for the Wissotzky Tea Company. Despite his differences with Herzl and the **World Zionist Organization**, Ha'am remained committed to and active on behalf of his notion of **Cultural Zionism**. In 1917, he supported the **Balfour Declaration** but urged greater consideration of the national rights of Arabs in Palestine. He immigrated to Eretz Israel in 1922 and spent the remainder of his life in Tel Aviv.

HA'AVARA. To circumvent Nazi Germany's strict limits on how much currency German Jewish emigrants could take with them, the Anglo-Palestine Bank negotiated the Ha'avara, or transfer, agreement with the German authorities in August 1933. The arrangement allowed Jewish funds in blocked German accounts to be used to pay for German exports to Palestine.

The **Revisionist Zionists** and many American Zionists opposed Ha'avara because it breached the international Jewish boycott of German products. Nevertheless, Ha'avara was approved by the 19th **Zionist Congress** (1935) and the Anglo-Palestine Bank gave the **Jewish Agency** full control of the program. Most of the 50,000 German Jews who immigrated to Palestine during 1933–1939 benefited from the Ha'avara arrangements, and the products imported from Germany aided in many Palestine development projects. The Ha'avara deal was terminated by the Germans upon the outbreak of World War II in September 1939.

HABONIM. Habonim (Hebrew for "The Builders"), the international youth movement of the **Labor Zionist** movement, became established at different times in different countries. It was founded in London, Great Britain, in 1928. In Germany five years later, two youth organizations, Kadimah and Berit Ha'olim, merged to become the local Habonim. It was established in North America in 1935. Habonim's main activity in the **Diaspora** consisted of Hebrew education and *hachshara*, preparatory programs for *aliya* and **kibbutz** life.

In 1958 the various Habonim organizations, as well as other Labor Zionist youth groups, merged to form Ihud Habonim. Headquartered in

Israel, it became the largest Labor Zionist youth movement, with more than 20,000 members in the 1960s. Its branches in many Diaspora communities run summer camps and other educational and community service programs, with particular emphasis on Habonim's primary values of Zionism, Judaism, and social justice that entails socialism. *See also* BERIT HA'OLIM; SOCIALIST ZIONISM.

HACHSHARA. A Hebrew word meaning "preparation," *hachshara* is a term adopted by many Zionist movements, especially youth movements, that incorporated specific programs that were viewed as training and anticipatory socialization for life in Eretz Israel in general, and especially **kibbutz** life. Zionist youth movements in the **Diaspora** would frequently hold summer camp programs for *hachshara,* in which the program would attempt to replicate, to the degree feasible, life in a kibbutz. *See also* LABOR ZIONISM; SOCIALIST ZIONISM.

HADASSAH. What began in the 1890s as a handful of women's Zionist study groups in New York and elsewhere, was by 1912–1913 transformed into Hadassah, the first national women's Zionist organization, under the leadership of **Henrietta Szold**.

Szold, a Zionist activist and educator from Baltimore, visited Palestine in 1909–1910 and was struck by the country's dismal health conditions, particularly those affecting children. Szold returned to the United States determined to organize American Jewish women to sponsor health-improvement programs in the Holy Land. The first small team of Hadassah nurses reached Jerusalem in 1913, where they set up a health station to provide maternity care and treat trachoma cases. It lasted until 1915. A much larger team of Hadassah doctors and nurses comprised the **American Zionist Medical Unit**, which, beginning in 1918, set up hospitals and clinics in many of Palestine's major cities.

Hadassah's health programs struck a responsive chord among American Jewish women, offering them a practical way to directly assist the development of the *yishuv*. Hadassah's membership rolls expanded quickly, as did its fundraising capabilities, enabling the organization to sponsor an ever-growing network of hospitals, infant health-care centers, playgrounds, and the like.

Until the late 1920s, Hadassah functioned as the autonomous women's division of the **Zionist Organization of America (ZOA)**. Differences with the ZOA leadership over administrative and financial practices, as well as the ZOA's reluctance to grant the women a greater say in the organization's decision-making process, led to the secession of Hadassah from the ZOA.

After the rise of Hitler in 1933, there were growing calls from the Hadassah membership for the organization to move away from its exclusive focus on medical projects in Palestine and to actively assist Jews in Nazi Germany. Hadassah president Rose Jacobs was dispatched to Palestine in 1935 to explore possible new directions for Hadassah activity there. Jacobs quickly became enamored of **Youth Aliya**, a project under the supervision of Henrietta Szold (who had settled in Palestine in 1920), which facilitated the emigration of young German Jews to the Holy Land. Hadassah soon adopted Youth Aliya, a decision that proved both a boon for fundraising and a source of inspiration for Hadassah activists during the Nazi era.

After its secession from the ZOA, Hadassah assumed an increasingly active role in the **World Zionist Organization** and Palestine-related political affairs. Hadassah opposed the British **Peel Commission**'s 1937 Palestine partition plan, protesting the small size of the territory allotted to the proposed Jewish state. Hadassah's Rose Jacobs was the only woman delegate to the **St. James Conference** in 1939, at which British, Arab, and Zionist leaders sought, unsuccessfully, to resolve the Palestine conflict.

In the wake of Palestinian Arab rioting and British restrictions on Jewish immigration in the late 1930s, Hadassah established a Committee for the Study of Arab–Jewish Relations, with Jacobs as its chair. It marked the first time that an American Zionist organization had taken an official interest in the problem of Arab–Jewish relations in Palestine. The committee, which operated until 1943, held private discussions on the subject and met with American experts on the Middle East and Zionist leaders from Palestine to discuss ways to alleviate Arab–Jewish tension.

Hadassah established a major medical center adjacent to the **Hebrew University** campus on Mount Scopus, Jerusalem, in 1939. The Allies used it for medical research and care during World War II. Dr. Haim Yassky, Hadassah's director in Palestine, and seventy-four other Hadassah staff members and Hebrew University faculty and staff members, were massacred when Arabs ambushed a Hadassah convoy heading to Mount Scopus in April 1948. The center ceased to function shortly thereafter.

Mount Scopus came under United Nations supervision as a result of the 1948 war and was inaccessible to Israelis during the Jordanian occupation of the surrounding parts of eastern Jerusalem during 1948–1967. Cut off from Mount Scopus, Hadassah established a major new hospital in Jerusalem's Ein Karem neighborhood in 1961, as well as a medical school in conjunction with Hebrew University. After Jerusalem was reunited in the Six-Day War, Hadassah rebuilt and expanded its facilities on Mount Scopus.

Hadassah currently boasts the largest membership of any American Jewish organization. It sponsors an array of educational and cultural programs related to Israel, encourages young American Jews to experience Israel via its Young Judea youth movement, and raises funds to support its medical facilities in Israel and its work with the **Jewish Agency** and Youth Aliya in assisting the absorption of new immigrants.

HAGANAH. Palestine's primary Jewish self-defense militia, the Haganah (Hebrew for "defense"), had its origins in the two hundred–member armed force organized by Zionist leaders **Ze'ev Jabotinsky** and **Pinhas Rutenberg** to protect Jerusalem's Jewish community against Palestinian Arab mob attacks in 1920. Many of the members had served in the **Jewish Legion**. Jabotinsky and a number of his men were sentenced to long prison terms for illegally bearing arms during the 1920 disturbances, but an international outcry prompted the British Mandate authorities to pardon them shortly afterward.

Hampered by a lack of financial resources and a meager arsenal of weapons, the Haganah was unprepared for the massive Palestinian Arab violence of 1929 and played only a modest role in combating the attackers. In the aftermath of the 1929 riots, the *yishuv* leadership invested substantial resources to significantly expand the Haganah, establish secret weapons-manufacturing sites, and develop young military leaders to turn the Haganah into the full-fledged military arm of the *yishuv* and the nucleus of the army of the future Jewish state.

While the Haganah was controlled by the **Labor Zionist**–dominated **Jewish Agency**, a second, smaller militia, known as Haganah Bet and also as the **Irgun Zvai Leumi** (National Military Organization), had been created in 1931 with the backing of the Revisionists, the **Mizrachi Religious Zionists**, and the **General Zionists**. When Palestinian Arab violence erupted anew in 1936, the Haganah opted for a policy called *havlaga*, or "restraint," which meant defending Jewish towns under attack but refraining from offensive strikes against Arab targets. The *havlaga* policy caused a split in the Irgun; a minority of its members merged with the Haganah in early 1937, while the majority opted to remain an independent force and launched their own counterterrorism actions against Arab targets.

The scope and duration of Palestinian Arab violence in the late 1930s, much of which was aimed at the British, forced the British Mandate authorities to cooperate with the Haganah despite the fact that the Jewish militia was technically illegal. The British established a 1,000-man Jewish police force in 1937 that was, in effect, controlled by the Haganah. It was enlarged to over 20,000 officers by 1939, many of whom were Haganah members who subsequently put their training and weapons at the disposal of the Jewish military. The Mandatory's Special Night Squads, consisting of Jewish fighters under the command of British captain Orde Wingate, carried out raids against Arab terrorists in 1938–1939 and provided the nucleus of the Haganah's future mobile strike force, the **Palmach**.

During World War II, many Haganah members volunteered to serve in the British Army. Some also served in the **Jewish Brigade**, the all-Jewish unit established by the English near the end of the war. Thirty-two Haganah members parachuted into Nazi-occupied Europe in 1944 on a variety of Allied missions.

Jewish Agency and Haganah leaders sought to persuade the Irgun to suspend the armed revolt against the British that the militants had launched in early 1944. The Jewish Agency and Haganah feared that anti-British violence would provoke the British to adopt an even more hostile attitude toward Zionism. When the Irgun persisted, the Haganah decided to collaborate with the British against the rebels. From late 1944 until mid-1945, the Haganah kidnapped members of the Irgun and its splinter, the **Lehi (Lohamei Herut Israel,** or **Stern Group)**, forcibly extracted information from them and transferred them to the British for imprisonment. This period, known as "The Season," brought the *yishuv* to the brink of civil war and aroused considerable public criticism of the Jewish Agency and Haganah.

The adoption of a sharply anti-Zionist policy by Great Britain's new Labour Party government, which came to power in July 1945, prompted the agency to abandon its war against the rebels and instead join their fight against the British. The United Hebrew Resistance, under a joint Haganah-Irgun-Lehi command, carried out attacks against British military and police targets throughout Palestine from the autumn of 1945 until the summer of 1946. A severe crackdown by the British, including the arrests of Jewish Agency leaders and thousands of activists and sympathizers on what came to be known as the "Black Saturday" of June 29, convinced the agency and Haganah to suspend their participation in the anti-British revolt.

During 1946–1947, the Haganah concentrated on smuggling tens of thousands of European Holocaust survivors to Palestine in defiance of British immigration restrictions. Although some of the shiploads of immigrants, such as the famous **S.S.** *Exodus,* were intercepted, their capture and forcible return to European or Cypriot detention camps outraged world opinion and increased pressure on the British to leave Palestine. At the same time, the Haganah also focused on improving its military capabilities and expanding its weapons arsenal, in anticipation of war with the Arabs in response to a declaration of Jewish statehood.

Violent Arab opposition to the prospect of a Jewish state intensified after the United Nations vote in November 1947, and the Haganah assumed the role of the de-facto army of the *yishuv,* battling the Arabs for control of towns and strategic sites throughout the country. The Haganah officially disbanded on May 31, 1948. Its leadership and rank and file comprised the bulk of the new Israel Defense Forces, successfully fought off the invading Arab armies, and secured the establishment of Israel.

HALUKA. *Haluka* (Hebrew for "distribution") was the name given to the traditional system of collecting and distributing donations from **Diaspora** Jewish communities to sustain impoverished Torah scholars in **Eretz Israel**.

As long ago as the Second Temple period, there existed a widespread practice in Diaspora communities of providing financial assistance to Jews living in the Holy Land. The practice was a means for those not yet willing or able to personally fulfill the biblical commandment of living in Eretz Israel to assist those who were. Throughout the centuries, emissaries, some of them prominent Talmudic scholars, were regularly sent from Palestine to the Diaspora to solicit donations. There was periodic friction between the Ashkenazi and Sephardi communities in Eretz Israel over the proportion of funds distributed to their respective followers.

In the eyes of the Zionist movement, the term *haluka* came to symbolize the old *yishuv* ways that Zionism strove to replace with a modern polity based on the principles of physical labor and economic self-sufficiency. With the emergence of the twentieth-century "new *yishuv,*" the segment of Palestine Jewry supported by *haluka* contributions was reduced to a tiny minority.

HALUTZ. *Halutz,* or "pioneer," is the Hebrew term used to refer to a young Zionist who immigrated to Palestine, especially during the late 1800s and early 1900s, to help develop the Jewish homeland through manual labor, most often involving agriculture. Although the *halutzim* constituted only a small minority of Palestine's growing Jewish population, the *halutz* image quickly became a staple of Zionist literature, art, and films, as the ideal to which young **Diaspora** Zionists should aspire. It glorified forsaking physical comforts and white-collar professions, in favor of a life of difficult physical toil and selfless devotion to the Zionist cause.

In many Zionist circles, *halutziyut,* "pioneering," was seen as a healthy corrective to the ghetto lifestyle, as well as an antidote to stereotypes of Jews as bookish and weaklings. Zionists also took special pride in the pioneers' willingness to engage in armed self-defense, in stark contrast with the traditional phenomenon of helpless Diaspora Jews being victimized by pogromists. *See also* LABOR ZIONISM; SOCIALIST ZIONISM.

HANOAR HALEUMI HA'OVED VEHALOMED. The **Revisionist Zionist** movement established Hanoar Haleumi Ha'oved Vehalomed (The Working and Studying Nationalist Youth) in 1949. Its branches throughout Israel sponsor educational and cultural activities.

HANOAR HATZIONI. Representatives of Zionist youth movements in a number of European countries met in Lvov, Poland, in 1931 to unite as Hanoar Hatzioni (The Zionist Youth). Emphasizing the values of **kibbutz** life, the movement encouraged its members to settle in Palestine. It established a number of kibbutzim, including En Hashelosha, Hasolelim, Kfar Glickson, Mei Ami, Nitzanim, Tel Yitzhak, and Usha, as well as youth villages to provide education for new immigrants. Hanoar Hatzioni was traditionally associated with the now-defunct Independent Liberal Party.

HAPOEL HATZAIR. The non-Marxist Socialist Zionist organization Hapoel Hatzair was founded in late 1905 by ten young people, four of them from Plonsk, Poland, who had come to **Eretz Israel** as part of the **Second Aliya.** By February 1906, it had grown to ninety members, and the following year it founded a newspaper by the same name, *Hapoel Hatzair.* Hapoel Hatzair was committed to the growth of Jewish labor and the Hebrew language, which its members viewed as prerequisites for the realization of Zionism. The organization's ideological father was **Aharon David Gordon,** a radical who believed in the spiritual value of physical labor, the "Religion of Labor" as he called it, and the establishment of a new Jewish, socially just society. It promoted the notion of **Practical Zionism,** that is, involvement in practical work in Eretz Israel. Although some of its members joined with some **Poalei Zion** members and others to form Ahdut Ha'avoda in February 1919, Poalei Zion itself refused to join because of Ahdut Ha'avoda's adherence to Marxist notions, especially its emphasis on class struggle. Subsequently, however, there was a decline in the emphasis on the class struggle in Ahdut Ha'avoda, and in 1930 Hapoel Hatzair and Ahdut Ha'avoda merged and became Mapai (Mifleget Poalei Eretz Israel). *See also* LABOR ZIONISM; SOCIALIST ZIONISM.

HASHOMER. Hashomer (Hebrew for "The Guardian"), the first Jewish self-defense militia in modern Palestine, was organized in 1909 by activists of the **Second Aliya** as an outgrowth of the quasi-military Bar Giora group that had been secretly established in Palestine two years earlier. Many of the Hashomer members had recently been involved in Jewish self-defense groups that fought against pogromists in Russia. Hashomer began as a regional defense organization for Jewish communities in the Galilee, each of which helped defray the group's expenses. It later branched out to provide protection to Jews in Hadera, Rehovot, Rishon le-Zion, Be'er Ya'akov, and other towns.

In 1913 Hashomer established its own settlement, Tel Adashim; it also founded Kfar Giladi in 1916 and Tel Hai in 1918. After the creation of the **Haganah** in 1920, Hashomer gradually disbanded, although small groups of Hashomer activists refused to merge with the **Haganah** and maintained local, independent defense groups until the late 1920s.

In addition to protecting Jewish communities against terrorists and thieves, Hashomer sought to instill in the Palestinian Arabs a respect for the ability of the newly emerging *yishuv* to defend itself. The Shomrim, Guardians, who never numbered more than a hundred, excelled in marksmanship and horseback riding and were often referred to by local Arabs as Moscoby, or "Russians," a term connoting courage and hunting skills. Hashomer's exploits were featured prominently in the **Diaspora** Jewish press, where its efforts to forge an image of a new, fighting Jew became a source of pride and inspiration to young Zionists.

HASHOMER HADATI. The American **Religious Zionist** youth organization Hashomer Hadati was founded in 1934. It conducted seminars, summer camps, and programs that prepared participants for *aliya,* immigration to Israel (*hachshara*). It subsequently transformed and became part of the international **Bnei Akiva** movement. *See also* MIZRACHI.

HASHOMER HATZAIR. Zionist youth organizations in Poland and Galicia united in 1913 under the name Hashomer Hatzair, or "Young Guardian," after the Palestine self-defense militia Hashomer. The mystical and romantic themes of the early twentieth-century German youth movement exerted considerable influence upon the founders of Hashomer Hatzair. Emphasizing the values of nature, pioneering, and settlement on **kibbutzim** in Palestine, Hashomer Hatzair dispatched its first group of settlers to **Eretz Israel** in 1919. By the time of the first international Hashomer Hatzair conference in Danzig in 1924, the movement had over 10,000 members.

During the late 1920s and early 1930s, Hashomer Hatzair formulated a distinct Marxist-Zionist ideology to which it would closely adhere in the decades to follow. Many of its leaders referred to the Soviet Union as their "second homeland" and envisioned a socialist Palestine working side by side with the Union of Soviet Socialist Republics to bring about a global workers' revolution. Hashomer Hatzair grew rapidly in the 1930s, expanding its membership to some 70,000 worldwide and establishing branches in the United States and South Africa, in addition to chapters throughout both Western and Eastern Europe. Recruits underwent extensive agricultural and ideological training on special Hashomer Hatzair farms in the **Diaspora** before immigrating to Palestine. There, the movement was also rapidly growing, from four kibbutzim in 1927 to thirty-nine on the eve of World War II.

Many members of the movement who had intended to settle in Palestine were trapped in Europe when war erupted and perished in the Holocaust. Some of them played a prominent role in the Warsaw Ghetto revolt and other Jewish armed rebellions against the Nazis, and many joined anti-Nazi partisan units. After the war, Hashomer Hatzair branches were reestablished in many countries, although on a smaller scale than previously.

Prior to 1948, Hashomer Hatzair favored the creation of a binational Arab-Jewish state in Palestine, rather than a specifically Jewish state. The credibility of the binationalist position was undermined, however, by the fact that even the Arabs rejected it, because it included provisions for substantial Jewish immigration to Palestine. As a result, Hashomer Hatzair was somewhat marginalized and exercised little influence on the political decision-making of the *yishuv* and the Zionist movement. In early 1948, Hashomer Hatzair joined with other left-wing political factions to establish Mapam, a **Socialist Zionist** party to the left of Labor.

Hashomer Hatzair remains active today on the Israeli scene, primarily as an educational movement. Members from the Diaspora spend periods of time working on the movement's kibbutzim, and small numbers settle there permanently. *See also* LABOR ZIONISM.

HATIKVAH. A stirring song about "the Jewish soul yearning" for the Land of Israel, "Hatikvah" ("The Hope") was composed by the Hebrew poet Naftali Hertz Imber, either in Romania in 1878 or, by some accounts, in 1882, when Imber was living in Rishon le-Zion. Comparable tunes have been located in the folk repertoire of Romania, Germany, Poland, Czechoslovakia, and among Sephardic Jews, leaving unsettled the question of the precise origins of "Hatikvah."

"Hatikvah" quickly gained popularity among the early settlers in Palestine during the 1880s and spread to Zionist groups in Europe during the 1890s, prior to the First **Zionist Congress**. The singing of "Hatikvah" became an emotion-laden staple of the Zionist Congresses, with enthusiastic delegates sometimes singing it over and over again.

The lyrics underwent slight modification over the years, while retaining their basic theme of Jews never relinquishing the hope of returning to **Eretz Israel**. Shortly after the establishment of Israel, "Hatikvah" was adopted as the official national anthem of the Jewish state. *See* APPENDIX 2.

HATZOFIM. Hatzofim ("The Scouts"), a Zionist version of the international scouting movement, was established in Palestine in 1919. It combined the ideology and symbols of scouting with the Zionist ideals of pioneering, self-reliance, and attachment to **Eretz Israel**. Since 1924, it has been associated with Young Judea, the youth movement of the American Zionist women's organization **Hadassah**. After the establishment of Israel, Hatzofim joined the world scouting movement. Later, in 1957, the Israeli girl scouts joined the World Girl Scout Federation.

HAVLAGA. The Hebrew term for "restraint," *havlaga* was the name that the **Haganah**, the **Labor Zionist** militia in Mandatory Palestine, gave to its strategy for responding to the Palestinian Arab violence that erupted in 1936. In practice, *havlaga* meant defending Jewish towns that were under attack but refraining from offensive strikes against Arab targets. The **Irgun Zvai Leumi (IZL)**, the Revisionist-aligned military force, denounced *havlaga* as a policy of weakness that would encourage Arab violence. This caused a split in the **Irgun**—a minority of its members merged with the Haganah in early 1937, while the majority opted to remain an independent force and launched their own counterterrorism actions against Arab targets.

As the Arab violence persisted, the Haganah loosened its *havlaga* policy. In 1938, it permitted the British military officer Charles Orde Wingate, a fervent **Christian Zionist**, to organize Special Night

Squads—mobile Haganah units that went on the offensive by launching attacks on Arab targets under the cover of darkness. Wingate's squads dealt a blow to the Arab terrorists and boosted the morale of the *yishuv*.

HAYCRAFT COMMISSION. Palestinian Arab rioters, including uniformed Arab members of the Palestine police force, attacked Jews in the city of Jaffa in May 1921, killing 47 and wounding 146. A number of Jewish women were raped, and Jewish shops in the city were looted. The British high commissioner for Palestine, Herbert Samuel, appointed Palestine's chief justice, Sir Thomas W. Haycraft, to head a commission of inquiry into the violence.

The final report of the Haycraft Commission, released in October 1921, criticized the Arabs' use of violence and confirmed that Arab policemen were "in some cases leaders of or participators in violence." But the report also charged that a May Day rally by Jewish Marxists had provoked the riots, and it stressed that "the fundamental cause" of the violence was Arab concern over Jewish immigration and colonization and British support for Zionism. Haycraft also concluded that the **World Zionist Organization** had been "a contributory cause of the disturbances" because it had "exercised an exacerbating rather than a conciliatory influence on the Arab population of Palestine."

High Commissioner Samuel used the Haycraft report as justification for his shift, already under way, to a more pro-Arab policy in Palestine. Samuel's actions included the first-ever restrictions on Jewish immigration as well as offers to allow the Arabs greater say in running the country, through participation in a Palestine legislative council. Zionist leaders were strongly critical of Haycraft's attempt to blame Zionism, and Great Britain's support for Zionism, as the cause of the violence. **Chaim Weizmann** decried the emphasis on blaming the Zionists as an indication of "a mentality which is worse than that of Russian officials in the Czarist regime," while **Ze'ev Jabotinsky** called on the British to disarm Arab members of the Palestine police force.

HAZOFIM. Disappointed by the 1926 decision of the German-Jewish youth movement **Kadimah** to devote greater attention to **Diaspora** concerns rather than to Zionism, young Berlin Zionists seceded from Kadimah to establish Hazofim ("The Scouts"). The group's membership, which never exceeded 150–200 and remained concentrated in Berlin, took part in scouting activities, sports, cultural events, and educational seminars. Members were strongly encouraged to personally settle in Palestine. Ideologically, Hazofim was **Socialist Zionist**. In 1931 the group's leaders dissolved Hazofim in order to join with a Kadimah faction in Berlin to establish the German division of **Hashomer Hatzair**.

HEBREW LABOR. Traditional Zionist ideology always emphasized the value of Jews personally tilling the soil of Palestine. Early Zionist thinkers were critical of what they regarded as the over-representation of **Diaspora** Jews in entrepreneurship, finance, and other "non-productive" occupations. They regarded the large number of Jews in such fields as a stimulus to anti-Semitism and an obstacle to the development of a "healthy" Jewish nation. Jewish physical labor was seen as a way to gain the respect of the non-Jewish world. Jewish labor in Palestine therefore became a way to simultaneously revamp the Jewish image and develop **Eretz Israel** into a modern Jewish homeland.

The young **Socialist Zionists** who came with the **Second Aliya** (1904–1914), and joined the **Poalei Zion** and **Hapoel Hatzair** movements, were particularly emphatic on this point, arguing that only those who cultivated the land could stake a moral claim to ownership of it. Many of them were attracted to the "religion of labor" philosophy of **Aharon David Gordon**, elevating the concept of labor nearly to the level of a religious faith and displaying such zeal that some historians have compared their passion to that of European Hasidim or American Puritans.

These young militants were deeply disappointed to discover, upon their arrival in Palestine, that a number of Jewish farming colonies employed Arab laborers. Thus was born their determination to undertake the "conquest of labor" (*kibbush ha'avoda*)—that is, exclusive Jewish control of the Jewish economic sector—and their slogans about hiring "Hebrew labor [*avoda ivrit*] only" and developing Palestine according to the theory of "two societies, two economies." Their initial protest actions, in 1908–1909, included instigating a strike in Sejera against Jewish employers who sought to hire Arabs, physically evicting Arab workers from the grounds of the Jaffa Hebrew High School, and digging up trees planted by Arab laborers in Ben-Shemen for the **Jewish National Fund**.

Because of the willingness of Arabs to work for wages far lower than those of Jewish laborers, the "Hebrew labor" zealots were unable to persuade significant numbers of Jewish employers to stop hiring Arabs. While continuing to advocate "Hebrew labor only" in principle, the young activists turned their attention to the establishment of self-sufficient Jewish communal settlements, known as *kvutzot* (later called **kibbutzim**), where they could control hiring practices and develop a Jewish economic sector independent of the Palestinian Arabs. *See also* LABOR ZIONISM.

HEBREW UNIVERSITY OF JERUSALEM. The main campus of the first Jewish university in Eretz Israel, the Hebrew University of Jerusalem, is located on Mount Scopus, just north of the Old City.

The idea of establishing a university in Jerusalem was raised at the **First Zionist Congress** in 1897, after it had been proposed at the Kattowitz [Kattowice] Conference of **Hovevei Zion** in 1884. A resolution for its establishment was adopted at the Fifth Zionist Congress in 1901, with Chaim Weizmann leading a move to make it a cornerstone of the Zionist movement. A branch of Hovevei Zion bought a tract of land on Mount Scopus in 1914, and on July 24, 1918, the foundation stones were laid. Lord Arthur Balfour presided over the formal inauguration on April 1, 1925. Among the many dignitaries present were General Edmund Allenby, **Hayim Nahman Bialik**, **Ahad Ha'am**, **Chief Rabbi Abraham I. Kook**, **Sir Herbert Samuel**, and **Chaim Weizmann**. **Dr. Judah L. Magnes** served as the university's first chancellor and president. Albert Einstein was a staunch supporter of the university and, prior to its formal opening, he lectured there in 1923.

The university was frequently attacked for several years prior to and during the 1948 War of Independence. The 1949 armistice agreement with Jordan left Mount Scopus a demilitarized Israeli area within Jordanian territory. The university relocated to Giv'at Ram, near the main entrance to the New City, and the School of Agriculture was opened in Rehovot. After the Six-Day War of June 1967, when Israel regained Mount Scopus, the main campus was reopened there.

The university, whose student body numbers more than 20,000 full-time students, has become an internationally respected multi-disciplinary institution of higher learning and research whose faculties include the humanities, social sciences, science, agriculture, medicine, nursing, pharmacy, public health and community medicine law, business administration, nutritional sciences, occupational therapy, and social work, among others.

The university is also the home of the Jewish National and University Library, the Institute for Advanced Studies, the Harry S. Truman Research Institute for the Advancement of Peace, and the Magnes Press.

HEHALUTZ. Zionist activists established Hehalutz ("The Pioneer") in Russia in the early 1900s for the purpose of organizing and training young pioneers for settlement and construction activity in Palestine. War hero **Yosef Trumpeldor** was elected president at the first major Hehalutz conference, held in Moscow in early 1919.

Following the death of Trumpeldor at the hands of Arab attackers in Palestine in 1920 and the intensifying anti-Zionism of the new Soviet authorities, Hehalutz split in two. One faction remained legal by adapting to Soviet ideology and pledging to oppose capitalism; the other went underground and continued its activities in secret. Some Hehalutz pioneers managed to make their way to Palestine before the Soviets fully consolidated their hold on power, but many others were jailed or exiled to Siberia.

In 1921 Hehalutz was formally recognized by the 12th **Zionist Congress** as an autonomous body within the **World Zionist Organization**. Because of Soviet persecution, Poland became the new center of the movement. Additional training facilities for aspiring pioneers were established in Romania, Lithuania, and Germany. In response to Palestinian Arab rioting in the 1930s, **Haganah** emissaries were sent to a number of Hehalutz camps to provide military training. During the interwar period, approximately 45,000 pioneers were sent to Palestine by Hehalutz.

Many Hehalutz activists perished in the Holocaust or were persecuted following the Soviet occupation of Eastern Europe. Those trapped in Warsaw and other ghettoes were active in Jewish armed resistance against the Nazis. After the war, Hehalutz members played a prominent role in the effort to bring Holocaust survivors to Palestine in defiance of British immigration restrictions. Hehalutz activists set up dozens of training camps in postwar Italy and were able to use Italian soil as a transit point for the smuggling of thousands of refugees to Eretz Israel. *See also* LABOR ZIONISM; SOCIALIST ZIONISM.

HEHAVER. Russian-Jewish students living in Switzerland established the Hehaver ("The Comrade") Zionist youth group in 1912. Branches were soon created at a number of universities in Western Europe as well as in Russia. Persecuted by the Soviet authorities in the early 1920s, Hehaver merged with other Zionist youth groups in 1924 as the United All-Russia Organization of Zionist Youth.

HERZL, THEODOR (1860–1904). The father of the modern Zionist movement, Theodor Herzl was born Binyamin Ze'ev in Budapest to a well-to-do, middle-class, and fairly assimilated family. He attended a Jewish elementary school that provided, in additional to the secular curriculum, a rudimentary Jewish education. His family moved to Vienna in 1878, and Herzl studied law at the University of Vienna, from which he graduated with a doctorate in 1884. Between 1885 and 1891, Herzl wrote plays professionally and in 1891 was appointed as the Paris correspondent for the *Neue Freie Presse,* a highly influential liberal newspaper in Vienna.

While covering the Dreyfus trial in Paris, Herzl came to the conclusion that the only solution to the Jewish problem was a political one. He first approached Baron de Hirsch, but the two came to no agreement. Herzl then brought his message directly to the Jewish masses in Eastern Europe, where he was met with resounding enthusiasm. He called for the establishment of a mechanism that would raise money through memberships from Jews around the world and would create the political and social infrastructure of "the Jewish state" (*Der Judenstaat,* 1896). Herzl organized the First **Zionist Congress** in Basle in August 1897 and established the Zionist Organization (which became known as the **World Zionist Organization**), the mechanism of which he had spoken earlier. He was so buoyed by the congress's success that he asserted, in his diary, "In Basle I created the Jewish State." Herzl was the unquestioned leader of the Zionist movement until the Sixth Zionist Congress in 1903, which was bitterly divided over the issue of the **Uganda Plan**. Herzl argued for accepting temporary Jewish shelter in Uganda, and the congress voted, 295 to 178, for the proposal to investigate its viability.

Shortly after a visit with the king of Italy and the pope, in which Herzl persisted in his efforts to gain support for a charter, he died in Edlach, Austria. Herzl passed away before the Uganda issue was finally resolved; the plan was resoundingly rejected at the Seventh Zionist Congress in 1905. He was buried in Vienna with a funeral procession normally reserved for heads of state. Herzl was reinterred on Mount Herzl in Jerusalem in 1949.

HERZL FOUNDATION. Founded in 1954, the New York–based Theodor Herzl Foundation sponsors a variety of cultural and educational programs on Israel, Zionism, and the Hebrew language, as well as the monthly Zionist journal *Midstream.* The Herzl Foundation's book division, Herzl Press, publishes books on Zionist topics. From 1958 to 1978, it also published the highly regarded *Herzl Year Book,* a collection of original research essays on Zionist history by prominent scholars.

HESS, MOSES (1812–1875). Early Zionist thinker Moses Hess was born in Bonn. Although the descendant of prominent rabbinical figures—his paternal great-grandfather was a rabbi in Mannheim and his maternal grandfather was a rabbi near Frankfurt—Hess was a secular Jew who, in his youth, became estranged from Jews and Judaism and married a non-Jewish woman of ill repute, Sybille Pesch. He was an editor of the *Rheinische Zeitung* (Rhein Newspaper) and has been called "the first German Communist." Hess developed a relationship with Karl Marx, who was a regular contributor to the *Rheinische Zeitung,* through their mutual interest in the philosophy of Hegel and socialist theory and praxis. Friends nicknamed Hess "the communist rabbi."

According to his own account, it was Hess's reaction to the Damascus blood libel of 1840 that led him to write his Zionist treatise, *Rome and Jerusalem,* which was first published in 1862. The book offered the revolutionary thesis that Jews are a national entity and advocated the establishment of a Jewish national home in **Eretz Israel**. After reading *Rome and Jerusalem* in 1901, **Theodor Herzl** remarked that all of his own plans were already in Hess's book. As a student of modern nationalist movements with a passionate interest in the ultimate liberation of the oppressed classes, Hess argued for Jewish national liberation with the same fervor he expressed for other oppressed nations.

Despite the vast differences in the backgrounds of Hess, **Zvi Hirsch Kalischer**, and **Yehuda Alkalai**, they shared a common belief—unusual for the mid-nineteenth century—in the approaching dawn of the messianic era. For Hess, that century marked the "springtime" of human history and was characterized by the liberation and rebirth of oppressed nations and classes. He was convinced it was the destiny of the Jewish people, in their own liberation and regeneration, to play a pivotal role in the universal process of national freedom. Few other secular Zionist leaders held such messianic notions.

Hess died in Paris and, according to his own request, was buried in the Jewish cemetery near Cologne. In 1961 his remains were reinterred in Israel, in the cemetery at Kibbutz Kinneret, near the graves of other founding fathers of **Socialist Zionism**, such as **Nahman Syrkin**, **Ber Borochov**, and **Berl Katznelson**.

HIBBAT ZION. As a result of the pogroms that followed the assassination of Czar Alexander II in 1881, Russian and Polish Jews established the Hibbat Zion ("Love of Zion") movement to promote settlement in Eretz Israel. The first leader of the Hovevei Zion ("Lovers of Zion"), as Hibbat Zion members were known, was **Leon Pinsker**, author of the tract *Autoemancipation,* which argued that Jews could never be safe until they acquired their own territory. Pinsker had previously advocated Jewish assimilation into Russian society, but the violence of 1881 and the subsequent anti-Semitic "May laws" of 1882 shattered his belief in the possibility of Jewish integration in Russia.

Hibbat Zion's Romanian branch established the towns of Rosh Pina in the Galilee and Zikhron Ya'akov on Mount Carmel in late 1882. Two years later, Polish Hovevei Zion founded the Galilee community of Yesud Hama'ala, while the Russian branch of the movement established Gedera. A group of Hovevei Zion members including **Rabbi Samuel Mohilever**, leader of the movement's sizable religious faction, founded the town of Rehovot in 1890. Mohilever was also instrumental in persuading Baron Edmond de Rothschild to provide financial support to the Hibbat Zion settlements in Palestine.

The Hovevei Zion initially functioned as small, independent societies in various European Jewish communities. An international conference of Hibbat Zion chapters and like-minded organizations was held in the city of Katowice in November 1884 for the purpose of welding the disparate groups into a single, unified movement. Subsequent national Hibbat Zion conferences were held in Druskenik in June 1887 and Vilna in August 1889. In addition to the movement's centers in Russia, branches were active in Germany, Austria, Romania, Poland, Serbia, Bosnia, Great Britain, and the United States. They raised money to support existing settlements in Palestine and encouraged their members to personally immigrate to the Holy Land, although only a small number did so.

Officially illegal during its first nine years, Hibbat Zion finally gained recognition by the Russian government in 1890 on condition that it restrict its activity to aiding existing settlements in Palestine and refrain from promoting the emigration of Russian Jews. The movement adopted a new name, "The Society for the Support of Jewish Farmers and Artisans in Syria and Palestine," which symbolized its shift to an emphasis on philanthropy rather than settlement. Although Hibbat Zion's practical achievements were modest, it did help pave the way for the rise of **Theodor Herzl**'s **World Zionist Organization**, which overtook and absorbed the Hovevei Zion after 1897.

HILFSVEREIN DER DEUTSCHEN JUDEN. The Hilfsverein der Deutschen Juden, or German Jews' Aid Society, was established in 1901 to provide assistance to downtrodden Jews around the world. It provided financial aid, sponsored schools, and lobbied foreign governments against anti-Jewish discrimination. During the early 1900s, the Hilfsverein assumed an active role in educational activities in Palestine, managing a network of kindergartens, elementary schools, a high school, and a teachers' training college.

In establishing the Haifa Technikum (later Technion) and its adjacent Reali High School, the Hilfsverein inadvertently sparked a national controversy in 1913 by insisting that all scientific and technical subjects at the schools be taught in German. The Hilfsverein saw the project as a philanthropic gesture, to help bring technical knowledge to a backward part of the world; but Zionist leaders viewed the establishment of modern Palestine's first major academic institution as an integral part of their dream of nation-building. Fearing the use of German in the new Haifa schools would interfere with their effort to develop a new Hebrew-based culture in Palestine, the Zionists organized teacher strikes against the Hilfsverein's institutions throughout the country. The protests and vigorous public debate that consumed Palestine during the ensuing months have come to be known as the "Language War." In the end, many teachers and students left the schools and established their own Hebrew-language institutions instead.

After the onset of British Mandatory rule in Palestine, management of the Hilfsverein schools was assumed by the government and the **World Zionist Organization**. In 1939, the Hilfsverein was abolished by the Nazi authorities in Germany.

HISTADRUT. The Histadrut (Hebrew for "Federation"), Israel's General Federation of Labor (Hahistadrut Hakelalit Shel Ha'ovedim Be-Eretz Israel) was founded in Haifa in December 1920, as a joint project of **Ahdut Ha'avoda**, **Hapoel Hatzair**, and a number of smaller left-wing parties, as the General Federation of Jewish Labor in Eretz Israel. It subsequently admitted Arabs to full membership and adopted its present name. It is the world's largest Jewish labor organization, having grown from an initial membership of 5,000 to more than 1,500,000 in 1990. **David Ben-Gurion** was the Histadrut's secretary general from 1921 to 1935.

The Histadrut's objective was not only to serve the interests of current workers but, even more, to foster the creation of a new, elite working class. This was perceived to entail the extensive resocialization, education, and training activities undertaken by the Histadrut. It also entailed political action, and the Histadrut became a very powerful political body that often engages in activities that in other countries are relegated to the domain of the government. Histadrut elections are on a political party–basis and are conducted every four years. The Labor Party controlled the Histadrut from its inception, and that control fostered Labor's domination of the country's political life until 1977.

The Histadrut functions as an umbrella group for the country's separate trade unions and offers health insurance as well as recreational, educational, and other services to its members, who include about 85 percent of the labor force. In addition to wage earners, **kibbutz** members are automatically members of the Histadrut.

Headquartered in Tel Aviv, it has pioneered the development of almost every industrial and commercial area. It operates the country's largest health-care organization, Kupat Holim Kelalit, and one of the country's largest retail cooperatives, Hamshbir Hamercazi. It also established Bank Hapoalim (Workers' Bank), which is currently rated as one of the world's largest banks. It currently owns about a quarter of Israel's farms, businesses, and industries.

As the country's economic structure changed dramatically since the late 1970s, a number of the Histadrut's largest companies experienced severe economic crises that in some cases resulted in bankruptcy and in others in radical reorganization. Also, its prestigious daily newspaper, *Davar,* was forced to close because of declining readership and financial burdens. All of this, as well as the growth of the politically conservative sector in Israel, has seriously undermined the power and prestige of the Histadrut during the decade of the 1990s. *See also* LABOR ZIONISM; SOCIALIST ZIONISM.

HITAHDUT. At a conference in Prague in March 1920, the European Labor Zionist groups Hapoel Hatzair and Zeirei Zion united to form the World Union (Hitahdut Olamit) of **Hapoel Hatzair** and Zeirei Zion, known as Hitahdut. At the movement's third annual conference in Berlin in 1926, the name was altered to the World Zionist Labor Party Hitahdut. The Hitahdut's youth movement was called **Gordonia**, based on the "religion of labor" principles of the Zionist philosopher **Aharon David Gordon**.

Hitahdut's branches varied in their attitudes toward socialism, with the Polish Hitahdut the most distant from traditional socialist ideology. The party as a whole advocated a socialist economy for the future Jewish homeland but opposed the concept of class struggle. In 1932 Hitahdut merged with the larger **Labor Zionist** movement **Poalei Zion** to form the Ihud Olami, or World Union of Zionists-Socialists.

HOVEVEI SEFAT EVER. The organization Hovevei Sefat Ever, or "Lovers of the Hebrew Language," was established in Russia in the early 1900s to popularize Hebrew as a spoken language. More than sixty chapters of the group in local Jewish communities throughout Russia sponsored educational and cultural activities in Hebrew. Some of them operated Hebrew-language kindergartens. Hovevei Sefat Ever was forcibly disbanded by the Communist regime that took power in 1917.

HOVEVEI ZION. *See* HIBBAT ZION.

-I-

IHUD. Judah Magnes, the **Hebrew University** president and advocate of a binational Arab-Jewish state in Palestine, was the driving force in establishing the Ihud organization in the summer of 1942, to promote binationalism as an alternative to the Zionist goal of Jewish statehood. The name Ihud, or "union" in Hebrew, alluded to the goal of union between Arabs and Jews in Palestine, and between Palestine and the neighboring Arab states. Ihud's founders also included the philosopher Martin Buber, the writer Moshe Smilansky, **Youth Aliya** leader (and **Hadassah** founder) **Henrietta Szold**, and officials of the Marxist Zionist youth movement **Hashomer Hatzair**.

Ihud was in some ways a reincarnation of **Brith Shalom**, which during 1925–1933 had advocated binationalism and initiated unsuccessful peace contacts with Palestinian Arab representatives. Buber had been Brith Shalom's ideological mentor. Magnes had played only a modest part in Brith Shalom, but he assumed the leadership of Ihud. Magnes's willingness to take a more active role reflected his anxiety over the May 1942 **Biltmore Conference** resolution urging "that Palestine be established as a Jewish Commonwealth," a declaration Magnes regarded as a recipe for Arab–Jewish conflict.

Although numbering less than one hundred individuals, Ihud gained disproportionate notoriety, thanks in part to generous news coverage of its activities by sympathetic segments of the American media. The prominence Ihud attained was a source of considerable frustration for Zionist leaders, who feared that the appearance of division within Jewish ranks would undermine their ability to win international support for the cause of Jewish statehood. Ihud's success in generating headlines did not translate into progress at the negotiating table. Its peace feelers were rebuffed by Palestinian Arab officials, who could not accept the Ihud position that additional Jewish immigration should be permitted until the *yishuv* achieved numerical parity with Palestine's Arab community.

Magnes received a sympathetic hearing when he testified before the **Anglo-American Committee of Inquiry** (1946). The committee's final report, recommending a United Nations trusteeship over Palestine rather than Jewish statehood, in some ways resembled Magnes's proposals. Magnes was less successful in his appearance before the **United Nations**

Special Committee on Palestine (1947), which recommended partition of Palestine into Jewish and Arab states. Magnes visited the United States in the spring of 1948, where he met with government officials, including President Harry S. Truman, in a futile bid to bring about an American trusteeship over Palestine instead of partition. In the wake of Israel's victory in the 1948 war and Magnes's death in October 1948, Ihud disbanded.

IMBER, NAFTALI HERTZ (1856–1909). The author of "**Hatikvah,**" which was the anthem of the Zionist movement and subsequently became Israel's national anthem, Naftali Imber was born in Zlotzhov, Galicia, and received a traditional Jewish education but not a secular one. As a youth he manifested his artistic talents; by the age of ten he had already composed a Hebrew song dedicated to the Austro-Prussian War.

There is some debate about when, precisely, Imber composed "Hatikvah." According to his own autobiographical account, he wrote the song "Tikvateinu" in 1878, to commemorate the founding of the Jewish settlement in Palestine of Petah Tikva, and the song was subsequently retitled "Hatikvah." Others, however, assert that "Hatikvah" was composed later, between 1882 and 1886, and that it was influenced by the Polish national anthem.

There is also some debate about the music to which the anthem is set. According to some, Imber himself set the poem to the music of a Slav folk song that he brought from Romania. Others, however, suggest that the music was composed by a cantor. In any case, the opening motif is clearly from Bedřich Smetana's *Vltava* ("The Moldau").

In 1882 Imber met and became close with Laurence Oliphant, a **Christian Zionist**, in Constantinople. He became Oliphant's secretary and adviser on Jewish affairs and accompanied him when he went to Palestine in 1882–1887, during which time Imber composed many songs. He left Palestine in 1887, and after brief stays in various countries, Imber arrived in London in 1888, where he met and became friendly with **Israel Zangwill**.

In 1892 Imber left for the United States, where he remained, except for a brief return-visit to London, for the next seventeen years, until his death. His life in America was materially miserable; he suffered from want and alcoholism. He was briefly married to Amanda Katie, a Christian physician who converted to Judaism in order to marry him. Throughout, he continued to be creative in literary endeavors. Imber served as poet, author, and, briefly, as editor of a periodical devoted to Kabbalah.

He also translated portions of F. Scott Fitzgerald's rendition of *The Rubiyat of Omar Khayyam* into Hebrew. Imber was erratic, a dreamer with mystical tendencies, and a somewhat unpolished poet who, nevertheless, wrote many poems, almost all of which appear in the volume *Kol Shirei Naftali Hertz Imber* ("The Complete Poetry of Naftali Hertz Imber," with a preface by Dov Sadan [Tel Aviv: Neuman, 1950]).

IRGUN ZVAI LEUMI (IZL). Militant members of the **Haganah**, Palestine's self-defense militia, broke away in 1931 to establish the Irgun Zvai Leumi, or National Military Organization. The immediate causes of the split were the militants' dissatisfaction over the Haganah's close ties to the **Labor Zionists** and the Haganah's policy of *havlaga,* or self-restraint, in response to Palestinian Arab violence. The Irgun's initial governing board was composed of representatives of the **Revisionist Zionists**, the **Mizrachi Religious Zionists**, and the **General Zionists**. In 1936 the Irgun formally became the armed wing of the Revisionist movement.

The eruption of nationwide Palestinian Arab violence in 1936 provoked a split in the Irgun's ranks. A minority returned to the Haganah, while the majority remained independent and launched a series of retaliatory attacks against Arab targets. In the course of one such raid, a young IZL member, Shlomo Ben-Yosef, was captured by the British and sentenced to death, the first Jew to be hanged in modern Palestine. At the same time, the Irgun took the lead in organizing **Aliya Bet**, the unauthorized immigration of European Jewish refugees to Palestine. This operation, under the command of Viennese Revisionist William Perl, brought an estimated tens of thousands of Jews to **Eretz Israel** during the late 1930s.

The IZL responded to the May 1939 British **White Paper**, which severely restricted Jewish immigration, with violent attacks on British targets throughout Palestine. But with the eruption of World War II in September 1939, the IZL suspended its military operations, and many Irgun members enlisted in the British armed forces to help fight against the Nazis. The Irgun's commander in chief at the time, **David Raziel**, was killed while participating in a British mission behind enemy lines in Iraq in May 1941. The Irgun's 1939 truce with the British prompted a minority of IZL members, led by a senior Irgun officer, **Avraham Stern**, to break away and form the Fighters for the Freedom of Israel (**Lohamei Herut Israel**, or **Lehi**). Stern's group continued to perpetrate anti-British violence in Palestine, albeit on a small scale.

In late 1942, **Menachem Begin**, the former leader of the Revisionist youth movement **Betar** in Poland, arrived in Palestine and soon assumed command of the Irgun. After more than a year of preparations, the IZL in early 1944 announced the launching of an armed revolt against the British forces in Mandatory Palestine. At first it seemed the 600 badly equipped Jewish guerrillas stood little chance of ousting a British occupation army of 80,000.

The Irgunists made the most of advantages such as the element of surprise, their intimate knowledge of the terrain, and the protective sympathy of a significant part of the local population. At the same time, the Jewish militants actively sought to reach influential segments of foreign public opinion. The democratic systems of government in Great Britain and the United States by their very nature enabled the Irgun to mobilize sympathizers in Parliament and Congress to press for a British withdrawal from Palestine.

Much of the international sympathy that aided the Irgun derived not so much from admiration for the underground's war against the British, but from sorrow at the suffering of European Jewry under the Nazis. Western public consciousness of the Nazi genocide fueled Western public support for the goal of a Jewish state in Palestine. Great Britain's policy of preventing shiploads of European refugees from reaching Palestine further intensified American public sympathy for the Zionist cause. Irgun emissaries in the United States, well aware of America's own history of battling British colonial rulers, peppered their newspaper advertisements with references to 1776, the Boston Tea Party, and the midnight ride of Paul Revere.

The revolt itself was very much a product of its era. Although the Irgun had been established prior to the onset of the Holocaust, it was the transformation of Nazi brutality from discrimination and sporadic violence to organized mass murder, combined with British immigration restrictionism, that were the decisive factors in igniting the rebellion. The Holocaust created the atmosphere of urgency, even desperation, that drove significant numbers of young Jews to join the underground. The Irgun's revolt against the British was often more of a psychological contest of wills than a battlefield struggle. The IZL did not possess the necessary manpower or other resources to achieve a conventional military victory over the much larger and superior British armed forces. The British, for their part, could have eliminated the rebels only by using methods too harsh to be acceptable to British public opinion. Operating within the parameters created by their own weaknesses as well as those of the British, the Irgun took aim at British pride as much as at British army bases, police stations, and government offices. Thus when the British, in June 1946, sentenced Irgun members Yosef Shimshon and Michael Ashbel to death, their comrades kidnapped five British officers and threatened to hang them if the sentences against Shimshon and Ashbel were carried out. Unable to locate the kidnap victims or to put an end to ongoing attacks by the Jewish underground, the humiliated Mandate authorities backed down and commuted the sentences. The officers' lives were saved, but the psychological effect of the Jewish guerrillas' victory was inestimable.

A similar triumph for the IZL wounded the British later that year. Two seventeen-year-olds convicted of Irgun activity, Binyamin Kimche and Yehuda Katz, were sentenced to lengthy prison terms plus eighteen lashes. Defying an IZL threat to subject British soldiers to retaliatory lashings, the British whipped Kimche. The next day, four British soldiers were seized at gunpoint, driven to remote locations along the coast, and given eighteen lashes each. The British amnestied the second IZL youth and abolished the practice of whipping.

In July 1946, Irgun bombers blew apart the southern wing of the King David Hotel in Jerusalem, which was used as the headquarters of the British military administration. Three months later, the Irgun demonstrated its ability to strike overseas as well, blowing up the British embassy in Rome. In late 1946 and early 1947, Jewish underground attacks in Palestine intensified. British airplanes were dynamited in their hangars. British troop trains were mined. British soldiers were gunned down in broad daylight. A brazen Irgun raid on the officers' club in Tel Aviv, Goldsmith House, left seventeen dead.

After the British hanged four Irgun members in the Acre Prison in April 1947, Irgun fighters dynamited their way through the prison's south wall, setting free hundreds of prisoners in what was portrayed by the international media as one of the most spectacular prison breaks of all time. The Acre raid, later immortalized in the film *Exodus,* dealt a shattering blow to British prestige and morale.

The **Jewish Agency**, the governing body of the *yishuv,* favored a policy of cooperation with the British and denounced the Irgun's revolt. In 1944–1945, the Agency leadership worked with the British to stamp out Irgun activity, by sending Haganah units to kidnap IZL members and turn them over to the British for imprisonment. In some cases, the Haganah captors used force on the Irgunists to extract information concerning the underground. This period, known as "The Season," came to a halt in mid-

1945 after the newly elected British Labour government refused to alter Great Britain's Palestine policy. The disillusioned Jewish Agency leadership forged an alliance between the Haganah, the Irgun, and the Lehi, with all three fighting under a joint command as the United Hebrew Resistance. The combined forces launched violent attacks on British targets in Palestine until mid-1946 when the Jewish Agency, under British pressure, withdrew from the alliance and undertook a second "Season" against the militants. By that time, however, the Irgun was much larger and stronger than during the first Season—it now numbered over 3,000 soldiers—and was able to both withstand the Haganah's attacks and escalate its own assaults on British targets.

The Irgun's war against the British climaxed in a battle of the gallows. In April 1947, the British hanged four Irgun men. While the Irgun was unsuccessfully seeking suitable British hostages, the authorities sentenced three more Irgun men to be hanged. The militants then managed to capture two British sergeants. The British, calling the Irgun's bluff, executed the three Jewish fighters; the Irgun responded by hanging the sergeants in a grove near Netanya. That same afternoon, the **S.S.** *Exodus,* having been turned away from Palestine by the British authorities, arrived back in France with its pitiful cargo of Holocaust survivors. Their tragic journey provided the poignant backdrop to the Irgun's unprecedented action.

The hanging of the sergeants was the straw that broke the camel's back. The expense of the Palestine occupation, especially the cost in British lives, demoralized the British public. The accumulation of humiliations—the bold attacks on major British targets, the prison breaks, the retaliatory whippings, and now the hangings—was too much for the British government, and the British public. Unable to defeat the rebels, the British returned the Palestine Mandate to the United Nations in the autumn of 1947 and prepared to withdraw from the Holy Land.

-J-

JABOTINSKY, VLADIMIR ZE'EV (1880–1940). The Zionist orator and activist Ze'ev Jabotinsky was raised in an acculturated, middle-class family in Odessa. As a young man, Jabotinsky exhibited skills as a multilingual essayist, poet, translator, and public speaker. He embraced Zionism in response to the rising tide of anti-Semitism in Russia, particularly the 1903 Kishinev pogrom, and soon earned a reputation as one of Russian Jewry's most dynamic Zionist speakers and leaders.

Jabotinsky's first major success as a Zionist activist was the establishment, under British auspices, of a **Jewish Legion** that helped capture Palestine from the Turks during World War I. The legion's contribution to the war effort made a profound impression upon some British cabinet ministers, helping to pave the way for the **Balfour Declaration** and the awarding of the Palestine Mandate to Great Britain.

The Palestinian Arab rioters who attacked Jews in Jerusalem in 1920 were confronted by a self-defense group, consisting largely of former Jewish Legionnaires who had been assembled by Jabotinsky and **Pinhas Rutenberg**. Many of the Jewish defenders, including Jabotinsky, were jailed by the British for unauthorized possession of weapons, but the resulting international outcry brought about their early release.

As continuing Arab opposition to Zionism caused a shift in British policy away from the cause of Jewish statehood, a militant faction within the Zionist hierarchy, led by Jabotinsky, argued—unsuccessfully—that only a more aggressive stance could prevent Great Britain from altogether abandoning the Zionist cause. By 1925, Jabotinsky established his own wing of the Zionist movement, the League of Zionist-Revisionists, so named because of their determination to revise the Zionist position vis-à-vis London.

Jabotinsky frequently shuttled back and forth from Jerusalem (until the British barred him from returning to Palestine in 1930) to Paris to London, to press the Zionist case in the halls of international power, with occasional forays into farther-flung corners of the **Diaspora**, such as South Africa and the United States. Jabotinsky's message of Jewish pride resonated among Eastern European audiences in particular. In the bleak interwar atmosphere of economic crises and rising anti-Semitism, Jabotinsky offered hope.

The **Arlosoroff Affair** of 1933–1934, with its accusations that Jabotinsky had incited the murder of a **Labor Zionist** leader, seriously tarred Jabotinsky's reputation. His successful negotiations with **David Ben-Gurion** on a peace pact between the **Revisionists** and Laborites could not gain the approval of the **Histadrut** rank and file in the atmosphere of post-Arlosoroff hostility.

Economic issues were another source of tension between Jabotinsky and the Labor Zionists. Jabotinsky rejected the socialists' concept of class war as a threat to Jewish national unity, insisting that labor disputes be subjected to compulsory arbitration. Pitched battles between Histadrut strike-enforcers and nonunion Revisionist workers became commonplace for a time in 1930s Palestine.

In many ways, Jabotinsky was a pessimist. He believed that Palestinian Arab opposition to Zionism was natural and inevitable. It could not be softened, in his view, so the only answer was to build an "iron wall" of Jewish determination. Jabotinsky also implored his European audiences to immigrate to Palestine, "to liquidate the Exile before it liquidates you." He anticipated that they would be crushed by anti-Semitism and economic discrimination, although he did not imagine physical annihilation.

Wary about Great Britain's faithfulness to the **Balfour Declaration**, Jabotinsky urged the adoption of extra-legal immigration as the "Jewish national sport." As a result, his Revisionist movement was the first to bring unauthorized boatloads of European refugees to Palestine in defiance of British restrictions.

By contrast with those Zionist leaders who feared that explicit demands for statehood would be strategically unwise, Jabotinsky pressed for an open declaration by the Zionist movement that its goal was a sovereign state. Although he did not call for a Jewish armed revolt against the British in Palestine—Jabotinsky still thought the British might be persuaded to re-embrace Zionism—after Jabotinsky's sudden death in 1940, his followers were convinced they were implementing the spirit of his ideology when they launched their revolt four years later.

JABOTINSKY INSTITUTE. The Jabotinsky Institute (Mahon Jabotinsky, in Hebrew) was established in 1935 as the central repository of manuscripts and documents pertaining to the history of **Revisionist Zionism** and its founder, **Ze'ev Jabotinsky**. The institute is located in a Tel Aviv building known as Metzudat Ze'ev (the Fortress of Ze'ev), which houses the Revisionist archives as well as the headquarters of the Likud Party. The Jabotinsky Institute also hosts a museum of the Palestine underground **Irgun Zvai Leumi** and a museum focusing on Revisionists who fought against the Nazis during the Holocaust. The institute's publications division publishes historical studies as well as a quarterly journal concerning the institute's archival collections.

JERUSALEM PROGRAM. The 23rd **World Zionist Congress**, held in Jerusalem in 1951, adopted the Jerusalem Program as its official platform. It replaced the outdated **Basle Program**, adopted at the First Zionist Congress, which had focused on the need to establish a Jewish homeland. That aim having been accomplished, the new Jerusalem Program briefly summarized the purpose of Zionism as "strengthening of the State of Israel, the ingathering of the exiles in **Eretz Israel**, and the fostering of the unity of the Jewish people."

A somewhat more detailed version of the 1951 platform was passed by the 26th Zionist Congress in 1961: "The aims of Zionism are: The unity of the Jewish people and the centrality of Israel in Jewish life; the ingathering of the Jewish people in its historic homeland Eretz Israel through *aliya* from all countries; the strengthening of the State of Israel which is based on the prophetic vision of justice and peace; the preservation of identity of the Jewish people through the fostering of Jewish and Hebrew education and of Jewish spiritual and cultural values; the protection of Jewish rights everywhere." It remains to this day the official credo of the world Zionist movement.

JEWISH AGENCY. When the League of Nations granted Great Britain the Mandate for Palestine in 1922, it called for the establishment of a "Jewish agency . . . as a public body for the purpose of advising and cooperating with the administration of Palestine in such economic, social, and other matters as may affect the establishment of the Jewish national home and the interests of the Jewish population in Palestine." In 1923 the **World Zionist Organization** requested that its president, **Chaim Weizmann**, create that agency, and in 1929, after years of intense negotiations, the Jewish Agency for Palestine was established in partnership with the president of the **American Jewish Committee**, Louis Marshall, and other prominent non-Zionists.

However, the Jewish Agency never was independent of the Zionist Organization and, in fact, since most of the non-Zionist representatives were actually quite sympathetic to Zionism, the Jewish Agency and the Zionist Organization have always worked as one. Formally, the Jewish Agency was responsible for the educational and social services to the Jews in Palestine, in addition to being the representative of organized Zionism and **Diaspora** Jewry in the creation of the Jewish national home, which included discussions with Great Britain, the League of Nations, and the United Nations. Although the mandatory government maintained that the Jewish Agency had no governmental authority in Palestine, the agency managed to set up a broad administrative structure and was, in fact, viewed by the Jews of Palestine as their government.

After the establishment of the State of Israel, the governmental functions were relegated to the state, and the Jewish Agency for Israel was given the principal tasks of immigration (*aliya*) and absorption (*kelita*). In 1950, the Knesset formally designated the World Zionist Organization-Jewish Agency as the unit responsible for immigration and absorption, as well as building support for Israel around the world. Ostensibly, the Jewish Agency carried out the work in Israel, while the World Zionist Organization operated in the Diaspora. Actually, however, from that point on, they have been formally recognized as one unit, the World Zionist Organization-Jewish Agency.

The strong pro-Israel sentiment aroused throughout the Jewish world by the Six-Day War galvanized efforts to find ways for Diaspora Jews to participate more fully in the workings of the World Zionist Organization-Jewish Agency. The Jewish Agency was formally reconstituted in 1970–1971 according to a formula that gave Diaspora Jewry, and especially "non-Zionists," a considerably larger role in its decision-making process.

JEWISH BRIGADE. Shortly after the outbreak of World War II, the **Revisionist Zionists** launched a public campaign in the United States and Great Britain to urge the Allies to establish a Jewish army that would take part in the war against Germany. Mainstream Zionist leaders proposed a more modest Jewish armed unit that would be based in Palestine to defend it against a possible Nazi invasion. The British resisted both proposals because of Arab objections.

When its private lobbying yielded no results, the Zionist leadership launched its own public campaign for a Jewish armed force. The cumulative pressure finally compelled the British, in the autumn of 1944, to organize the Jewish Brigade, an infantry force of five thousand soldiers. In deference to Arab concerns, the unit was slated to fight in Europe only and would have no connection to Palestine.

The Jewish Brigade, which was based in Italy, began organizing and training in October 1944 and fought with distinction against the Germans in March 1945, near the war's end. Many veterans of the Jewish Brigade took part in organizing the postwar unauthorized immigration of Holocaust survivors to Palestine. A number of former brigade members also put their military training to use in the Jewish revolt against the British in Palestine and subsequently in Israel's 1948 War of Independence.

JEWISH COLONIAL TRUST. The Jewish Colonial Trust Ltd. was the first financial institution of the **World Zionist Organization**. At **Theodor Herzl**'s initiative, it was approved by the Second **Zionist Congress** in 1898, established in 1899, and registered in London. Its designated objectives were to foster the economic development of and immigration to Palestine. However, the geographic limits of the trust's mission were not explicitly defined, and thus for a number of years, it was a source of contention for those, such as **Ahad Ha'am**, who feared that the Zionist Organization would establish a Jewish state elsewhere if its leaders concluded that establishment of a state in **Eretz Israel** was unfeasible. In 1905 the Seventh Zionist Congress, which rejected the **Uganda Plan**, also explicitly limited the trust's mission to Palestine and Syria.

The Jewish Colonial Trust established a subsidiary, the Anglo-Palestine Company Ltd., which was reorganized in 1933 and became the Anglo-Palestine Bank Ltd., acting as the official bank of the Jewish community in Palestine. With the establishment of the State of Israel, the Anglo-Palestine Bank became Bank Leumi Le-Israel, and in 1955 the trust, which was the holding company for the bank's shares, became an Israeli company, Ozar Hityashevut Hayehudim.

JEWISH COLONIZATION ASSOCIATION (JCA; in Yiddish, ICA). The Jewish philanthropist Baron Maurice de Hirsch established the Paris-based Jewish Colonization Association in 1891 to help resettle Russian Jews in agricultural communities in Argentina. Beginning in 1896, the JCA also provided assistance to Jewish settlements in Palestine. As of 1900, the JCA assumed the role of sponsor and overseer of agricultural communities that had been established in Palestine during the previous decade by Baron Edmond de Rothschild.

The strict control that Rothschild's administrators exercised over the settlements, and their lack of sympathy for the settlers' Zionist idealism, had provoked conflicts between the pioneers and the administration. The JCA alleviated the tension by granting the settlers more autonomy and shifting their focus to crops that gave them increased financial independence. The JCA subsequently established a number of its own agricultural villages in Palestine and helped sponsor the founding of a number of **kibbutzim**—including Kfar Giladi, Tel Hai, Ayelet Hashahar, and Mahanayim—in the northern Galilee. In contemporary Israel, which is the primary site of JCA activity today, the association sponsors schools specializing in agricultural training and finances agricultural research projects.

JEWISH DEFENSE LEAGUE (JDL). Meir Kahane, an Orthodox rabbi and former activist in the **Revisionist Zionist** youth movement **Betar**, established the Jewish Defense League in New York in 1968, in response to rising black anti-Semitism and dangers facing Jews in deteriorating urban neighborhoods. The JDL organized armed patrols to protect Jews in such areas. The league's willingness to use force, an unprecedented departure from the previous tactics utilized by American Jewish organizations in responding to anti-Semitism, was strongly denounced by mainstream Jewish leaders. The JDL soon broadened its agenda to include protests on behalf of Israel and, especially, the plight of Jews in the Soviet Union. The league's harassment of Soviet diplomatic personnel and violent attacks on Soviet offices became a source of tension between the United States and the Union of Soviet Socialist Republics during the early 1970s. The JDL's use of violence was criticized by other Jewish groups, although the militants were credited by many for attracting international attention to the plight of Soviet Jewry.

The ideology of the JDL contained a strong Zionist component. In his writings, Kahane argued that *aliya* was a religious commandment incumbent upon every Jew. He also predicted that rising anti-Semitism would eventually compel many American Jews to seek refuge in Israel. Kahane himself settled in Jerusalem in 1971, and many other JDL activists followed suit.

In Israel, Kahane and the JDL campaigned against Christian missionary activity and lobbied the Israeli government to use more forceful tactics in combating Arab terrorism. Shortly after the 1972 massacre of Israeli athletes at the Munich Olympics, Kahane and several colleagues were arrested for attempting to smuggle weapons from Israel to Europe for use in retaliatory attacks on Arab targets.

In the 1973 Knesset elections, Kahane headed a list of candidates called HaLiga ("The League"), which narrowly missed winning one seat. The movement subsequently changed its name to Kach ("Thus" in Hebrew), derived from the motto of the 1940s **Irgun Zvai Leumi** underground, "Rak Kach" ("Only Thus"). Kach argued that Israel should annex the territories captured in the 1967 war, both because of their religious significance and as a buffer against future Arab attacks. Kach also proposed that the Arabs in the territories, as well as Israeli Arabs, be offered financial incentives to emigrate, in order to ensure perpetual Jewish demographic superiority in Israel.

Kach's campaigns for the Knesset in 1977 and 1981 were likewise unsuccessful. In 1984, however, it won one seat, which Kahane occupied. Kach was disqualified from the 1988 Knesset race because of its proposals concerning the Arabs. Kahane was assassinated by an Arab terrorist in New York in 1990. After his death, a number of the remaining JDL chapters in the United States disbanded. In 1994 the Israeli government outlawed Kach and a splinter group, Kahane Chai, after a Kahane supporter, Dr. Baruch Goldstein, killed twenty-nine Arabs in Hebron.

JEWISH LEGION. After Turkey entered World War I on the side of the Central Powers in 1914, Zionist leader **Ze'ev Jabotinsky** began urging the Allies to establish a Jewish military force to take part in the liberation of Palestine from Turkish rule. Jabotinsky, together with the Russian Zionist activist **Yosef Trumpeldor**, recruited a five-hundred-man volunteer force from among the thousands of Palestinian Jews expelled by the Turks to Egypt. The British offered to have them perform auxiliary duties rather than go in to combat, and not on the Palestine front. Trumpeldor accepted the proposal and led the Zion Mule Corps, as it was called, in the Gallipoli campaign. Jabotinsky refused to take part and resumed his lobbying efforts for a full-fledged Jewish military force.

Many Zionist leaders opposed Jabotinsky's activity, fearing the Turks would retaliate against Palestine Jewry. British Jewish anti-Zionists lobbied against the Jewish army proposal because they believed such a military force would call too much attention to Jewish separateness. The British cabinet, however, gradually came to see such a force as a way to recruit Russian Jewish immigrants in Great Britain to fight for the Allied cause.

In the summer of 1917, the British assented to the formation of the Jewish Legion, officially known as the 38th Battalion, Fusiliers. Its members included many Zion Mule Corps veterans who had re-enlisted. Later, two additional battalions, the 39th and 40th, were added to the legion when over 1,000 Palestinian Jews signed up. A large number of American Jewish volunteers also joined the force. Commanded by the famed soldier and lion-hunter Lt. Col. John Henry Patterson, with Jabotinsky serving as a lieutenant, the Jewish Legion assisted in the British conquest of Palestine in the autumn of 1918.

Anti-Zionist officials within the British administration in Palestine insisted on the quick demobilization of the Jewish Legion. Some of the veterans remained in the country to take part in settlement activities, although many who had come from the West to serve in the legion opted to return to their native countries. One result was that only a small number of Legionnaires were still armed and available to help defend against the Arab riots of 1920 and 1921. Repeated appeals by the **World Zionist Organization** that the legion be maintained as part of the British army in Palestine went unheeded. The legion was gradually disbanded, prompting the *yishuv* to organize the **Haganah** in its stead. Some ex-Legionnaires later put their British military training to good use in the Haganah and, subsequently, in the Israeli army.

JEWISH NATIONAL FUND (JNF). The Jewish National Fund (Keren Kayemet Le-Israel) was established by the Fifth **Zionist Congress** in 1901, as a fund for the purpose of purchasing and developing land in Eretz Israel. Originally stationed in Vienna, the JNF established a worldwide fundraising network. One of its innovative techniques, the blue and white coin collection box, became an international Zionist symbol. In 1904 the JNF purchased its first land, at Kfar Hittim in the lower Galilee, and in 1908 it planted its first forest.

By 1939, more than 60 percent of all Jewish-owned land was held by the JNF. When the State of Israel was established in 1948, the JNF held some 232,000 acres. Since 1948, its major activity has been the planting of forests.

In 1960 the JNF and the Israeli government signed an agreement establishing the Israel Land Authority to administer both government and JNF land. The bulk of the JNF's budget still comes from voluntary contributions.

JEWISH STATE PARTY. The small minority of **Revisionist Zionists** who favored remaining part of the **World Zionist Organization (WZO)** when their movement seceded from the WZO in 1933, broke from the Revisionist party and established the Jewish State Party. The split represented a division of tactics, not ideology; the new State Party remained loyal to the ideas of Revisionism's founder, **Ze'ev Jabotinsky**.

In the elections to the 1933 **Zionist Congress**, the Jewish State Party won eight seats, while the Revisionist Party won forty-five. At its first world conference, held in Paris in the summer of 1937, the Jewish State Party split in two over the British plan for the establishment of a Jewish state in only a small portion of a partitioned Palestine. Supporters of the British plan resigned from the party, while the majority, who opposed partition, elected Meir Grossman their leader and joined the anti-partition forces at that year's World Zionist Congress. In 1946, the Jewish State Party reunited with the Revisionist movement as the World Union of Zionist-Revisionists.

JEWISH TERRITORIAL ORGANIZATION (JTO; in Yiddish, ITO). The Jewish Territorial Organization was established in 1905 by supporters of the plan to establish a temporary Jewish homeland in East Africa (the **Uganda Plan**), who seceded from the **World Zionist Organization** after the Seventh **Zionist Congress** repudiated the Africa proposal. **Israel Zangwill**, the early British Zionist activist and playwright, was elected president. Dozens of chapters were established in Russia in the wake of the 1905 pogroms, and branches were also founded in Western European countries and the United States.

The Territorialists were convinced that because of the country's underdevelopment as well as Arab opposition, Palestine was not a feasible destination for large numbers of Jewish refugees. Nor were they impressed by Jewish historical or spiritual ties to the Holy Land. Their goal was to find territories where a substantial number of Jews could find speedy relief from Eastern European oppression.

In 1906 Zangwill relocated the headquarters of the JTO, as the organization was known, from Warsaw to London and sought to persuade the British government of the viability of the East Africa scheme. When that failed, the JTO examined the possibility of Canada or Australia as sites of Jewish settlement and sent exploratory delegations to Cyrenaica (Libya), Mesopotamia (Iraq), and Portuguese Angola, but in each case, insurmountable political or economic obstacles arose. In the end, the JTO's only practical settlement project was its involvement in the Galveston Plan, which diverted some nine thousand New York–bound Eastern European Jewish immigrants to the port of Galveston, Texas, for settlement in towns in the southwestern United States.

The **Balfour Declaration** and the subsequent awarding of the Palestine Mandate to Great Britain convinced Zangwill and many JTO activists to return to the Zionist fold. The JTO was officially disbanded in 1925.

JUDISCHE VOLKSPARTEI (JV). Pro-Zionist German Jewish groups established the umbrella organization Judische Volkspartei, or Jewish People's Party, in Berlin in 1919. The JV was active in local Jewish communal affairs and held a majority of the seats on the Jewish community council of Berlin from 1926 to 1930. When the Nazis drastically reduced the size of the Jewish communal leadership in 1935, the JV was deprived of its seats, and no further elections were held.

JUNG ISRAEL. One of the earliest modern Zionist organizations, Jung Israel ("Young Israel") was established in Berlin in 1892. Its Zionist educational work, particularly on German university campuses, continued until 1897. It was succeeded by the Berliner Zionistische Vereinigung ("Berlin Zionist Association").

JUNG JUDISCHER WANDERBUND (JJWB). Young German Jewish hiking enthusiasts established the Jung Judischer Wanderbund (Association of Young Jewish Outdoorsmen) in 1922. Patterned on the highly popular German Jewish youth movements of that era, the JJWB emphasized the value of nature. It gradually embraced **Socialist Zionism**. In 1925 the JJWB merged with the Germany Zionist youth group **Berit Ha'olim**, and many of its members settled in the early **kibbutzim** in Palestine during the interwar years.

-K-

KADIMAH. Jewish students established the Kadimah organization in Vienna in 1882, to oppose assimilation and promote Jewish nationalism and settlement in Eretz Israel. The famous Hebrew writer **Peretz Smolenskin** assisted the group and gave it its name, which means "Forward" or "Eastward." A number of Kadimah members later worked closely with **Theodor Herzl** and the **World Zionist Organization**.

KALISCHER, ZVI HIRSCH (1795–1874). Religious Zionist philosopher Zvi Hirsch Kalischer was born and raised in Leszno in western Poland and later moved to Germany, where he studied with the most prominent scholars of halakhah of the late nineteenth century. He soon emerged as one of the most learned Orthodox rabbis of his generation. He was, however, atypical, in that he did not adopt the characteristic Eastern European Orthodox approach of rejecting modernity out of hand. Kalischer spoke the language of modernists and maintained close relationships even with those who rejected Orthodoxy.

Perhaps the most novel aspect of Kalischer's worldview was his conviction that the Messiah would arrive through natural processes. To this end, he attempted to interest Muhammad Ali, the Egyptian ruler who then controlled **Eretz Israel**, in permitting Jewish land purchases in order to develop the Holy Land for the return of the exiled Jewish masses. Kalischer also became active in Dr. Chaim Lurie's Society for the Colonization of Palestine, in Frankfurt on the Oder.

In 1862 Kalischer published *Derishat Zion* ("Zion's Call"), a seminal work in the literature of Religious Zionism. In it, he systematically explained the natural process of the redemption, combining his vision with pragmatism by suggesting specific ways to settle the land. Two of his suggestions, the establishment of an agricultural cooperative as the economic foundation of settlement and the establishment of an agriculture school in Eretz Israel, were both seconded by **Moses Hess** and eventually materialized. The latter was realized when the **Alliance Israélite Universelle** founded the well-known agricultural school Mikveh Israel in 1870, and the former, with the adoption by the Palestine Office of **World Zionist Organization** of an emphasis on agricultural development in the early 1900s.

Kalischer did not live to realize his plan to make *aliya*. He died in Toruń, central Poland. Tirat Zvi, a religious **kibbutz** in the Bet She'an Valley, is named for him.

KALLEN, HORACE MEYER (1882–1974). American Zionist philosopher Horace Kallen was born in Berenstadt, Silesia, Germany, to a rabbinic family. His parents immigrated to the United States with him when he was five years of age. Kallen graduated from Harvard University in 1903 and taught English at Princeton University from 1903 to 1905. He then returned to Harvard for his doctorate in philosophy and taught there from 1908 to 1911 and at Clark College in 1910. Kallen then taught at the University of Wisconsin from 1911 to 1918, during which time he published a number of significant works in philosophy. One of the founders of the New School for Social Research in New York in 1919, Kallen taught there from 1919 to 1952, serving as dean of the Graduate Faculty of Political and Social Science from 1944 to 1946 and as research professor from 1952 to 1965. In 1965, at age 83, he accepted a teaching appointment at Long Island University.

Kallen was active in the **American Jewish Congress**, the American Association for Jewish Education, and YIVO Institute for Jewish Research. He also served on many general committees and organizations dedicated to civil and minority rights, including the Presidential Commission on Higher Education, the New York City Commission on Intergroup Relations, the International League for the Rights of Man, and the Society for the Scientific Study of Religion.

Kallen is probably best known for his social philosophy of "cultural pluralism." In contrast to the dominant cultural ideology of the "melting pot," he argued that American culture is enriched by its variety and that all ethnic groups, including Jews, should have group pride because each contributes in its unique way to the richness of American culture. Kallen specifically argued for Jews' right of and need for a homeland in **Eretz Israel**.

KATZNELSON, BERL (1887–1944). **Labor Zionist** leader Berl Katznelson (née Beeri) was born in Bobruysk, Belarus, to a wealthy family. Berl's father was a member of **Hovevei Zion** and the youth was educated by private tutors. He studied well and was able to complete the required curriculum to pass the exams required to be certified as a tutor, a vocation that Katznelson practiced briefly, both privately and in a girls' school in his native town, where he taught Jewish history and literature. He was also a very popular librarian in the Hebrew-Yiddish library that had been established in the town.

As a youth, Katznelson was interested in socio-political issues, especially as they affected the Jews. He grew increasingly skeptical of the future of Jewish life in the **Diaspora**; thus, he was attracted to **Socialist Zionism**. He developed a strong desire to live in **Eretz Israel** and in 1908, after poor health removed any danger of his being drafted into the army, Katznelson went on *aliya*. Upon arriving in Eretz Israel, he worked near Petah Tikvah and became acquainted with **Aharon David Gordon** and **Yosef Hayim Brenner**, who quickly became his closest friends. He also became politically involved with **David Ben-Gurion** and **Izhak Ben-Zvi**. Katznelson was a firm believer in the "conquest of labor," that is, the central role of Jewish labor in a Jewish society, and he urged all Jewish employers in the *yishuv* to hire Jewish workers.

Katznelson joined Kinneret, a **kibbutz** in the Galilee in 1911 and soon became secretary of the Council of Galilean Agricultural Workers, during which time he began to formulate the notion of a workers' union. After a short tenure, he became critical of the Zionist movement, including much of Socialist Zionism, because its members in the Diaspora tried to control the *yishuv*. Katznelson aspired to a movement of individuals personally committed to *aliya* and labor. He served in the **Jewish Brigade** in 1918 and, two years later, helped found the **Histadrut** trade union federation. One of the founders of Hamashbir and Kupat Holim, Katznelson was in 1925 named editor of *Davar,* the Histadrut daily. He also founded the Labor publishing house Am Oved. Katznelson was appointed to head the **Jewish National Fund** and held that position for the remainder of his life.

A vigorous opponent of **Ze'ev Jabotinsky** and the **Revisionist Zionists**, Katznelson believed their actions were irresponsible and could spell disaster for the welfare of Jews.

At the same time, Katznelson broke with **Chaim Weizmann** and Ben-Gurion on the issue of partition, opposing the **Peel Commission** partition proposal of 1937 on the grounds that Zionism must demand all of Palestine. He later advocated active struggle against the mandatory authorities and was a driving force for "illegal" immigration. During the Nazi period, Katznelson encouraged his younger followers to parachute into occupied Europe to save Jews.

In contrast to most of his Socialist Zionist colleagues, Katznelson advocated the observance of Sabbath, festivals, and dietary laws in the Histadrut kitchens, and he wanted young people to respect and appreciate their Jewish religious heritage. Katznelson was buried in the Kinneret cemetery. The Histadrut college, Beit Berl, in Kfar Sava and Kibbutz Beeri in the Negev are named in his memory.

KEREN HAYESOD. The Keren Hayesod, or the Palestine Foundation Fund, was established in 1920 to serve as the chief fundraising arm of the **World Zionist Organization (WZO)**. The fund became the focal point of controversy when **Justice Louis D. Brandeis** and other American Zionist leaders charged their European WZO counterparts with financial mismanagement of Palestine development projects. A showdown between Brandeis and supporters of WZO president **Chaim Weizmann** ended with the defeat of the Brandeis group, and the Keren Hayesod emerged as the WZO's preeminent financial arm. It soon assumed responsibility for the entire operating budget of the Jewish Agency.

During the British Mandate years, Keren Hayesod played a major role in financing immigration, absorption, education, housing, and development for the *yishuv*. It also purchased arms and paid for other expenses involved in the 1948 War of Independence. Since the establishment of Israel, Keren Hayesod has raised funds to assist in immigration and absorption activities and to aid underprivileged Israelis through programs such as Project Renewal, which rebuilds deteriorating neighborhoods with funds raised in part by **Diaspora** Jewish communities.

KIBBUTZ. Kibbutz (also *kevutza;* pl., kibbutzim, *kevutzot*) is the generic term used to identify a collective community in Israel. Favored by **Socialist Zionists** as the most effective way to settle the land and build a new society, the first kibbutz had its origins in the founding, in December 1909, of an experimental collective settlement in the Jordan River Valley, just off the southern shore of the Kinneret (Sea of Galilee). Although the experiment proved successful, its original members dispersed shortly thereafter, and it was taken over by a group of pioneers (*halutzim*) from Russia who named it Degania.

The various streams of Socialist Zionism devised different types of collectivism but, at least originally, all adhered to the basic tenets of collectivism, namely, that all property was communal and the kibbutz provided for the needs of all of its members (*haverim*). Everyone worked in and for the kibbutz and all jobs were, ostensibly, of equal status. Members shared in the goods and services according to their needs, as defined by the democratically decided criteria. The kibbutz functioned as a popular democracy, with all members having equal voice in the operation of the community. Until the 1970s, kibbutzim were overwhelmingly involved in agricultural production.

In the more ideologically socialist kibbutzim, there was strong age-segregation, with adults and children, even young infants, living separately not only during the daytime hours but at night as well. An original motivating factor for this type of living arrangement was to foster the notion that the kibbutz was more important than the family. Over time, commitment to this ideology dwindled and traditional family patterns, including that of children living with parents, reasserted themselves in the overwhelming majority of kibbutzim.

Some other basic tenets have likewise undergone radical transformation, such as the commitment to agricultural production and the ban on the employment of nonkibbutz members. Kibbutzim are now heavily engaged in manufacturing, and some have opened large shopping centers.

Never comprising more than approximately 4 percent of the Israeli population, the kibbutz has been promoted as the elite of Israeli society. The kibbutz was presented as the model of the new, egalitarian society and became one of most effective fundraising symbols among **Diaspora** communities. It has always been a priority sight-seeing attraction for visitors from abroad, and a prominent American Jewish social scientist once quipped that there were probably many more books and articles written about them than there were actual kibbutzim. Undoubtedly true, this statement indicates the exalted status of the kibbutz and its members, in a society whose political elite viewed the kibbutz as most beneficial to the country's development.

KING-CRANE COMMISSION. Henry C. King, president of Oberlin College, and Charles R. Crane, a businessman and former U.S. diplomat, co-chaired the American section of the Inter-Allied Commission on Mandates in Turkey, which was established by the 1919 Paris Peace Conference. Great Britain and France opposed an American proposal to have the commission visit the formerly Turkish territories of Palestine and Syria to recommend the disposition of those areas. Ignoring his allies' objections, President Woodrow Wilson dispatched King and Crane to scout out the region.

Within days of their arrival in Palestine in June 1919, King and Crane cabled a warning to Wilson that Zionist aspirations could be implemented only through the use of "a large army," thus indicating the commissioners' predisposition against Zionism. After three weeks of meetings with an array of representatives of local political and religious groups, they filed a preliminary report from Beirut. It proposed that a single mandate, consisting of Syria, Lebanon, and Palestine, be granted to the United States or, if it declined, to Great Britain. Emphasizing the Wilsonian principle of national self-determination and Palestinian Arab opposition to Zionism, King-Crane urged the Allies to accept no more than "a greatly reduced Zionist program," according to which limited Jewish immigration would be permitted to Palestine, but no Jewish state would be established against the desires of Palestine's Arab majority.

The commission's final report, reiterating these points, was delivered to the U.S. delegation to the Paris Peace Conference in August. Two Middle East experts who accompanied King and Crane disagreed with some of their conclusions and filed their own reports, one sympathetic to Zionism and the other differing on the issue of a single, unified mandate.

The King-Crane report did not reach President Wilson until after his medical collapse in September, and many historians believe he never even read it. It was not made public until 1922. Consequently, the report had no influence on the disposition of Palestine, the Mandate over which was granted to Britain at the April 1920 **San Remo Conference** and ratified by the League of Nations in July 1922.

KOLLEK, TEDDY. *See* SONNENBORN, RUDOLPH GOLDSCHMIDT.

KOOK, ABRAHAM ISAAC HACOHEN (1865–1935). **Religious Zionist** philosopher and future chief rabbi of Palestine, Abraham Isaac Kook was born in Latvia. Kook's early education was in the local *heder,* the Jewish day school. His father was a scholar who imparted to him a great love for **Eretz Israel**. As a teenager, Kook studied privately with several well-known scholars and, subsequently, in the yeshiva in Volozhin. In addition to traditional Talmud learning, he studied literature, philosophy, and Kabbalah—Jewish mysticism—and began writing original works of Talmudic literature, philosophy, and poetry. Kook served as rabbi in Lithuania from 1888 to 1904, when he immigrated to Eretz Israel and was appointed rabbi of Jaffa. His enthusiastic support of Zionism, which he perceived as part of messianic redemption, antagonized much of the Orthodox rabbinic leadership, whose members were religiously opposed to both the notion and the movement.

In 1914 Kook traveled to Europe and, prevented from returning by the outbreak of World War I, assumed the temporary position of rabbi in a

London congregation. While there, he also attempted to establish a movement for spiritual renewal, Degel Yerushalayim ("Flag of Jerusalem") to supplement the secular Zionist movement. He returned to Eretz Israel after the war and was appointed chief rabbi of Jerusalem. When the mandatory rabbinate was instituted in 1921, Kook was selected as the Ashkenazi chief rabbi of Palestine.

Kook's personal warmth and his interaction with all Jews, regardless of religiosity, as well as his attribution of holiness to all participants in the Zionist endeavor, became legendary and won him admiration even among the most secular Zionists. Some, no doubt, mistook his openness to them as acceptance of their secularism in principle. Although firmly entrenched in traditional learning, Kook was also well-versed in modern Western thought. He simultaneously manifested the sensitivity of the mystic and an intellectual sharpness that took cognizance of the rational. As a communal rabbi, he was attuned to the difficulties of the day and attempted to accommodate his rabbinic decisions to what he perceived as the authentic principles of religio-legal decision making as well as the contemporary situation. This was, at times, another source of tension in Kook's relations with the sectarian Orthodox community.

Another manifestation of his relatively modern perspective was his view of higher Jewish education. Kook established a yeshiva, Mercaz Harav, which was unique in that it incorporated the study of the Bible and Jewish thought and promoted a deep commitment to Zionism, in addition to traditional Talmud study. The yeshiva was small and remained so after his death, when it was headed by his son, Rabbi Zvi Yehuda Kook, and his son-in-law, Rabbi Shalom Natan Raanan. It became a major institution and the center of the messianist ideology that fostered **Gush Emunim** after the Six-Day War of June 1967.

Although Kook's voluminous writings are readily available in Hebrew, only a minute portion of his works has been translated into English.

KOOK, HILLEL (PETER BERGSON) (1915–). Born to a prominent rabbinic family in Lithuania, Hillel Kook grew up at a time of widespread pogroms carried out by rival armies amid the turmoil of the Russian civil war. Kook's childhood memories of **Diaspora** Jewish weakness and suffering would help shape his future political perspective. The Kook family's plans to emigrate to Palestine were delayed when Kook's father was imprisoned by the Soviet authorities because of his Zionist activities. After his release, the Kooks settled in Palestine in 1925, where Hillel's uncle, **Rabbi Abraham Isaac Hacohen Kook**, had recently been named chief rabbi.

As a teenage student in his uncle's yeshiva, Kook became friendly with **David Raziel**, an older student who shared Kook's strong Zionist sentiment. Both young men were admirers of **Ze'ev Jabotinsky**, the founder of **Revisionist Zionism**. Kook and Raziel remained close friends even after Kook, unlike Raziel, left the yeshiva and abandoned religious observance. Kook's sister once described Raziel as Hillel's "*rebbe*" (his personal and spiritual mentor). After the Palestinian Arab pogroms of 1929, Kook followed Raziel into the ranks of the **Haganah**, the Jewish community's self-defense militia.

As students at **Hebrew University** in the early 1930s, Kook and Raziel joined El-Al, a nationalist-activist fraternity. When the Haganah split in 1931, Kook and Raziel went with the more militant underground faction, which would soon be known as the **Irgun Zvai Leumi (IZL)** (National Military Organization); Raziel would eventually become its commander. Kook took part in secret military training, which he put to use as the leader of an IZL unit that combated Palestinian Arab rioters during the nationwide wave of violence that erupted in 1936.

The Irgun sent Kook to Warsaw in 1937 to raise funds, seek support from Polish Jewry as well as the Polish government, and help organize unauthorized Jewish immigration (**Aliya Bet**) to Palestine. In the summer of 1938, the IZL decided to transfer Kook to Revisionist headquarters in London, where he could work closely with Jabotinsky and play a more central role in the movement's leadership. Stationed in the British capital as a leader of a militant underground outlawed by the British, Kook began using an alias, "Peter Bergson," to avoid arrest.

After the outbreak of World War II, Jabotinsky led a delegation of Revisionist and Irgun activists to the United States to launch a propaganda campaign for the creation of a Jewish army to fight alongside the Allies against Hitler. Kook, continuing to use the name Bergson, joined Jabotinsky in New York in May 1940. After the Revisionist leader's sudden death that summer, Bergson and a handful of his friends seceded from the official Revisionist movement and established a succession of Jewish activist groups, most notably the Committee for a Jewish Army of Stateless and Palestinian Jews, the Emergency Committee to Save the Jewish People of Europe, the American League for a Free Palestine, and the Hebrew Committee of National Liberation, which were often referred to collectively as the **Bergson Groups**.

As leader of the Hebrew Committee of National Liberation in 1944, Bergson began advocating a new theory of Jewish identity, according to which Jewish residents of Palestine and European Jews who intended to settle there would adopt the nationality-based identity of "Hebrews," while other **Diaspora** Jews would retain the religion-based designation "Jews." The theory reflected, in part, the influence on Bergson of the poet Yonatan Ratosh, leader of the Canaanite Movement, who argued that the Jews in Palestine constituted a new nation, culturally and spiritually distinct from Diaspora Jewry. Bergson's attempts to promote the "Hebrews" concept met with widespread derision in the American Jewish community.

Immediately after the establishment of Israel in May 1948, Kook— now resuming his real name—returned to the Holy Land. He was one of many Irgunists arrested in the aftermath of the **Altalena Affair** and spent two months in detention. Kook was elected to the First Knesset as a representative of **Menachem Begin**'s Herut Party, but personal and ideological differences led to a split between Kook and Begin, and Kook resigned from Herut in 1950. He returned to the United States the following year, where he took up commodity trading. Kook resettled in Israel in 1968 but never reentered the political arena. He today lives in retirement in the Tel Aviv suburb of Kfar Shmaryahu.

-L-

LABOR ZIONISM. The first Labor Zionist organization, known as Poalei Zion and based on the principles of **Socialist Zionism**, appeared in Minsk, Russia, in 1900. Additional Poalei Zion groups arose elsewhere in Europe and they formed a single international organization at a convention in the Hague in 1907. Internal conflicts in the world socialist movement, especially concerning the movement's relationship with the Soviet Union, led to a division within Poalei Zion. Two rival factions arose at the world Labor Zionist conference in Vienna in 1920.

The more conservative Right Poalei Zion faction merged with **Hapoel Hatzair** to form **Ahdut Ha'avoda**. The Left Poalei Zion was explicitly Marxist, viewing **Ber Borochov** as its ideologist. It remained apart from organized Zionism, including the **Zionist Congresses**, and was hardly involved in the activities of **Practical Zionism**. It concentrated on the socioeconomic, economic, and cultural life of the Jewish communities in the **Diaspora** and on broader societal issues of social justice.

In 1930 Ahdut Ha'avoda and Hapoel Hatzair merged to become Mapai, an acronym for Mifleget Poalei Eretz Israel (Israel Workers' Party). A split emerged in 1944, and an opposition Faction B (Si'ah Bet) seceded from Mapai and took the name Ahdut Ha'avoda. A year later, in 1945, it merged with the Left Poalei Zion, and in 1948 it merged with Hashomer Hatzair as Mapam. Subsequently, in 1954, ideological differences again led it to secede, whereupon it again took the name Ahdut Ha'avoda. In 1965 Ahdut Ha'avoda again joined Mapai to form the Israel Labor Party, and after the Six-Day War, in 1968, they were joined by Rafi, the splinter party created in 1965 by **David Ben-Gurion** and a small group of Knesset members after the Lavon Affair. Since 1969, there has been a Labor Alignment (Ma'arach), which affiliates the Israel Labor Party and Mapam. However, each retains its organizational and party distinctness. *See also* ARLOSOROFF AFFAIR; GORDONIA; HABONIM; HACHSCHARA; HAGANAH; HALUTZ; HEBREW LABOR; HISTADRUT; HEHALUTZ; KIBBUTZ; NA'AMAT; PALMACH.

LAW OF RETURN. The Law of Return was passed by Israel's parliament, the Knesset, in 1950. Its rationale was that Israel is a Jewish state and the state of the Jews. The law, therefore, proclaimed the right of every Jew to come to Israel as an *oleh,* an immigrant with immediate and complete rights of Israeli citizenship. The law was amended in 1954, for clarification purposes but without significant change. In 1965 it was further amended to exclude those for whom there are public documents indicating that they are not Jewish. In 1970 an amendment extended citizenship rights under the law to spouses and children of Jews, even if they are not Jewish.

There have been calls for repeal of the law by some non-Zionists and others who view it as discriminatory. From their perspective, Israel should be a state like any other modern state and should not have laws that discriminate on the basis of religion or ethnicity.

Some Orthodox leaders have called for an amendment to the law that would precisely define a Jew as one born of a Jewish mother or one who converted according to Orthodox tradition. It is the call for this amendment that has given rise to the question "Who is a Jew?" sparking passionate debate, both in Israel and the **Diaspora,** over definitions of Jewish identity and arousing strong opposition from the Reform and Conservative movements.

LEAGUE OF BRITISH JEWS. British Jewish opponents of Zionism established the League of British Jews in 1917 to counter the Zionist lobbying efforts that eventually resulted in the **Balfour Declaration.** The league included a number of prominent British Jews and was chaired by Lionel de Rothschild. Another of its leading members was Laurie

Magnus, editor of the *Jewish Guardian,* which served as a voice of the anti-Zionists. The league disbanded in 1929.

LEHI. *See* LOHAMEI HERUT ISRAEL.

LEVIN, SHEMARYAHU (1867–1935). Russian Zionist activist Shemaryahu Levin was born in Svislovitch, Belarus, where he received a traditional Jewish education. He also received a secular education in the school in Minsk. Levin joined the **Hibbat Zion** movement as a young man and was one of **Ahad Ha'am**'s most dedicated protégés. He joined the **Benei Moshe** society and then studied at the University of Berlin at Berlin's college for the science of Judaism (*wissenschaft des Judentums*) and became a member of the Russian-Jewish Scientific Society, a group that propagated Jewish nationalism. Levin was appointed a rabbi (*Kazyonny ravvin*) in Grodno in 1896, in Yekatrinoslav in 1898, and in Vilna in 1904. In all of his pulpits he spread the idea of Jewish nationalism. Levin was a charismatic orator and a thoughtful journalist who was fluent in both Hebrew and Yiddish, as well as Russian. Youths were especially attracted to his powerful lectures on Jewish historical-cultural themes.

In 1903 Levin was one of the leaders at the Sixth **Zionist Congress** in opposition to the **Uganda Plan**. He helped found the League for the Attainment of Equal Rights for the Jewish People in Russia in 1905 and the following year was elected to the Duma on the Jewish National List in Vilna. Levin left Russia and settled in Berlin in 1908, where he worked for a German-Jewish organization, championed the founding of the Technion in Haifa, and raised money for it. Levin also urged that its language of instruction be Hebrew and, when the suggestion was rejected, he, Ahad Ha'am, and several other Hebraists resigned from the Board of Governors. Elected a delegate to a number of Zionist Congresses, beginning with the Fourth in London in 1900, Levin was an advocate of **Practical Zionism**. He was elected to the Zionist Executive at the Tenth Zionist Congress in 1911.

During World War I, Levin lived in the United States, where he was a prominent Zionist publicist, orator, and proponent of Hebrew culture. He co-edited a weekly Hebrew periodical, *Hatoren* ("The Mast"), and regularly penned its lead article. After the war, Levin returned to Berlin where he joined **Hayyim Bialik** in the founding of the Dvir publishing house. In 1920, he was appointed to head the information services of Keren Hayesod, where Levin was pulled into the **Chaim Weizmann-Louis Brandeis** rift. He remained loyal to Weizmann throughout and orchestrated the victory of the Weizmann faction at the **Zionist Organization of America** convention in Cleveland in 1921. Levin settled in Eretz Israel in 1924. The village of Kfar Shemaryahu, in the southern Sharon, is named for him.

LILIENBLUM, MOSHE LEIB (1843–1910). Early Zionist author and activist Moshe Lilienblum was born in Kedainiai, near Kaunas (Kovno), Lithuania, and received an intensive Orthodox Jewish education. As a young man, he was attracted to the secular Hebrew literature of the Enlightenment and to socialism, believing that it would solve the problem of anti-Semitism. Lilienblum sharply criticized traditional Judaism and wrote articles that harshly rejected Orthodoxy as a stifling relic that has no place in modern culture.

In 1881 Lilienblum underwent a change with respect to socialism and the redemptive power of progress, and he came to view Zionism as the answer to anti-Semitism. Retaining his hostility toward Orthodoxy and its rabbis, he argued that Jews will always remain aliens in the **Diaspora** and they need their own land. He joined **Hibbat Zion,** he was a delegate at its conference held in Katowice in November 1884, and, when the **World Zionist Organization** was founded, he became an active ideologist of **Practical Zionism**.

LIPSKY, LOUIS (1876–1963). American Zionist leader Louis Lipsky was born in Rochester, New York, to immigrants from Poland. Lipsky served as editor of various English-language Jewish periodicals, including *Shofar, The Maccabean, The New Palestine,* and *The American Hebrew,* all of which were implicitly or explicitly Zionist.

Chosen chairman of the **Federation of American Zionists (FAZ)** Executive Committee, Lipsky later served as president of the **Zionist Organization of America (ZOA)** between 1921 and 1930. He was close to **Chaim Weizmann** and was a staunch defender of his policy in the **Weizmann–Brandeis** debate, which, at the 1921 ZOA convention in Cleveland, was decided in Weizmann's favor.

Lipsky was active in the founding of **Keren Hayesod** in the United States and, for a number of years, served as its chief executive officer. He was one of the founders of the World Jewish Congress, a vice president of the **American Jewish Congress**, and president of the **United Jewish Appeal**. During World War II, he played a significant role in garnering American Jewish support for a Jewish state in **Eretz Israel**. He was chairman of the **American Zionist Federation** from 1949–1954.

LOHAMEI HERUT ISRAEL (Lehi). Members of the **Irgun Zvai Leumi (IZL)** underground in Palestine who disagreed with the organization's decision to suspend anti-British actions for the duration of World War II, broke away from the IZL in 1940 to establish a separate Jewish underground movement aspiring to drive the British out of Palestine. The new group, led by senior IZL officer **Avraham Stern**, initially called itself the Irgun Zvai Leumi B'Israel but was known as the Stern Group or, to its detractors, the Stern Gang. In 1941 it changed its name to Lohamei Herut Israel ("Fighters for the Freedom of Israel"), or Lehi.

Lehi's early actions included bank robberies to finance small-scale anti-British attacks. Stern was captured by the British police in February 1942 and executed on the spot. His death led to the temporary disintegration of Lehi.

In mid-1943, Lehi was reorganized under the command of Yitzhak Yezernitzky (later **Shamir**), Israel Scheib (later **Eldad**), and Natan Friedman-Yellin (later Yellin-Mor). Handicapped by their modest numbers—never more than several hundred—and limited arsenal, Lehi concentrated on assassinations of British officials rather than on the larger-scale military attacks launched by the **Irgun**, its partner-in-revolt as of 1944. In November 1944, Lehi members Eliahu Hakim and Eliahu Bet-Zouri killed Lord Moyne, the top British official in the Middle East. The Moyne assassination triggered the first "Season," the **Haganah**'s campaign against the militant Jewish underground. The Haganah focused on the IZL, however, after agreeing to ignore Lehi in exchange for a cessation of Lehi activities.

Lehi resumed the armed struggle when it joined with the IZL and Haganah in the United Hebrew Resistance (UHR), which fought the British from October 1945 until July 1946. When the UHR dissolved, Lehi returned to independent action, sometimes taking part in joint operations with the Irgun, such as attacks on British police and military positions. A Lehi member captured in one of those assaults, Moshe Barazani, was sentenced to death by the British but cheated the hangman by blowing himself up, together with a death-row inmate from the Irgun, Meir Feinstein, in April 1947.

Lehi, like the IZL, was absorbed into the new Israeli army in mid-1948. Nonetheless, Lehi members carried out the assassination of United Nations mediator Count Folke Bernadotte in September 1948, to scuttle his plan to pressure Israel into making substantial territorial concessions to the Arabs. The Israeli government responded by formally outlawing Lehi and placing many ex-members in temporary detention. Yellin-Mor and another Lehi official, Mattitiyahu Shmulevitz, were prosecuted and jailed for their roles in the assassination.

Lehi's three commanders went in different directions after the group's dissolution. Yellin-Mor campaigned in the 1949 Knesset elections from his jail cell; his "Fighters" list won enough votes for one seat, and he was set free to serve in Parliament. Eldad became a prominent Israeli political commentator, writing a column for the Hebrew press and authoring a number of books. Shamir opted for a career in the Mossad, Israel's secret intelligence service. In the 1970s, he became active in the Likud, rose to become foreign minister under **Menachem Begin**, and eventually served as prime minister from 1983–1984 and 1986–1992. *See also* REVISIONIST ZIONISM.

LOWDERMILK, WALTER CLAY (1888–1974). In late 1938, U.S. Secretary of Agriculture Henry Wallace sent Walter Clay Lowdermilk, his assistant chief of soil conservation, to Africa, Europe, and the Middle East to examine whether climactic changes or human mistreatment of the soil were responsible for the transformation of ancient fertile regions into modern deserts. Lowdermilk had previously spent time in northern China and was convinced that local farmers' misuse of the land was to blame for the silt problems in the Yellow River that had caused devastating floods and famine.

Lowdermilk was delighted to discover in Palestine that the Zionist pioneers were carefully practicing soil conservation efforts as they sought to reclaim barren areas of the country. In a radio broadcast from Jerusalem, Lowdermilk dedicated to the pioneers what he called the Eleventh Commandment: "Thou shalt inherit the holy earth as a faithful steward, conserving its resources and productivity from generation to generation. . . ." Lowdermilk's Methodist upbringing had already instilled in him a measure of sympathy for the Jewish rebuilding of the Holy Land. His encounter with the modern *yishuv* sealed his commitment to the Zionist cause.

Lowdermilk's final report of his journeys, completed in the spring of 1939, argued that Palestine could absorb as many as four million Jewish refugees if it used modern scientific methods to irrigate its desert regions, such as hydroelectric power and the diversion of water from the Jordan River. To that end, he recommended the establishment of a Jordan Valley Authority, modeled on the U.S. government's Tennessee Valley Authority.

Lowdermilk's conclusions were utilized by the Zionist movement to combat British claims that Palestine contained an insufficient amount of fertile land to absorb large numbers of immigrants. **Justice Louis D. Brandeis** characterized Lowdermilk's final report as "the best argument for Zionism I have ever read." The **American Zionist Emergency Council** provided him with research assistants and financial backing to facilitate the publication of a book based on his report. *Palestine: Land of Promise* reached the best-seller list in 1944. It eventually went through fourteen printings and was translated into seven languages. Lowdermilk and his wife, Inez, wrote and lectured widely on the Holy Land's future, and Inez even founded a **Hadassah** chapter in Berkeley, California, where they resided.

Lowdermilk's arguments played an important role in the November 1947 debate within the Truman administration over whether or not the Negev desert should be included in the territory that the United Nations had recommended become a Jewish state. **Chaim Weizmann** convinced President Harry S. Truman to support Jewish retention of the Negev by showing him *Palestine: Land of Promise* and arguing that the desert region could be made fertile through methods recommended by Lowdermilk. Many years later, Israeli foreign minister Yigal Allon remarked that Lowdermilk's work had been "instrumental" in securing the Negev for the Jewish state.

On his first visit to the new State of Israel, in 1949, Lowdermilk was troubled to find the Israeli government too overwhelmed by its immigrant absorption problems and national security concerns to pay sufficient attention to the country's agricultural needs. At Chaim Weizmann's request, Lowdermilk spent two years in Israel (1951–1953) as special adviser on soil conservation to the Israeli government. In that capacity, he established the Israeli Soil Conservation Service, created the country's first land-use conservation program, and developed its master water plan.

Returning to Israel in 1954, Lowdermilk developed a school of agricultural engineering at the Haifa Technion, where he served as professor of soil conservation until 1957. Lowdermilk visited Israel again in 1964, to witness the inauguration of the project to use the headwaters of the Jordan River for irrigating desert areas around the southern city of Beersheba, a partial realization of the ideas he had presented twenty years earlier in *Palestine: Land of Promise*.

-M-

MAGNES, JUDAH (1877–1948). American Zionist leader, and later president of **Hebrew University** in Jerusalem, Judah Magnes was born in San

Francisco to German-Jewish immigrants. Magnes received rabbinic ordination at Hebrew Union College in Cincinnati in 1900 and then studied
at the University of Berlin and University of Heidelberg, where he received a doctorate in philosophy. While studying in Europe, he became
aware of Eastern European Jewry and sympathetic to the Zionist movement. He was named rabbi of New York's prestigious Reform congregation Temple Emanuel in 1906. However, his traditionalism as well as
his Zionism caused conflict with the more powerful modernist members
of the congregation and forced him to resign in 1910. He was active in
the small group of Reform rabbis who rejected the anti-Zionist stance
of classical Reform Judaism. His marriage to the sister-in-law of Louis
Marshall, a prominent figure in American Jewry, brought Magnes close
to many American Jewish leaders. He was among the founders of the
American Jewish Committee, was a delegate to the **Zionist Congress**
in 1905, and from 1905 to 1908, was secretary of the **Federation of
American Zionists**.

Magnes was the major force behind the bold experiment to organize
the Jewish community of New York City, the Kehillah, of which he served
as president from its inception in 1908 until its demise in 1922. During
the years of its existence, the Kehillah dealt with religious matters, Jewish
education, and labor relations issues. In the final analysis, despite the
tireless efforts of Magnes, the modern character of American society that
emphasizes the individual over the collective and personal achievement
over ascribed status rendered his dream of creating an organic communal structure unfeasible and unrealizable.

During the World War I years, Magnes was distinctly unpopular in the
American Jewish community because of his deep pacifist convictions,
which were probably rooted in more basic anti-imperialist convictions.
Never one to be swayed because his views were not in vogue, he did not
waver from his pacifism until Hitler rose to power, after which he announced the change in his thinking.

Although he considered himself a Zionist, Magnes did not subscribe
to a notion that became a doctrine of much of Eastern European Zionism, namely, the "negation of the **Diaspora**" (*shelilat hagola*). He viewed
Jewish life as important, whether it be in **Eretz Israel** or in the Diaspora.
His conception was one of the Jewish people with two centers, Israel and
the Diaspora, rather than one of an Israeli center and a Diaspora periph-
ery. Even when, in 1922, Magnes personally went on *aliya,* it was not
out of any belief in an imperative of *aliya* but, rather, as a voluntary personal decision of his own.

Magnes's major activity in Palestine consisted of building the Hebrew University and working toward Arab–Jewish cooperation. In 1923 he was involved in opening the university and establishing an institute for Jewish studies there. He was named chancellor in 1925 and president in 1935, a position that he held until his death. The university's press was named for him. He also served as the chairman of an Emergency Council of **Hadassah** in Palestine and as chairman of the Middle East Advisory Council of the **American Jewish Joint Distribution Committee**, an organization that he had helped found in 1914.

Magnes opposed the establishment of a Jewish state in Palestine. Instead, he advocated a binational state of Palestine in which Jews and Arabs and, indeed, all its citizens would enjoy equal rights. He was one of the founders, in 1925, of **Brith Shalom**, a small group, primarily of intellectuals, that included such personalities as Hans Kohn, **Arthur Ruppin**, Samuel Hugo Bergman, and Gershom Scholem, who held similar convictions on binationalism and Arab–Jewish relations. Magnes was at the center of a major controversy in 1948 when he cooperated with the U.S. State Department in efforts to forestall the establishment of Israel. He died during a visit to New York in October 1948 and was buried in Jerusalem.

MAHAL. Mahal is an acronym for Mitnadevei Hutz La-aretz and refers to volunteers from abroad. Originally, it referred to those 3,000–5,000 **Diaspora** Jews who, in 1947–1948, volunteered and fought in Israel's War of Independence. Many of them had previous military experience and were a significant military resource. Those who did not were provided with basic training as rapidly as possible, sometimes even before their arrival in the country, and they were immediately integrated into units of the Israel Defense Forces (Tzahal). Because of their experience, socioeconomic background, and dedication, they often played significant roles. More than a hundred of these volunteers were killed in action, among the most famous being Colonel Mickey Marcus.

Since American immigration laws began to be interpreted as allowing for volunteering for a foreign country's military service, a very small number of American youth who go to Israel for a year or two of study, with eyes to their own *aliya* several years hence, have begun volunteering for the more recent Mahal program of the Israel Defense Forces.

MAIMON (FISHMAN), JUDAH LEIB (1875–1962). **Religious Zionist** activist Judah Leib Maimon was born in Marculeshti, Russia, and educated at Lithuanian yeshivot. From 1905 to 1913, he was rabbi in Ungeni,

Russia. As a youth, Maimon joined **Hovevei Zion**. After meeting **Rabbi Isaac Jacob Reines**, he became active in the effort to create a Religious Zionist movement and was a participant in the founding conference of **Mizrachi** in Vilna in 1902 and in its first international conference in Pressburg in 1904. From then on, he participated in every **Zionist Congress**. Maimon also spearheaded Zionist educational campaigns in southern Russia, for which he was arrested.

Maimon went on *aliya* in 1913 and settled in Tel Aviv, where his major efforts were devoted to establishing a Religious Zionist educational system in **Eretz Israel**. During World War I, he was deported by the Turkish authorities and opted to move to the United States, where he was soon elected to the central committee of the American Mizrachi organization. Maimon returned to Palestine in 1919, on the first ship to reach its shores after the war. There he headed Mizrachi; edited its newspaper, *Hator* ("The Turtledove"); and, together with **Rabbi Abraham Isaac Kook**, helped establish the Chief Rabbinate of Eretz Israel. Maimon was elected Mizrachi's representative to the Jewish Agency Executive in 1935 and the following year established Mossad Harav Kook, a publishing house that specializes in rabbinic literature. He also founded its journal, *Sinai,* which he edited until his death.

Maimon maintained a strong position with respect to the conflict with the British and, though he remained within the organized Jewish community, he expressed sympathy for such dissident organizations as the **Irgun Zvai Leumi (IZL)** and the **Lohamei Herut Israel**. When the **Haganah** embarked on a campaign of suppression against the IZL, Maimon publicly expressed his opposition. At the same time, he remained a close ally of **David Ben-Gurion** and, at the beginning of the War of Independence, took an active part in the negotiations between the **Jewish Agency** and the IZL. When Israel was established, Maimon was a signatory to its Declaration of Independence.

In 1947 Maimon, Ben-Gurion, and **Yitzhak Gruenbaum** sent a letter in the name of the Jewish Agency to leaders of **Agudat Israel,** pledging that in the State of Israel religious matters would be governed as before, with freedom of religion in the private sphere and traditional Judaism in the public sphere. This agreement, which came to be known as the **Status Quo Agreement**, has been a source of controversy ever since in the struggles between religious and secular factions in Israel.

Maimon served as Israel's first minister of religion until 1951. During his tenure, he advocated the reestablishment of the Sanhedrin, the ancient religious high court, with the authority to improvise and "update" traditional Judaism in light of the new realities, especially of a Jewish state. Maimon and his proposal were sharply denounced in many religious quarters, especially among the *haredim* (ultra-Orthodox). The Sanhedrin dispute worsened relations between Maimon and the *haredim,* which were already tense due to Maimon's criticism of *haredi* anti-Zionism.

Maimon authored numerous works, including biographies of prominent scholars, memoirs, and books on Religious Zionism.

MAPAI. *See* LABOR ZIONISM.

MAPAM. *See* LABOR ZIONISM.

MEIR (MEYERSON), GOLDA (1898–1978). **Labor Zionist** activist and future prime minister of Israel Golda Meir was born Golda Mabovitch in Kiev, Russia. Her family resettled in Milwaukee, Wisconsin, in 1906, where she joined **Poalei Zion** while in high school. After working as a school teacher for several years, Golda and her husband, Morris Meyerson, settled in **Eretz Israel**, in Kibbutz Merhavia, in 1921. She soon became active in the *yishuv's* labor movement. She and her husband moved to Tel Aviv in 1924, where she took a position with the **Histadrut's** construction corporation, Solel Boneh, but returned to the United States for the period of 1932–1934 as a Labor Zionist emissary to the Pioneer Women organization. Meir later served as secretary of the Histadrut's Action Committee and policy section and in 1946, when the mandatory authorities arrested and imprisoned many *yishuv* leaders, she was named in place of **Moshe Sharett** as head of the Political Department of the **Jewish Agency**.

In 1948 Meir was appointed to **David Ben-Gurion's** Provisional Government. After the establishment of the State of Israel, she was elected to the Knesset, served as ambassador to Moscow, and then served in the cabinet as minister of labor from 1949 to 1956 and as foreign minister from 1956 to 1966. Meir was secretary-general of Mapai from 1966 to 1968 and, upon the death of Levi Eshkol in 1969, she became interim prime minister and remained in the position after the October 1969 elections.

The Yom Kippur War broke out during Meir's premiership. Her decision to refrain from launching a preemptive strike against the Arab armies on the eve of the war stirred considerable controversy. After the war, the Israeli government–appointed Agranat Commission concluded that Chief of Staff Moshe Dayan and the government had seriously misjudged Arab intentions. The Labor Party won the elections in December 1973, but Meir resigned in April 1974 after two unsuccessful attempts to form a coalition.

MIZRACHI. When the Fifth **Zionist Congress** in 1901 resolved to enter the educational sphere, many religious members of the **World Zionist Organization (WZO)** who believed that secular nationalism was antithetical to Judaism refused to acquiesce to a program of secular Zionist education. Under the leadership of **Rabbi Isaac Jacob Reines**, the Mizrachi movement was founded in Vilna in 1902 as the **Religious Zionist** organization within the World Zionist Organization. It was the first recognized separate federation within the WZO. The name is an acronym for *mercaz ruhani* (spiritual center), and its banner was "The Land of Israel for the people of Israel according to the Torah of Israel." In 1904 a world conference of Mizrachi was convened in Bratislava, Czechoslovakia (then Pressburg, Hungary), and the Mizrachi World Organization was founded with the objective of educating and promoting Religious Zionism in all religious Jewish circles. The first convention of the American Mizrachi Organization was convened in 1914 under the guidance of **Rabbi Meir Bar-Ilan (Berlin)**, its general secretary.

After World War I, a faction of Religious Zionists with a special interest in settlement and labor formed the Hapoel Hamizrachi (Mizrachi Labor) Organization, which went on to found a series of religious **kibbutzim** and *moshav* settlements. Although Hapoel Hamizrachi worked closely with Mizrachi, the two were separate, autonomous organizations and initially remained so when they were transformed into political parties in the Israeli Knesset. They merged in 1956 and became the National Religious Party (NRP). From 1951 to 1977, they jointly occupied ten to twelve seats in the Knesset.

Although the Mizrachi-Hapoel Hamizrachi movement played a major, if not the most significant, role in establishing the public religious character of Israel in its initial decades, its power and prestige declined notably by the fourth decade of Israel's statehood. In 1981 the party lost half of its twelve seats, and it declined from its representation of two-thirds of the combined religious parties to less than half. It lost even further in 1984 and 1988, declining to less than a third of the combined religious parties' votes. The decline of the NRP has been attributed to a variety of factors, including the perceived accommodative stance of the Likud to religious tradition; ideological confusion, stagnation, and an absence of leadership development within the NRP; and a move to the religious right that led many former Mizrachi loyalists into the more sectarian religious parties such as Agudat Israel and Shas. The 1992 elections gave the NRP a very modest gain of one seat, but that only brought it back to the number of seats it had held in 1981. The NRP's increase to nine seats in 1996 proved to be only a temporary surge, as it dropped to five seats in the 1999 elections. *See also* EMUNAH; BACHAD; HASHOMER HADATI.

MOHILEVER, SAMUEL (1824–1898). Early **Religious Zionist** philosopher Samuel Mohilever was born in a small town near Vilna. He studied at and, in 1842, received ordination at the prominent yeshiva in Volozhin. He served as rabbi in a number of cities in the Polish-Russian region: Glubokoye, 1848–1854; Szaki, 1854–1860; Suwalki, 1860–1868; Radom, 1868–1883; and finally, Bialystok, 1883. Most of his scholarly writings were destroyed in the pogroms of 1906. He founded the Bnai Zion club, which advocated settlement in **Eretz Israel**.

In each of his rabbinic positions, Mohilever was active in community affairs and sought to bridge the growing gap between religious traditionalists and modernists. He was an early member of **Hovevei Zion** and a pioneer of Religious Zionism. At a time when most of his Orthodox colleagues withdrew from the movement because of its growing secular influence, Mohilever remained supportive. Indeed, he encouraged **Leo Pinsker** and **Moshe Lilienblum** in their efforts to organize the various local Hovevei Zion groups into a single organization, **Hibbat Zion**, and he immediately joined that organization. He attributed much greater significance to the modest sums given to Hovevei Zion than to the huge sums that Baron Hirsch dedicated to the establishment of Jewish settlements in Argentina, which Mohilever viewed as dangerous.

In the early 1880s, Mohilever led a group of Hovevei Zion members and influenced Baron Edmond de Rothschild to support the establishment of early settlements in Eretz Israel, especially Rishon le-Zion, Zikhron Ya'akov, Ekron, and Petah Tikvah, to which Rothschild responded very generously. In 1884 Mohilever was named honorary president of the Hovevei Zion conference, and he was chairman of the 1887 and 1889 conferences. In 1890 he led a Hovevei Zion group on a tour of Eretz Israel and, upon his return, issued a public call for physical and financial support of settlement. He also encouraged his Orthodox colleagues to lend their support as well.

Under Mohilever's influence, a rabbinic board was named to ensure that settlement work in Eretz Israel would be carried out in accordance with Jewish tradition, and he issued a responsum that permitted the Jewish farmers in Eretz Israel to work their land during the "seventh year" (*shemita*), when biblical law would appear to prohibit it.

In 1893, at a meeting of Hovevei Zion, Mohilever proposed fostering a movement that would be a *mercaz ruhani*, a "spiritual center" within Zionism. His proposal was adopted and led to the founding of the **Mizrachi** movement; the name, Mizrachi, was adopted as an acronym for *mercaz ruhani*.

Mohilever was an enthusiastic supporter and member of the **World Zionist Organization**. Although he was not able, due to poor health, to attend the First **Zionist Congress** in Basle in 1897, Mohilever did write a stirring letter that was read at the congress. In recognition and appreciation of his activity, he was elected as one of four Russian representatives to the Zionist Executive. In his last letter to the Jews of Russia, Mohilever implored them to tolerance and to participate to the fullest in the settlement of Eretz Israel, "the foundation of the existence of our people."

On his seventieth birthday, an orchard named Gan Shmuel was planted near Hadera in Mohilever's honor and in recognition of all of his activities on behalf of settlement and Zionism.

MONTEFIORE, MOSES (1784–1885). The sponsor of nineteenth-century Jewish settlement efforts in Palestine, Moses Montefiore was born in Leghorn, Italy, while his parents, who lived in Kensington, England, were there on business at the time. The family was of Spanish origin and of modest means. Moses studied at a small commercial school and, upon graduation, went into business as a stockbroker. He was married in 1812 to Judith Barent Cohen, whose father was a wealthy merchant and was related by marriage to the Rothschilds. Montefiore, however, prospered on his own, succeeding in a number of highly lucrative stock market ventures. In 1830, he purchased East Cliff, Ramsgate, as his residence and proceeded to build a synagogue there.

Montefiore's first of seven trips to Jerusalem was in 1827. He went with his wife and, in the course of the trip, also visited Egypt, where he met with Muhammad Ali. In 1836 he was elected president of a group representing the Jewish communities of Great Britain and, from then on, became the spokesman of masses of Jews around the world. In 1840 Montefiore was very active in behalf of the Jewish community of Damascus, which was pillaged in a pogrom emanating from an especially vicious blood libel. Montefiore visited Czarist Russia on at least two occasions for the purpose of seeking to alleviate the plight of Russian Jews. In 1858 a Jewish child, Edgar Mortara of Bologna, Italy, was abducted from the home of his parents, Girolamo Mortara Levi and Marianna Padovani Levi, by a Catholic nurse and was hidden in a convent. According to evidence, the abduction took place with the approval of the archbishop of Bologna, and it was subsequently endorsed by Pope Pius IX. The entire incident was a major cause célèbre in Jewish communities around the world, and Montefiore played a pivotal role in efforts on behalf of the child and his parents.

In his ninetieth year, in 1875, Montefiore undertook efforts to improve the dismal economic condition of the *yishuv* in **Eretz Israel** and to enable it to become economically productive, especially in agriculture and crafts. He established numerous health and social welfare institutions in the *yishuv;* sponsored the first neighborhood outside of the walls of the Old City in Jerusalem, Mishkenot Shaananim; and built the building that houses Rachel's Tomb in Bethlehem.

Montefiore was buried in Ramsgate, England, next to his wife. A number of neighborhoods in Jerusalem are named for him.

MOSHAV. The *moshav* (plural, *moshavim*) is a community in Israel based on agriculture, which has some of the characteristics of the **kibbutz**, in that it is a cooperative but is also based on private farming. The idea of the *moshav* was formulated in 1919 by Eliezer Jaffe. Like the kibbutz, the *moshav* was viewed as a pioneering institution. It provided an economic structure that its members favored and it facilitated mass settlement. The first *moshavim,* Nahalal and Kfar Yehezkel, were founded in 1921 in the Jezreel Valley, and they became the models for the *moshav 'ovdim,* the workers' collective.

The *moshav* leases land from the Israel Lands Authority or the **Jewish National Fund** and that land is then divided among the settlement's members, who typically number approximately 60 families. Prior to the Six-Day War, the *moshav* ban on hired labor was widely upheld. Since then, however, *moshavim* have increasingly come to rely on Arab labor as an integral part of the moshav economy.

Another kind of *moshav,* the *moshav shitufi,* or collective settlement, was established by those who wished to combine what they viewed as the best of the kibbutz and the *moshav,* while not being, as they viewed it, overly collective, as in the kibbutz, or overly individualistic, as in the *moshav 'ovdim.* The first two *moshavim* of this type, Kefar Hittim and Moledat, were established in 1936–1937 in the Galilee.

By 1970, there were over 300 workers' *moshavim,* with a population of more than 100,000, and 22 collective *moshavim,* with a population of approximately 4,200. By 1991, the latter grew to 46 collective *moshavim,* with a total population of 12,600.

MOTZKIN, LEON (ARYE LEIB) (1867–1933). Early Zionist author and activist Leon Motzkin was born in a small town near Kiev and studied at a traditional Jewish primary school (*heder*). As a young teenager he witnessed a pogrom in Kiev, an event that was to profoundly affect the future course of his life. In 1889 Motzkin was among the founders of the Russian Jewish Academic Association. He also wrote articles in Jewish periodicals that advocated the return to Zion and the national revival of the Jewish people. He was one of the founders of the first nationalist Jewish student society.

During that period, Motzkin met and became friendly with **Chaim Weizmann**, who viewed Motzkin as his mentor in Jewish nationalism. Motzkin was a harsh critic of **Hovevei Zion**, favoring instead the approach of **Theodor Herzl** and **Political Zionism**. He was active at the **First Zionist Congress** and participated in the drafting of the **Basle Program**. He was one of the founders of the **Democratic Faction**, which rallied for the democratization of the **World Zionist Organization** and for its inclusion of a cultural agenda in its activities.

In 1911–1913, while Mendel Beilis was on trial in the famous blood libel case in Russia, Motzkin actively provided information to world capitals and encouraged public figures to publicly protest against the false allegations. He was also a staunch advocate of Hebrew as the national language of the Jews.

During World War I, he headed the Zionist Organization's Copenhagen office, which served as a liaison between the various Zionist organizations in the warring countries. At the end of 1915, Motzkin went to the United States to garner support for Jewish war victims and to ensure equal rights for the Jews of Russia. While there, he became active in the movement to convene the **American Jewish Congress**.

Motzkin was elected to the Zionist Executive in 1921–1923 and, for the last several years of his life, served as president of the Zionist Congresses, which, de facto, he headed since the 12th Congress. He was an early advocate for the establishment of a World Jewish Congress to represent and advance Jewish interests in international forums. This objective was fulfilled with the convening of the first **World Jewish Congress** in 1930, three years before his death. He died in Paris and was reinterred on the Mount of Olives, in Jerusalem in 1934.

-N-

NA'AMAT (Working and Volunteering Women). The Israel-based women's **Labor Zionist** movement, Nashim Ovdot u-Mitnadvot, is better known by its acronym, Na'amat. It lobbies for women's rights, sponsors vocational training for girls, runs child-care centers, and provides various forms of assistance to working mothers. Pioneer Women, the **Diaspora** support group for Na'amat, raises funds for the movement's projects in Israel.

NATIONAL RELIGIOUS PARTY (NRP). *See* MIZRACHI.

NEGATION OF THE DIASPORA. The negative view of the **Diaspora**, a prominent theme in modern Zionist thought, was originally expressed in religious thought. A strong religious rejection of the Diaspora, *Galut,* was a major theme of most Jewish philosophers. Although there were differences among scholars-rabbis in terms of the degree to which they explicitly emphasized the negative nature of Diaspora existence and, concomitantly, the degree to which they emphasized the drive to return to **Eretz Israel**, there was virtually no Jewish religious authority until the modern era who even remotely suggested *Galut* existence as an ideal. Without exception, *Galut* was defined as an ultimately negative existence; Zion was the unequivocal ideal.

The ideological negation of the exile (*shelilat hagola*) is, to one degree or another, an explicit or implicit assumption of all varieties of Zionism. It flows from the premise that there can be no future for the Jewish people without the center in Eretz Israel.

NES ZIONA. Religious Zionist students from the Volozhin yeshiva who joined the **Hovevei Zion** movement established their own faction within the movement, known as Nes Ziona, in 1885. It was specifically Orthodox and had, among its explicit objectives, the goal of developing rabbis, orators, writers, and other intellectuals who would influence the masses and bring them closer to the movement to settle **Eretz Israel**. Similar to other groups at the time, Nes Ziona was a semi-secret, underground group because it had no government authorization. Its elaborate oath of allegiance was a source of controversy among its members and, in 1887, jeopardized the group's future when some members threatened to leave unless the oath was modified. Lengthy deliberations resulted in new leadership for the group and created a heightened pace of activity, most of which was directed at propaganda, especially in the distribution of rabbinic Zionist literature. Books, periodicals, and a letter by the revered Rabbi Naphtali Zvi Judah Berlin ("Netziv") that was emphatically supportive of **Hibbat Zion** were widely circulated. A strong letter of support from thirteen of Eastern Europe's most prominent rabbis gave Nes Ziona a significant boost.

The group was eventually exposed when a letter written by one of its members to a periodical fell into the hands of the Russian police, who promptly shut the group down. Many of Nes Ziona's members subsequently joined the **Benei Moshe** group, while a small core reorganized, calling themselves "Netzach Israel," with virtually the same objectives as its predecessor. However, when the yeshiva in Volozhin closed in the winter of 1892, the group's members dispersed and it ceased to exist.

NETANYAHU, BENZION (1911–). **Revisionist Zionist** activist and Jewish history scholar Benzion Netanyahu is the eldest son of Russian Zionist activist and Orthodox rabbi Nathan Mileikowsky. Benzion came to Palestine with his family in 1920, at age nine. During the early 1930s, he became active in the Revisionist Zionist movement, joining its Central Committee in 1933 and founding the Revisionist daily newspaper *Hayarden* ("The Jordan") the following year. After his father's death in 1935, Benzion memorialized him by adopting a Hebraized version of his father's first name as his new family name.

Netanyahu's strong interest in Jewish historical scholarship was reflected in a series of literary projects he undertook during 1935–1940, including his editing of the collected writings of Zionist leaders **Theodor Herzl**, **Max Nordau**, and **Israel Zangwill**.

In the spring of 1940, Netanyahu joined **Ze'ev Jabotinsky**'s delegation to the United States, where he worked to revive Revisionism's American wing. He was one of the initiators of the campaign to create a Jewish army to fight alongside the Allies, a proposal that eventually led to the British establishment of the **Jewish Brigade** in 1944.

Netanyahu became executive director of the New Zionist Organization of America (NZOA), the U.S. wing of the Revisionist movement, in early 1942. He helped raise the group's profile and influence by organizing public rallies and authoring newspaper advertisements calling for Jewish statehood in Palestine. Netanyahu also spent considerable time lobbying on Capitol Hill, where he established the first serious relationships between the Zionist movement and Republican members of Congress. When the NZOA was admitted, in 1946, to the **American Zionist Emergency Council (AZEC)**—the coalition of major U.S. Zionist groups—Netanyahu served as its representative in AZEC deliberations.

At the same time, he completed his doctorate at Dropsie College in Philadelphia, specializing in the history of Spanish Jewry.

After the establishment of Israel, Netanyahu settled in Jerusalem and became editor of the *Encyclopedia Hebraica*. In 1960 he accepted a teaching post at Dropsie and later served on the faculties at the University of Denver and Cornell University, before returning to Jerusalem in 1979. He has authored several scholarly works, most notably his 1995 magnum opus, a 1,300-page study of the Inquisition.

Netanyahu's eldest son, Jonathan, was killed leading the Entebbe rescue raid in 1976. His second son, Benjamin, was elected prime minister of Israel in 1996 as leader of the Likud Party. His youngest son, Ido, is a radiologist and novelist.

NETUREI KARTA. Neturei Karta is a sect of *haredi* (ultra-Orthodox) Jews whose name is Aramaic for "Guardians of the City." Its founders seceded from **Agudat Israel** in 1935 because the group totally disavows the Zionist movement, not only because it opposes the secularism of modern Zionism, but because it defines all forms of Zionism as well as any other human endeavors to end the Divinely decreed Exile as inherently Satanic. In Neturei Karta's view, the dispersion was ordained by God and the redemption can only come about through His intervention. A vehement early advocate of this perspective was the Munkaczer Rebbe, Rabbi Chaim Elazar Shapira, one of the first and fiercest opponents of both Zionism and non-Zionism in the early part of this century. As he saw it, Zion was always the focus of a great struggle between the forces of light and those of darkness, between God, on the one hand, and the Evil Inclination (*yetzer hara*), on the other. Thus, in our day it is not only God Who delights to dwell in the Holy Land and the Holy City, but also "the new ones, who came but lately" (Deuteronomy 32:17), those who seek to force Zion to submit to them and make it the center of their sacrilegious enterprise.

Neturei Karta opposed the establishment of the State of Israel and Israeli sovereignty over Jerusalem. Centered in the Meah Shearim area of Jerusalem, it rejects the validity of Israel's existence, does not participate in its political process, maintains its own autonomous religio-communal structure, views itself as the sole authentic protector of the religious nature of the city, and frequently demonstrates against what it views as violations of that nature. A number of individuals claiming to represent it have made various overtures to the Palestine Liberation Organization (PLO). One in particular, Rabbi Moshe Hirsch, is frequently referred to in the Israeli media as the PLO's Jewish foreign minister. The much larger Satmar Hasidic group is supportive of Neturei Karta and often serves as its voice in Jewish communities outside Israel. Both groups have undertaken numerous public demonstrations against Zionism and Israel.

NETZER OLAMI. Headquartered in Jerusalem, Netzer Olami (Hebrew for "Eternal Crown") was established in 1980 as the international Reform Zionist Youth Movement, with branches in North America, Europe, South Africa, and Australia. It sponsors educational meetings, tours of Israel, and summer and winter camps.

NEUMANN, EMANUEL (1893–1980). American Zionist leader Emanuel Neumann was raised in a home steeped in Zionism and Hebrew culture. His father established the first school in the United States in which Hebrew was the sole language of instruction, and Hebrew was the language spoken in the Neumann home.

Beginning in his teenage years, Neumann was a seminal figure in a wide variety of American Zionist endeavors. At seventeen, he helped establish the Zionist youth movement Young Judea and later edited the group's magazine. He was education director of the **Zionist Organization of America** (1918–1920), cofounder and national director of the U.S. division of the **Keren Hayesod** (1921–1925), a founder and chairman of the executive committee of the **United Palestine Appeal** (1925–1927), president of the **Jewish National Fund** (1928–1930), and first organizer of the **American Palestine Committee** (1931).

Neumann spent 1932–1934 in Jerusalem as director of the **Jewish Agency**'s Economic Department. During that period, he also undertook secret negotiations with Abdullah, Emir of Transjordan, to allow Jewish settlement in that region. He remained in Palestine until 1939, taking part in various business ventures. Neumann also became active with the **General Zionist** party, which put him at odds with the *yishuv*'s **Labor Zionist** leadership for many years afterward.

When American Zionist leaders decided, on the eve of World War II, to intensify their political action efforts, Neumann was dispatched to the United States to take charge of the Public Relations and Political Action Department of the **Emergency Committee for Zionist Affairs**. He revived the American Palestine Committee, which recruited politicians, intellectuals, and other public figures to support the Zionist cause.

Disappointed by the U.S. Zionist leadership's reluctance to adopt a more activist approach, Neumann resigned in late 1942. He then worked to facilitate the appointment of **Rabbi Abba Hillel Silver** as co-chairman of the **American Zionist Emergency Council (AZEC)** in the summer of 1943, resulting in the implementation of activist policies. After Silver resigned in late 1944 over differences with the more cautious **Stephen Wise**, Neumann worked successfully to bring Silver back to power the following year. Throughout this period, Neumann served as Silver's senior aide, director of political action for the AZEC, and a primary spokesman for the American Zionist movement. At the same time, Neumann served as a member of the Jewish Agency Executive, chaired the Committee on Political Resolutions of the **World Zionist Congress**, and testified before the U.S. Congress and the **Anglo-American Committee of Inquiry on Palestine**.

In 1947 Neumann was elected president of the **Zionist Organization of America (ZOA)**, a crowning achievement after nearly forty years of professional Zionist activity. During his two years as president, the ZOA, working closely with Silver and the AZEC, played a key role in the mobilization of American Jewry, Congress, and public opinion on behalf of Jewish statehood.

After Israel's establishment, Neumann remained active in Zionist affairs. Along with Silver, he left the Zionist leadership in 1949 in a dispute over the Israeli government's involvement in **Diaspora** organizational matters. He returned to the Jewish Agency Executive in 1951, however, and chaired its American Section during several periods in the 1960s and early 1970s. He was elected to another term as president of the ZOA, from 1956 to 1958, while also serving as president of the **World Union of General Zionists** throughout the 1950s and 1960s. Neumann's interest in Zionist cultural affairs remained keen. He established the Jewish Agency's adult education division in New York, the **Theodor Herzl Institute**; helped found the Tarbuth Foundation for the Advancement of Hebrew Culture in America; chaired the editorial committee of the first *Encyclopedia of Zionism and Israel;* and authored numerous essays on Zionist topics for Jewish publications.

NEW ISRAEL FUND. Left-of-center American Jews established the New Israel Fund in northern California in 1979 to raise funds for like-minded Israeli political, social, and religious movements. The fund subsequently shifted its headquarters to New York City and established branch offices in numerous U.S. cities, as well as Canada and Jerusalem.

The New Israel Fund's beneficiaries include Israeli groups involved in civil rights litigation, environmental activism, women's rights, Jewish–Arab social interaction, and lobbying for Israeli governmental recognition of Reform and Conservative Judaism. The fund has attracted some criticism in the Jewish community because its largest beneficiary, the Association for Civil Rights in Israel, provides legal assistance to, among others, imprisoned Arab terrorist suspects.

In addition to its grants program, the New Israel Fund annually awards endowed prizes to selected organizations promoting education for democracy; working in the field of community relations; furthering democratic values; and improving Jewish–Arab relations. An Israel Women's Leadership Award is given each year to a leader of the Israeli women's rights movement. The fund's annual award to a journalist for the best coverage of issues in Israel was discontinued after several of the award recipients were criticized for being unsympathetic to Israel.

Despite the controversies it has stirred, the New Israel Fund has grown steadily over the years, from an annual income of less than $100,000 at its inception to more than $17 million by 1997.

NEW JEWISH AGENDA (NJA). After the dissolution of the **Breira** organization in 1978–1979, left-wing American Jews regrouped to establish New Jewish Agenda, which was intended to provide "a Jewish voice among progressives, a progressive voice among Jews."

Regarding Israel, New Jewish Agenda called for an Israeli–Arab settlement based on withdrawal to Israel's pre-1967 borders and the establishment of a Palestinian state, with Jerusalem to be shared between Israel and the new state. Unlike Breira, which focused almost exclusively on the Middle East, NJA was also active on a broad range of other issues, including support for feminism, gay rights, superpower disarmament, and Central American liberation movements.

The NJA's sharp criticism of Israel, its meetings with officials of the Palestine Liberation Organization, and its willingness to cooperate with Arab-American groups that were unfriendly to Israel aroused opposition in the Jewish community. The NJA's Western States division stirred further controversy by opposing "Operation Exodus," the mainstream community's campaign to finance Soviet Jewish immigration to Israel, on grounds that it might impinge on Arab rights.

The NJA's attempts to gain representation on local Federation-sponsored Jewish Community Relations Councils were rebuffed in some cities but successful in others. The movement failed, however, to attract either a broad base of popular support or substantial financial backing and in 1993 announced the shutdown of its national headquarters in New York City. Individual NJA chapters in some parts of the United States continue to function independently.

NILI. In 1915 a small group of Zionist activists in Palestine organized an espionage ring to provide Great Britain with intelligence information that they hoped would assist in the British conquest of the Holy Land. The group called itself Nili, a Hebrew acronym for the biblical verse (I Samuel 15:29) "The Eternal One of Israel will not lie." The internationally acclaimed agronomist **Aaron Aaronsohn** and a colleague at the Atlit agricultural experiment station, Avshalom Feinberg, founded and led Nili. Its forty or so members included Aaron's siblings, Alexander and Sarah.

Aaronsohn managed to reach Egypt in the summer of 1916, where he established a relationship with British military headquarters. Subsequently, a British ship stationed off the Palestine coast was employed to receive information gathered by Nili concerning military, political, and economic conditions in Palestine, which was used to great effect in Britain's capture of the Holy Land. In addition, Aaronsohn's meetings with British cabinet officials in London contributed to the Zionist lobbying effort that eventually resulted in the **Balfour Declaration**. Nevertheless, most leaders of the *yishuv* opposed Nili, for fear that its activities would unleash the Turkish authorities' wrath upon all of Palestine Jewry.

In October 1917, the Turks uncovered Nili. The activists who were captured were treated harshly, including Sarah Aaronsohn, who committed suicide after three days of torture so as to avoid the risk of breaking down and informing on her colleagues. Two Nili members were executed for treason; others were deported. This debacle, combined with the British conquest of Palestine and the death of Aaron Aaronsohn in a 1919 plane crash over the English Channel, ended Nili's brief but turbulent history.

NON-ZIONIST. Just as there are varying conceptions of Zionism, there are varying conceptions of non-Zionism. A non-Zionist may be one who rejects the entire notion of Jewish nationality, such as those who adhered to classical Reform Judaism; those who reject the notion of Jewish self-determination, such as the **Neturei Karta**; those who reject the singularity of Zion as the Jewish homeland, such as the **Territorialists**; and/ or those who reject the notion of a Jewish homeland, such as Simon Dubnow and the Autonomists. In the formal vocabulary of Jewish organizational life, the term *non-Zionist* refers to those who refuse to join the **World Zionist Organization** even though they may strongly support the notion of Jewish statehood. Most typically, the latter non-Zionists are Jews in Western countries, especially the United States, who are staunchly pro-Israel but reject the Zionist Organization's tenets of the centrality of Israel in Jewish life, because they view Jewish life in their country as at least on par with that of Israel, and reject the notion of *aliya*, immigration to Israel, as an imperative for all Jews.

Although the Zionist Organization and many of Israel's early leaders were at least implicitly deprecatory toward non-Zionism, it had already attained a significant role in Zionist affairs by virtue of the 1929 Pact of Glory, which gave non-Zionists a prominent role in the leadership of the **Jewish Agency** in exchange for their commitment to substantial fundraising for *yishuv* development projects. The continuing friendly relationship between Zionists and non-Zionists is a reflection of both changes in the ideological perspectives of Zionists and the increasing pro-Israelism of non-Zionists.

NORDAU, MAX (1849–1923). Zionist leader Max Nordau was born in Budapest, Hungary. His father, Gabriel Suedfeld (or Suegfeld), was ordained as an Orthodox rabbi and scholar and provided Max (Simha Zelig) with a traditional Jewish education. By age eighteen, however, Nordau rejected religious traditionalism, became a naturalist and evolutionist, and went on to study medicine, which he practiced for a number of years. He also engaged in journalism, changed his name, and acquired a reputation as a controversial intellectual and social critic, writing in a number of languages, primarily German. During the years 1880–1914, Nordau lived in Paris. In 1896 he married Elizabeth Dons-Kaufman, a Christian woman who was the widow of the Danish writer Richard Kaufman.

Like **Theodor Herzl** and others, Nordau's sense of Jewishness was profoundly affected by the rising tide of European anti-Semitism during the 1880s. As a journalist in Paris, he was witness to the Dreyfus trial, which apparently sparked his initial interest during the early 1990s in the projects of Baron Hirsch. Nordau first met Herzl in 1892, and when, in 1895, Herzl presented him with his plan for the Jewish state, Nordau was taken with it. He gave his pen and his reputation to the effort, became Herzl's partner in the Zionist movement, and helped mold the **Basle Program** for presentation at the First **Zionist Congress**.

Nordau served as vice president of the first six congresses and was president of the Seventh–Tenth Congresses. He defended the **Uganda Plan** at the Sixth Zionist Congress, which he defined as a temporary *nachtasyl* ("night shelter"). He also staunchly defended Herzl's **Political Zionism** and was sharply critical of **Ahad Ha'am**'s **Cultural Zion-**

ism, which he characterized as "Judaism without Jews." When, at the 11th Zionist Congress in 1911, David Wolffsohn was shunted aside by the **Practical Zionists**, Nordau joined the opposition. That was the last Zionist Congress he attended.

During World War I, Nordau insisted that the **Zionist Organization** maintain neutrality, and he urged that it present three Jewish demands to the Peace Conference: civil rights, cultural-national autonomy, and free immigration, settlement, and self-administration in **Eretz Israel**.

After the war, Nordau remained aloof from the Zionist Organization, believing that it was not the movement Herzl hoped it would become. **Chaim Weizmann** made several attempts to bring him back in, but he refused. He was skeptical of the **Balfour Declaration**, urging the Zionist Organization, instead, to bring half a million Jews from Europe to Eretz Israel. Nordau indicated that he planned to move to Eretz Israel, but he died in Paris without realizing that dream. He was reinterred in Tel Aviv in 1926.

-O-

ORDER OF ANCIENT MACCABEANS. Early British Zionist activists, including Herbert Bentwich and Ephraim Ish-Kishor, established the Order of Ancient Maccabeans in 1891. Rivalry between the order and the larger **Zionist Federation of Great Britain and Ireland** was eventually resolved through the creation of a Joint Zionist Council in 1912. Among the order's notable activities were its 1897 pilgrimage to Palestine by twenty-one prominent British Zionists and its post–World War I purchases of land in Palestine for Zionist settlement.

-P-

PALMACH. The Palmach (Hebrew acronym for Plugot Mahatz, or "shock units") was the mobile strike force of the **Haganah**, Palestine Jewry's self-defense militia. The Palmach was established by the Haganah high command in May 1941 to undertake special missions, including assisting in the British conquest of Syria and Lebanon that summer. In mid-1942, faced with the prospect of a German invasion of Palestine, British experts trained the Palmach in guerrilla warfare tactics. During the war, thirty-two Jewish parachutists from Palestine, most of them Palmach members, landed behind Nazi lines in Europe to aid the Allied war effort and make contact with persecuted Jewish communities. Toward the war's end, however, British Mandate authorities, fearing that the Palmach would eventually be used against them, turned against the Jewish strike force.

Palmach soldiers, one-third of whom were women, were stationed on **kibbutzim**, where they worked part time while continuing their military service. A small number were trained as pilots and later served in the Israeli Air Force. Others manned the Palmach's naval unit, the Palyam, and formed the core of the future Israeli Navy.

Palmach units played a leading role in the Haganah's campaign against the **Irgun Zvai Leumi (IZL)** and **Lehi** (Stern Group) undergrounds in 1944–1945 and in 1948 sank the IZL ship *Altalena,* which **Prime Minister David Ben-Gurion** feared was carrying weapons that might be used to overthrow his government. On the other hand, the Palmach cooperated with the IZL and Lehi as part of the United Hebrew Resistance movement that attacked British targets in Palestine during 1945–1946. After the alliance broke up in mid-1946, the Palmach concentrated its efforts on bringing shiploads of unauthorized Jewish immigrants from Europe to Palestine. Palmach frogmen repeatedly sank British ships that were used to deport immigrants to Cyprus.

The Palmach played a major role in the 1948 War of Independence, capturing Tiberias, Safed, Kastel, and other key areas, and taking part in the conquest of Beersheba, Lydda, and Ramleh, as well as in the counter-offensives against Egypt in late 1948 and early 1949. More than one-sixth of the Palmach's five thousand soldiers were killed in action. Fearing that the Palmach's independence of mind could pose a threat to his power, Ben-Gurion ordered the force dissolved shortly after the conclusion of the war. *See also* LABOR ZIONISM.

PEACE NOW. Critics of Israeli prime minister **Menachem Begin** launched the Peace Now movement in the spring of 1978, with an open letter signed by 350 army reserve officers, urging Begin to make more concessions to the Arabs.

During the 1980s, Peace Now gradually emerged as Israel's largest extraparliamentary protest movement, attracting large numbers of young Labor and Mapam activists who felt frustrated by their parties' inability to influence the course of events. Peace Now organized demonstrations, petitions, and newspaper advertisements urging Israel to make more concessions in the Israeli–Egyptian negotiations and opposing the establishment of Jewish communities in the Israeli-administered territories. Peace Now's activities were denounced by those who feared its public opposition to the Israeli government would undermine Israel's negotiating posture. Arab leaders' praise of Peace Now further fueled such resentment.

Peace Now's criticism of Israeli conduct in the 1982 Lebanon war was particularly controversial, since it was the first instance of significant public opposition to government policy during wartime. The mass rallies organized by Peace Now after the Christian Lebanese killings in the Sabra and Shatila refugee camps in September 1982 were a major impetus to the establishment of the Israeli Commission of Inquiry into that episode.

The signing of the 1993 Oslo accords by Israel and the Palestine Liberation Organization was seen by many Peace Now members as the fulfillment of their goals. One consequence is that Peace Now's ranks have dwindled in recent years, as has its influence, although the movement continues to undertake a variety of political and educational activities both in Israel and in the **Diaspora**. *See also* WHITE PAPERS.

PEEL COMMISSION. Responding to the eruption of sustained Palestinian Arab violence in April 1936, the British government announced the appointment of a Royal Commission, headed by former cabinet minister Lord Peel, to examine the causes of the violence and offer policy recommendations. When the violence finally subsided in November, the commission visited Palestine, where it spent nine weeks hearing testimony from Arab and Jewish representatives. The commissioners also briefly visited Transjordan to meet with its ruler, the Emir Abdullah.

In July 1937, the Peel Commission issued its 400-page final report, which was authored primarily by Oxford University professor Reginald Coupland. It recommended partition of Palestine into separate Arab and Jewish states, with the borders to be drawn largely according to demographic considerations. Thus the small Jewish state would encompass the Jezreel Valley, the Galilee, and part of the coastal strip, while the much larger Arab state would include the rest of the country. The British would maintain control over Haifa, Acre, Jerusalem, the area south of Jerusalem reaching Bethlehem, a corridor from Jerusalem to Jaffa, and an area adjacent to Aqaba. The plan also provided for the relocation of 225,000 Arabs from the Jewish area to the Arab state, in order to ensure that the Jewish state would have a Jewish majority.

Arab leaders rejected the plan unequivocally. The Zionist movement was deeply divided. At the August 1937 World Zionist Congress, **Chaim Weizmann** and **David Ben-Gurion** led the supporters of partition. Some Labor Zionists, many General Zionists, the Mizrachi Religious Zionists, and the **Jewish State Party** opposed the Peel plan because of the small amount of territory allotted to the Jews; the left-wing **Hashomer Hatzair** opposed the Peel plan because it preferred a binational Arab-Jewish state. By a vote of 300 to 158, the congress adopted a compromise resolution criticizing Peel's proposed borders but authorizing negotiations with the British to clarify the details of the plan. The British government, for its part, accepted the Peel Commission's recommendations, but in the face of renewed Arab violence during the year to follow, London gradually abandoned the plan.

PINSKER, LEON (JUDAH LEIB) (1821–1891). Russian Zionist leader Leon Pinsker was born in Tomaszów, Poland (now called Tomaszów Mazoweicki), and received his Jewish education in the school run by his father, Simcha Pinsker (1801–1864). He studied law in Odessa and medicine at the University of Moscow. Subsequently, he practiced medicine in Odessa in 1849, where he was one of the founders of and regular contributors to a Russian-language Jewish weekly. He also was involved with the local branch of the Society for the Dissemination of Enlightenment (Hevrat Mefitzei Haskala), which specialized in presenting Jewish culture in Russian. After the pogrom in Odessa in 1871 challenged his faith in the Enlightenment, Pinsker ceased his cultural work and concentrated on professional medicine.

Disheartened by the pogroms of 1881 and the blatant anti-Semitism of the regime, Pinsker met with a variety of European Jewish leaders and intellectuals—including Vienna's chief rabbi, Adolf Aaron Jellinek; the British jurist and head of the Board of Deputies of British Jews, Arthur Cohen; and the heads of the **Alliance Israélite Universelle**, to discuss his ideas concerning the need to organize the migration of Russian Jewry and the need for an autonomous national Jewish center. Almost all of those with whom he met rejected his notions. Cohen, however, was much more receptive, and he encouraged Pinsker to publish his views, which he did anonymously in a pamphlet, written in German, entitled *Auto-emancipation*. Written passionately by "a Russian Jew," Pinsker asserted that Jews constitute a unique ethnic entity that will not and cannot be assimilated into any other society and that the only solution to anti-Semitism and the Jewish problem is for them have their own country and be a nation like all others. In short, he asserted the necessity and inevitability of territorial independence in a Jewish homeland, and he called for its immediate realization, without, however, specifying its geographic location. The pamphlet was enthusiastically endorsed by **Hovevei Zion**, widely discussed by others, and heatedly debated in Russia and beyond.

Subsequently, Pinsker became increasingly active in **Hibbat Zion**, and in 1884 he helped organize a convention of Hibbat Zion, of which he was elected chairman and at which he delivered a speech that emphasized the importance of hands-on agricultural work. In 1887, at the second convention, a bitter dispute erupted between the secularist intellectuals (*maskilim*) and the religionists, led by Rabbi Samuel Mohilever. Pinsker remained and, at the behest of the secularists, continued to serve as the movement's leader. However, he did not attend the convention, which took place in Vilna in 1889, nor was he elected to the executive committee.

In 1890 Hovevei Zion was granted formal permission to establish the Society for the Support of Jewish Farmers and Artisans in Palestine, and Pinsker was elected its chairman. Concurrently, due to worsening conditions for Russia's Jews, the Hovevei Zion movement gained followers, and the *aliya* notion gained momentum. However, due to the Ottoman authorities' ban on immigration, no significant flow of *aliya* followed. The Society was thrown into crisis by its acquisition of huge debts and the annulment by the Ottoman authorities of many of its land purchases. Pinsker was at the time physically weak, and he grew increasingly pessimistic about the possibility of establishing a meaningful Jewish homeland in **Eretz Israel**. He came to believe that Eretz Israel could be no more than a spiritual center for Jews and shifted his support to Baron de Hirsch's **Jewish Colonization Association**, which promoted the settlement of Jews in Argentina.

Pinsker died and was buried in Russia in 1891. He was reinterred in 1934 in Nicanor's Cave, near Mount Scopus in Jerusalem.

PITTSBURGH PLATFORM. Nineteen prominent American Reform rabbis, meeting in Pittsburgh in November 1885, issued a statement of religious principles that later came to be known as the Pittsburgh Platform. It was intended as Reform Judaism's retort to its two main theological rivals—Felix Adler's Ethical Culture movement, which sought to attract American Jews to universalism, and traditional Judaism, which sought to preserve practices and beliefs that the Reform movement regarded as outdated.

The Pittsburgh Platform reflected the optimism of its era. It reveled in "the spirit of broad humanity of our age" and averred: "We recognize in the modern era of universal culture of heart and intellect the approaching of the realization of Israel's great Messianic hope for the establishment of the kingdom of truth, justice and peace among all men." The platform argued that modern Jews should discard the "primitive" ideas of their ancestors and concentrate on facilitating the arrival of the messianic era of universal brotherhood.

The Pittsburgh Platform asserted that "only the moral laws" of the Bible remain binding. It rejected all other traditional religious legislation, specifically citing those laws that "regulate diet, priestly purity and dress" as irrelevant to modern Jewry. On the question of Jewish nationalism and territorial aspirations, the fifth of the Pittsburgh Platform's eight planks declared: "We consider ourselves no longer a nation, but a religious community, and, therefore, expect neither a return to Palestine, nor a sacrificial worship under the sons of Aaron, nor the restoration of any of the laws concerning the Jewish state."

The Pittsburgh Platform's anti-Zionism remained the official position of the Reform movement until the 1937 convention of the Central Conference of American Rabbis, meeting in Columbus, for the first time formally expressed sympathy for the idea of Palestine as a Jewish refuge, although it did not embrace the Zionist goal of Jewish statehood. *See also* COLUMBUS PLATFORM.

POALEI AGUDAT ISRAEL (PAI). Poalei Agudat Israel was founded in Poland in 1922. It was an affiliate of **Agudat Israel** but was frequently at odds with the parent organization because of its emphasis on social and economic justice and its more favorable disposition to Zionism.

There were initial attempts, which proved to be short-lived, to establish PAI in **Eretz Israel** in 1925, but it became successfully established in 1933 and in 1944 founded its first **kibbutz**, Hafetz Hayyim. Subsequently, it created a second, Kibbutz Sha'alvim, as well as several *moshavim*. In 1946, in what was viewed as independence from Agudat Israel, the World Union of Poalei Agudat Israel was founded. PAI manifested further independence from its parent body when its members fought in the **Haganah**.

In almost every election from 1949 to 1960, PAI was a loyal political partner of Agudat Israel and followed the edicts of the Aguda's Council of Torah Sages (Mo'etzet Gedolei Hatora). That partnership was severed in 1960, however, when PAI ignored an edict of the Council of Torah Sages and joined the government. Throughout the 1960–1980 period, PAI consistently achieved less than 2 percent of the votes in national elections, and it held two Knesset seats. In 1980 PAI merged with a number of other religious-nationalist groups to form Morasha, which achieved 1.6 percent of the vote in 1984 but subsequently disintegrated.

Although no longer a political party, PAI continues as an Israel-based movement and has a number of branches worldwide. It also retains its youth organization, Ezra, which joined PAI in 1948.

POALEI ZION. *See* LABOR ZIONISM.

POLITICAL ZIONISM. Political Zionism was the approach taken by **Theodor Herzl** and his disciples toward achieving the Zionist goal. It emphasized the need to secure international political recognition of the claim for a Jewish homeland. Herzl viewed the Jewish problem as political in nature. His position was incorporated into the **Zionist Organization**'s **Basle Program**, which stated that the objective of Zionism is a publicly recognized and legally secured homeland in Palestine for the Jewish people. This contrasted with the objectives of others, such as the **Practical Zionists**, who stressed settlement activities, and **Cultural** (or Spiritual) **Zionists**, who aimed for a spiritual center in Eretz Israel.

POST-ZIONISM. *Post-Zionism* is a term of recent vintage that is used with a variety of meanings. In its most common and controversial sense, it reflects the view, more prevalent among secular Israelis, that Israel is and should be a state like any other—that is, a "state of all its citizens," Muslims and Christians as well as Jews. Some of the roots of this type of post-Zionism may be traced to the 1940s platform of Yonatan Ratosh and the **Canaanites**. Those committed to this version of post-Zionism advocate, among other things, the abolishment of the **Law of Return**, the replacement of "**Hatikvah**" as Israel's national anthem, and the severing of official links between Israel and world Jewry. They also advocate changes in the vocabulary of social discourse that they view as ideologically tainted. For example, they urge ceasing to speak of *aliya* and *yerida* and instead to speak of "migration."

Surveys indicate that the number of Israelis adhering to post-Zionism of this type is small. However, these adherents are visible and articulate, and their passionate political agenda provides them with the impetus to air their ideas in the most public and challenging ways. As a result, the term *post-Zionism* is increasingly found in popular discussions, and ideas related to it are frequently debated in the Israeli mass media. Also, many of the proponents of post-Zionism are prolific writers whose works appear not only in scholarly but also in popular intellectual media in

Israel and around the Western world. Their writings are welcomed abroad and give the appearance of representing a growing sector of Israeli society.

PRACTICAL ZIONISM. Practical Zionism was a stream within the Zionist movement that struggled with the overtly political interpretation given to Zionism by **Theodor Herzl** and his followers. Practical Zionism had its roots in **Hibbat Zion** and emphasized achieving the goals of Zionism though such practical measures as *aliya* and the establishment of rural settlements and educational institutions in **Eretz Israel**. In contrast to **Political Zionism**, the Practical Zionists argued that political activity would be useless without the practical settlement of Eretz Israel. Political Zionists, on the other hand, asserted that settlement would be to no avail unless it was rooted in political sovereignty.

The struggle between the Practical and Political Zionists persisted for many years and, at the Eighth **Zionist Congress** in 1907, **Chaim Weizmann** proposed a synthesis in which they were not to be viewed as contrasting conceptions of Zionism but, rather, as complementary ones.

PROTESTRABBINER. Fearing that the scheduled convening of the First **Zionist Congress** in Munich would raise questions as to the loyalties of German Jewry, a group of prominent German rabbis, Reform and Orthodox alike, issued a public statement in July 1897 condemning the planned congress. Speaking on behalf of the executive committee of the German Rabbinical Association, they called the Zionist goal of a Jewish state "antagonistic to the messianic promises of Judaism" and emphasized that Judaism obligates Jews to "serve the country to which they belong with the utmost devotion." The rabbis did, however, praise as "noble" the "colonization of Palestine by Jewish agriculturists, as they have no relation whatsoever to the founding of a National State." The declaration concluded with an appeal to the Jewish public to boycott the forthcoming Zionist Congress.

Responding in the pages of his Vienna-based Zionist weekly *Die Welt,* **Theodor Herzl** wrote that the rabbinical critics "at least enable us to distinguish between real rabbis and those salaried employees of the synagogue who fight against the redemption of their own people. Let us call them Protest Rabbis [*protestrabbiner*]."

The declaration of the *protestrabbiner,* combined with similar proclamations by other Jewish organizations in Munich, persuaded Herzl to shift the location of the Zionist Congress to Basle, Switzerland.

PROVISIONAL EXECUTIVE COMMITTEE FOR GENERAL ZIONIST AFFAIRS. At the initiative of the visiting Russian Zionist activist **Shemaryahu Levin**, American Zionist leaders in 1914 established the Provisional Executive Committee for General Zionist Affairs. Its aim was to reinvigorate American Zionism, to serve as a temporary international center for the Zionist movement, and to raise funds for war-torn European Jewish communities and the *yishuv*. The willingness of the famous attorney—and later Supreme Court justice—**Louis D. Brandeis** to serve as its chairman lent the Provisional Committee considerable prestige in the American Jewish community and beyond. Conceived from the start as a temporary body to meet the war emergency, the committee was dissolved at war's end. *See also* ZIONIST ORGANIZATION OF AMERICA.

-R-

RADICAL ZIONISTS. Polish Zionists who were critical of the leadership of **Chaim Weizmann** joined forces at the 13th **Zionist Congress** (1923) to establish an opposition faction that would eventually become the Radical Zionists. Originally known as Al Hamishmar ("On the Watch"), the dissidents criticized Weizmann's attitude toward the British as too compromising and opposed his plan to include wealthy **Diaspora non-Zionists** in the leadership of an expanded Jewish Agency. Ironically, the Al Hamishmar activists were inspired by the principles of the **Democratic Faction** that Weizmann himself had helped organize in 1901.

At a conference in Berlin in June 1925, the Al Hamishmar group merged with Zionist groups from Europe and Palestine to establish the Union of Radical Zionists, with Polish Zionist leader **Yitzhak Gruenbaum** as president. The similarities between the Radical Zionists and the recently founded **Revisionist Zionists** led to discussions about possible collaboration, but the alliance never materialized because of differences over the Radical Zionists' more sympathetic attitude toward the **Histadrut** and **Labor Zionist** settlement activity.

The Radical Zionists received enough votes for fifteen delegates at the 14th Zionist Congress in 1925. Its representation ranged from eight to fifteen delegates at the congresses of 1927, 1929, 1931, and 1933. After Gruenbaum, the party's driving force, joined the **Jewish Agency** Executive (1933) and then settled in Palestine (1935), the Radical Zionists merged with a faction of the General Zionists to become the **World Union of General Zionists**, also known as "**General Zionists A**."

RAZIEL, DAVID (1910–1941). A leader of the Palestine Jewish underground group **Irgun Zvai Leumi (IZL)**, David Raziel, born Rossensohn, was brought from Russia to Ottoman Palestine at age four, in 1914. Just four months after the family's arrival, however, the Rossensohns were among those expelled to Egypt by the Turks and did not return to Palestine until 1923. Raziel graduated from the Tahkemoni High School in Tel Aviv, then enrolled at **Hebrew University** and Mercaz Harav, the Jerusalem yeshiva of the chief rabbi, **Abraham Isaac Kook**.

One of the first members of the original IZL, Raziel, along with fellow Irgunist **Avraham Stern**, co-authored the first Hebrew-language military training manual. Raziel emerged as a central figure in the organization in 1937, when it split over the **Haganah**'s policy of *havlaga,* self-restraint, in the face of Arab terrorism. Some Irgunists joined the Haganah, while Raziel became leader of the remaining members and personally led the first counterterrorism raid against Arab targets in November 1937. He was named commander in chief of the IZL the following year.

Following the publication of the May 1939 **White Paper** and the Irgun's initiation of violent protests, Raziel and other Irgun members were jailed by the British. Upon the outbreak of World War II in September, Raziel and his comrades pledged to cease anti-British actions for the duration of the war. As a result, they were released from prison. Raziel's insistence on the cease-fire led to the secession of Avraham Stern and his followers from the Irgun and the creation of the **Lohamei Herut Israel**, or Lehi.

In May 1941, Raziel accepted a British request to lead an Irgun squad that would undertake sabotage missions against the pro-Nazi regime that had taken power in Iraq. As part of the deal, the British agreed to let the Irgunists independently attempt to kidnap the Mufti of Jerusalem, Haj Amin el-Husseini, who was then residing in Baghdad. Before they could act, however, Raziel was killed in a chance German air raid outside the Iraqi capital.

REINES, RABBI ISAAC JACOB (1839–1915). **Religious Zionist** leader Isaac Reines was born in Karlin, Belarus, to a rabbinic family. Reines studied at prominent yeshivot, authored a number of scholarly works, and served in a number of rabbinic positions. Early on, he developed a strong attachment for **Eretz Israel**—initially through his father, Shlomo Naftali, who had gone on *aliya* a number of years before Isaac Jacob was born and had settled in Safed, where he established a publishing company for Hebrew books. While he was on a trip, much of Safed was destroyed in an earthquake and Rabbi Shlomo Reines lost his entire family as well as all of his material possessions. He was forced to return to live in Karlin, where he remarried and established a new family, which included Isaac Jacob.

Reines joined the **Hibbat Zion** movement at its inception and was actively engaged in the promotion of Jewish settlement of Eretz Israel. In 1887 he met the head of the movement, **Rabbi Samuel Mohilever**, and presented him with a broad plan for the establishment of settlements accompanied by a multilevel national-religious school system. Mohilever, however, deemed the plan to be unrealistic and unworthy of support.

Reines did not participate in the First **Zionist Congress** in 1897 because, among other issues, he had questions about Zionism's congruency with his own religious views. Nevertheless, he was very impressed with **Theodor Herzl**, and when he concluded that Zionism's legitimacy lies in its goal to resolve the physical and material problems of the Jewish people, he joined the movement with a passion. He supported Herzl's call to "conquer the communities," issued at the Second Zionist Congress in Basle in August 1898. In 1902 Reines published a major work, *Ohr Hadash 'al Zion* ("New Light of Zion"), which presented his views on Zionism from a religious perspective and his refutation of the religious opposition to Zionism, including the arguments against cooperating with secularists.

Reines was avidly opposed to the **Zionist Organization**'s undertaking of cultural work and, when it formally adopted the task, Reines organized a separate movement within the organization, **Mizrachi**, the Religious Zionist movement; he was its unquestioned leader. Nevertheless, Reines continued to support Herzl. He was a staunch supporter of the **Uganda Plan**, which emerged in 1903, and his loyalty to Herzl remained firm throughout his lifetime.

RELIGIOUS ZIONISM. The origins of contemporary Religious Zionism may be traced to the prevalent air of messianic anticipation that pervaded early nineteenth-century Jewry. Several of the movement's founding fathers, especially **Rabbi Zvi Hirsch Kalischer**, **Rabbi Yehuda Chai Alkalai**, and Rabbi Samuel Mohilever, emerged as authoritative critics of the popular notion that the Messiah would arrive suddenly through a momentous act of Divine intervention. They asserted, by contrast, that the Messiah would come through a natural process and that the Jewish people themselves must redeem **Eretz Israel** and settle it. From their biddings, Religious Zionism emerged as a synthesis of Judaism and Jewish nationalism that strives to institute Jewish national life in Eretz Israel in accordance with Jewish religious law as prescribed in the Torah and halakhah.

Although the Religious Zionist movement, Mizrachi, was not officially founded until 1902, the initiative for it that was adopted was proposed by Mohilever in 1893. He died in 1898, four years before the movement was officially established as part of the **World Zionist Organization (WZO)**.

Within Mizrachi, there were two divergent approaches to Zionism, in general, and to **Theodor Herzl**, in particular. To **Rabbi Isaac Jacob Reines** (1839–1915), under whose leadership Mizrachi was in 1902 organized as a faction within the World Zionist Organization, Judaism based on the commandments is a sine qua non for Jewish national life in the homeland, but he viewed Zionism solely in pragmatic terms, that is, as a movement whose objective it is to guard and enhance the physical well-being of Jews. Under Reines's influence, Mizrachi initially supported the **Uganda Plan**.

On the other hand, Reines's close colleague, who subsequently became the first chief rabbi of Eretz Israel and spiritual leader of Mizrachi, **Rabbi Abraham Isaac Kook**, viewed the contemporary period as *ikveta demeshikha,* "the footsteps of the Messiah," and Herzl as a semi-messianic figure. Under Rabbi Kook's influence, Mizrachi reneged and rejected the Uganda Plan, and the messianic perspective gradually became the dominant one within Mizrachi. His son, Rabbi Tzvi Yehuda Kook, succeeded his father as the head of the first explicitly nationalist yeshiva, Mercaz Harav, and ultimately became the spiritual leader of the **Gush Emunim** movement.

Following the Six-Day War and the Yom Kippur War, organized Religious Zionism came to be dominated by territorial maximalists for whom retention of Judea and Samaria, the West Bank, and Gaza Strip regions administered by Israel after the Six-Day War became primary. A minority of Religious Zionists viewed these developments, as well as what they perceived to be a growth of religious fundamentalism within mainstream Religious Zionism, as antithetical to Jewish tradition and the historic principles of Religious Zionism. Accordingly, in 1975 they founded Oz Veshalom and Netivot Shalom, two Religious Zionist peace movements that ultimately merged.

Meimad is another reaction to Mizrachi's moves to the nationalist and religious right. Broader in scope than Oz Veshalom-Netivot Shalom, it initially formed as a political party with a more moderate approach to the territories than that of the National Religious Party. Although it failed to gain sufficient votes for a Knesset seat in the 1988 elections, Meimad ran for the Knesset in 1999 as part of the Labor Party–led "One Israel" coalition, and as a result Meimad leader Rabbi Michael Melchior was appointed to the Israeli cabinet as minister for Diaspora affairs.

Religious Zionists are united in their belief that religious Jews should participate in all aspects of Israeli society, and the movement fostered programs within which religious young men could combine military service with their yeshiva studies and religious young women could perform civilian as well as military service without violating their religious scruples.

Religious Zionism has been generally supportive of the authority of the chief rabbinate and initiated the system within which family law and personal status fall within the jurisdiction of the religious courts. *See also* AMIT; EMUNAH; BACHAD; HASHOMER HADATI.

REVISIONIST ZIONISM. Russian Zionist leader **Ze'ev Jabotinsky** launched Revisionist Zionism in 1925, as a militant faction within the world Zionist movement. Jabotinsky's theme was the need to revise the Zionist movement's strategy for achieving a Jewish national home in Palestine, a strategy he regarded as excessively cautious.

Jabotinsky, a member of the World Zionist Executive, had been jailed by the British in 1920 for organizing armed Jewish self-defense against Palestinian Arab mob attacks. The episode convinced Jabotinsky that British policy was turning against the *yishuv* and that the Zionist movement should actively resist London's shift. When his colleagues in the Zionist leadership rebuffed his calls for a more militant posture, Jabotinsky founded the Revisionist faction, known by its Hebrew acronym Hatzohar.

Revisionism had particularly strong appeal among Eastern European Jewish youth, and its youth movement, **Betar**, attracted substantial numbers of adherents, especially in Poland. Their themes of Jewish nationalist pride and *aliya* as the answer to inevitable **Diaspora** anti-Semitism resonated in Jewish communities suffering from poverty and anti-Jewish discrimination. As hardships intensified, increasing numbers of European Jews found themselves in accord with the Revisionist view of the Jewish people as being trapped in a hostile world where survival depends upon strength and assertiveness.

The Revisionists opposed the socialist economic theories of **Labor Zionism** and the **Histadrut** trade union. Jabotinsky argued that in view of the worsening crises faced by world Jewry, the *yishuv* should seek greater unity by employing compulsory arbitration in place of divisive strikes as a means of settling labor disputes. The Revisionists created their own labor union, the National Workers Federation (Histadrut Ha'ovdim Haleumit) to compete with the Histadrut. The Revisionists also established an international fundraising arm, the Tel Hai Fund, as well as high school, collegiate, and women's divisions, and a sports league, Nordia. *Rassviet* ("Dawn"), a Russian-language newspaper published in Paris with Jabotinsky as editor, was the de facto organ of the movement.

The Revisionist movement was dealt a serious blow when several of its members were arrested in connection with the June 1933 assassination of a senior Labor Zionist official, **Haim Arlosoroff**. Although the suspects were eventually cleared of these charges, the controversy in the meantime ignited a bitter and sometimes violent campaign by **Labor Zionists** against the Revisionists in Palestine and in Europe. Labor newspapers declared the suspects guilty even before their trials, and the Revisionist movement as a whole was accused of having inspired the murder. The controversy affected the outcome of the 1933 elections to the **World Zionist Congress**, with Labor's share of the vote increasing to 44 percent from its previous 29 percent, while the Revisionists dropped from 21 percent to 14 percent.

In an effort to ease tensions between the two camps, Jabotinsky and Labor Zionist leader **David Ben-Gurion** met in late 1934 and negotiated a peace pact. The agreement was endorsed by an international Revisionist conference but rejected in a referendum among Histadrut members, a majority of whom believed the deal made too many concessions to the Revisionists.

Following the collapse of the peace treaty initiative, a referendum among Revisionists in 1935 won overwhelming approval for Jabotinsky's proposal to secede from the **World Zionist Organization** and establish the New Zionist Organization. A small group of Revisionists who opposed secession broke from Jabotinsky and created their own **Jewish State Party**.

Revisionism emphasized the value of military strength, and Betar's training camps included paramilitary training and preparedness. The movement also ran a maritime training facility in interwar Italy and an aviation school on Long Island, New York. Many Betar graduates became active in the Revisionist movement's underground, the **Irgun Zvai**

Leumi (IZL). As the Haganah gradually came under the control of the Labor Zionist–dominated **Jewish Agency**, the Revisionists backed the establishment of their own militia, the Irgun (initially known as Haganah Bet), in 1931. When Palestinian Arab violence erupted anew in 1936, the IZL launched its own counterterrorism actions against Arab targets, rejecting the Haganah policy of *havlaga,* or restraint.

At the same time, the IZL began transporting unauthorized European Jewish immigrants to Palestine in defiance of British quota restrictions. Tens of thousands of such immigrants were brought to Eretz Israel by the Revisionists during the years immediately preceding the outbreak of World War II.

The war years dealt Revisionism a series of devastating blows. Jabotinsky, pledging the movement's support for the British war effort against the Nazis, traveled to the United States to seek support for the establishment of a Jewish army to fight alongside the Allies. He died there in the summer of 1940. Jabotinsky was never replaced as head of the Revisionist Party; instead, a presidium of senior activists ruled by consensus. Betar members figured prominently in armed resistance against the Nazis in a number of ghettoes in Europe, including the Warsaw Ghetto uprising, but the majority of Betar members in Europe perished in the Holocaust.

Polish Betar leader **Menachem Begin**, reaching Palestine in 1942, assumed the leadership of the IZL. At the beginning of 1944, the IZL launched an armed revolt against the British occupation forces in Eretz Israel. The Revisionist Party, a legal and above-ground political movement, retained no formal connection to the illegal militant underground, although it strongly sympathized with the revolt. In 1946 the Revisionists, having reunited with the Jewish State Party under the banner of the World Union of Zionist-Revisionists, rejoined the World Zionist Organization.

After the ouster of the British and the establishment of the State of Israel, Begin became chairman of the new Herut (Freedom) Party, which pledged allegiance to Jabotinsky's ideas and declared its candidacy for the elections to the first Israeli Knesset in 1949. A rival list of candidates offered by the Revisionist Party failed to gain any seats in parliament, and Begin's Herut emerged as the official representative of Revisionist ideology on the Israeli political scene. Negotiations between Herut and the World Union of Zionist-Revisionists brought about a merger of the two in 1951. In 1965 Herut allied itself with the Liberal Party to form the Gahal bloc, and in 1973 Gahal and several smaller nationalist parties united as the Likud Party.

The contemporary Likud officially regards itself as the heir to Jabotinsky's ideology. Although the influence of traditional Revisionist principles on today's Likud leaders is not always apparent, one may find echoes of the classic Revisionist-versus-Labor debates of the 1930s and 1940s in the disputes between the Israeli right and left over issues such as the disposition of territory, economic policy, and approaches to international relations. *See also* HANOAR HALEUMI HA'OVED VEHALOMED; IRGUN ZVAI LEUMI; JABOTINSKY INSTITUTE; LOHAMEI HERUT ISRAEL.

RUPPIN, ARTHUR (1876–1943). Zionist activist and settlement director Arthur Ruppin was born in Prussia to an affluent family that fell on bad times. Ruppin left high school at age fifteen to work. He subsequently completed high school externally, studied economics and law at the University of Berlin, and earned a doctorate in law. After working in the legal field for several years, Ruppin became director of the Bureau for Jewish Statistics and Demography in Berlin, a position that he held from 1902 to 1907.

A pioneer in the field of the sociological study of Jewry, in 1904 Ruppin published *Die Juden der Gegenwart,* which set out his framework for the sociology of the Jews. He subsequently revised and expanded the work in various editions, and it appeared in English as two volumes, *The Jews in the Modern World* (1934) and *Jewish Fate and Future* (1940).

Although he was not initially a formal Zionist, as soon as Ruppin was recognized as a prominent sociologist and demographer of Jews, he was sent to Palestine by the **Jewish Agency** in 1907 for the purpose of exploring the opportunities to implement the **Zionist Organization**'s activity there. Shortly thereafter, he immigrated and was appointed director of the Palestine Office of the Zionist Organization in Jaffa. He devoted the rest of his life to purchasing and settling the land throughout Palestine. A champion of **Practical Zionism**, his priority was obtaining land and systematically settling the country with a network and variety of economically viable urban and rural communities, including, in addition to cities, **kibbutzim** and *moshavim.* He played a central role in the establishment of Tel Aviv and major areas in Jerusalem and Haifa, as well as in the settlement of large portions of the Jezreel Valley. He was instrumental in the life of the *yishuv* from the Second to the **Fifth Aliya**, and his initial work in enabling its survival and growth is recognized as his greatest achievement.

A staunch believer in Arab–Jewish cooperation, Ruppin was one of the founders, in 1925, of **Brith Shalom**, a small organization that called for the establishment of a binational Jewish-Arab state in Palestine. He headed the organization until 1929 when, after the Arab riots in 1929, he came to view the necessity for a Jewish state that, in time, would be able to coexist with its Arab neighbors.

In 1926 Ruppin became a member of the faculty of **Hebrew University**, where he taught the sociology of the Jews. During the 1930s, he played an important role in the absorption of the masses of both German and Yemenite immigrants.

RUTENBERG, PINHAS (PIOTR) (1879–1942). A prominent *yishuv* leader and founder of the Palestine Electric Company, Pinhas Rutenberg was born in Romny in the Ukraine. He studied engineering at the Technological Institute of St. Petersburg and served as the foreman at the large metallurgical factory Putilov. While a student, Rutenberg first became active in the Social Democrat party and then in the Social Revolutionary party. In 1905, he was among the organizers of the workers' march to the Czar's castle on "Bloody Sunday," along with Father Gapon, who led the march of industrial workers on Russia's intellectual center and the Czar's capital. The march, which was unsuccessful, led to the persecution of many of the protesters, and Gapon was suspected by his comrades of being a spy for the police. Rutenberg was among those who organized Gapon's execution.

Between 1907 and 1915, Rutenberg worked in Italy as an irrigation engineer and developed a new method for constructing dams that preserved water and provided electrical power.

At the outbreak of World War I, Rutenberg became interested in his Jewish identity, founded an organization for Jewish affairs, and in 1915 traveled to London to present to Zionist leaders his arguments for the establishment of a **Jewish Legion**. He met with **Ze'ev Jabotinsky** in Italy to discuss the idea of a Jewish army and authored a pamphlet, "The National Revival of the Jewish People," which he signed under the pen name "Pinhas Ben–Ami." Continuing on to the United States, Rutenberg consulted with **David Ben-Gurion** and **Izhak Ben-Zvi** about the Jewish Legion campaign and became active in the campaign to establish the first **American Jewish Congress**.

After the Mensheviks succeeded in overthrowing the Czar in 1917, Rutenberg returned to Russia and was appointed by Alexander F. Kerensky, the head of the provisional government, as deputy governor of St. Petersburg for civilian affairs. After the October 1917 Bolshevik revolution, Rutenberg was imprisoned for six months. Following his release, he went to the Ukraine where he briefly served as deputy minister for supplies in the White Russian government until the area was conquered by the Bolsheviks. By 1919, convinced of the inevitability of anti-Semitism, Rutenberg settled in Palestine.

There Rutenberg devoted himself to a survey of the country's water resources, as a prerequisite to obtaining the legal right to establish an electrical power company. In response to the Palestinian Arab riots of 1920, he organized, with Jabotinsky, a self-defense militia in Jerusalem from which the **Haganah** later grew. When Jabotinsky was jailed, Rutenberg was left as its leader. Rutenberg led the Haganah forces in Tel Aviv during the May 1921 Arab riots, but after a subsequent conflict with members of Hashomer, he opted to devote himself primarily to establishing the electrical power company. His dreams were realized in 1923 when, despite fierce opposition from a number of British members of Parliament, he was granted the rights to establish the Palestine Electric Company, with such personalities as Lord Melchett (Alfred Mond), Lord Herbert Samuel, and Lord Reading, among others, serving on the board. In 1928, work on the power station in Naharayim began, and it went into service in 1932.

During the crisis caused by the Palestinian Arab riots of 1929, Rutenberg was named head of the **Va'ad Leumi** and, in 1930, he was appointed chairman of the Security Committee. Following the **Arlosoroff** assassination, he attempted to reach an accord between the **Revisionists** and the **Histadrut**. In 1934 Rutenberg helped bring Jabotinsky and David Ben-Gurion to an agreement, which was subsequently rejected by the Histadrut.

During the 1930s, Rutenberg took part in efforts aimed at Arab–Jewish rapprochement. He presented to the Jewish Agency a memo on the subject, in which he suggested a number of compromises on the issue of Arab labor and worked closely with the binationalists **Judah Magnes**, Moshe Novomeysky, Moshe Smilansky, and the jurist Gad Frumkin. Their efforts were ultimately unsuccessful.

In 1940 he was again selected to head the Va'ad Leumi, but his failing health permitted him to serve only briefly. In his last will and testament, he called for national unity and for the education of youth in that spirit. Rutenberg designated his possessions to youth activities, and his house on Mount Carmel, Haifa, now serves as a youth center.

-S-

SABRA. Sabra is a derivative of an Arabic term for a prickly pear that was believed to be indigenous to the Middle East. In fact, it is indigenous to Central America and was imported to the Middle East in the eighteenth century. It has become the term applied to native Israelis, symbolizing their being, as is the sabra fruit, hard on the outside but sweet on the inside. In Zionist ideology, the Sabra was of especially lofty, heroic status, frequently portrayed as the brave, altruistic defender of Israel. With the increasing questioning of Zionist mythology, the image of the Sabra has undergone extensive transformation and some Israelis, especially **post-Zionists**, now question the validity of the heroic image of the Sabra.

SAN REMO CONFERENCE. Representatives of the victorious Allied Powers met in San Remo, Italy, in April 1920 to discuss issues arising from World War I, including the future of territories they had captured from Turkey and Germany. Zionist officials were on hand at the conference, lobbying for a British mandate over Palestine based on the **Balfour Declaration**. The San Remo conferees agreed to award the mandate for Palestine—including the area later known as Transjordan—to Great Britain, specifying that the Holy Land was to be administered in accordance with the terms of the Balfour Declaration. The San Remo decision on Palestine, which was reiterated in the August 1920 Treaty of Sevres and would be formally endorsed by the League of Nations in 1922, was hailed by Zionist leaders and denounced by the Arabs.

SHALIACH. *Shaliach* is a Hebrew term meaning "emissary." In its original context, it referred to the millennia-old tradition of emissaries from **Eretz Israel** who traveled around the world to involve Jews in **Diaspora** communities in the support of Jewish communities of the Holy Land. Typically, they came to raise money for Jewish institutions abroad or for themselves, while at the same time imparting Jewish learning among those whom they solicited. They frequently served as itinerant rabbis in small and distant Jewish communities that had no resident rabbinical leadership.

For example, in the early New World communities in what is now the United States, Rabbi Moses Malki, from Safed, was with New York's

Congregation Shearith Israel for four months in late 1759 and then went to Newport for a brief stay. In 1761 another emissary from Safed, Chaim Muddahy, arrived in New York to raise funds for the relief of those who suffered from the earthquake in Safed on October 30, 1760. The most notable among the early emissaries from the Holy Land was Rabbi Chaim Isaac Karigal from Hebron, who in 1772 spent a month in Philadelphia, almost half a year in New York, and then stayed in Newport from March through July 1773. One of his sermons, preached in Newport on the first day of the Jewish holiday of Shavuot, became the first Jewish sermon published in America. During the course of his stay in Newport, Karigal developed a close relationship with the Rev. Ezra Stiles, a local Congregationalist minister who later was to become president of Yale University. Following the efforts of these emissaries, correspondence between Jews in Eretz Israel and Jewish communities in North America, in which the former solicited funds from the latter, became a fairly regular phenomenon.

The **Hibbat Zion** movement adopted the institution of support for new Jewish settlement in Palestine, and the **World Zionist Organization (WZO)** institutionalized it. The various movements, especially the youth movement, within the organization sent *shelichim* (emissaries) to enlist support for their work. With the decline of the role of such movements in Western society, the *shaliach* is typically an emissary for the WZO itself, and his or her role is a multifaceted one. When *aliya* was a major goal of Zionism, significant efforts were expended on recruiting potential *olim* (immigrants) from the Diaspora communities. As a result of the lower priority placed on *aliya* within the Zionist movement, *shelichim* serve as teachers of Hebrew and Zionist education, as well as cultural emissaries. The *shaliach* is expected to be, in the broadest sense, a "social-cultural ambassador" of Israel, the personification of Israel in his or her host-community, representing the totality of Israeli society and culture.

SHAMIR, YITZHAK (1915–). A leader of the Palestine Jewish underground group **Lohamei Herut Israel (Lehi)** and later Prime Minister of Israel, Yitzhak Shamir was born Yitzhak Yezernitsky in Rozinai, Poland, in 1915. After graduating from a Hebrew high school in Bialystok, Yezernitsky studied law in Warsaw, where he became active in the **Revisionist Zionist** youth movement **Betar**. He moved to Palestine in 1935, enrolled at **Hebrew University**, and, two years later, joined the **Irgun Zvai Leumi (IZL)**. Shamir, as he was known by this time, was among the minority of IZL members who split from the movement in 1940 and joined the faction headed by **Avraham Stern**, soon named the *Lohamei Herut Israel* ("Fighters for the Freedom of Israel").

After Stern's death, Shamir, along with **Israel Eldad** and Natan Yellin-Friedman, comprised the ruling triumvirate of Lehi. Shamir was responsible for organization and operations. He was arrested by the British in 1946 and deported to the African territory of Eritrea, but he escaped in January 1947 by smuggling himself out of the prison camp in an empty oil barrel. He made his way to Ethiopia, then France, and returned to Palestine to resume his active leadership of Lehi.

After Israel was established, Shamir initially eschewed politics, working in private business until 1955, then serving in the Mossad, Israel's secret service, for ten years and returning to the business sector in 1965. In 1969, however, Shamir joined **Menachem Begin**'s Herut Party as chairman of its immigration and organization department. He was first elected to the Knesset in 1973, was chosen speaker of the Knesset in 1977, and became foreign minister in 1980. Following the resignation of Prime Minister Begin in 1983, Shamir served as prime minister from 1983 to 1984 and again from 1986 to 1992.

SHARETT (SHERTOK), MOSHE (1894–1965). **Labor Zionist** leader and later prime minister of Israel, Moshe Sharett was born in Kherson in the Ukraine. His father, Jacob, was one of the first members of the **Bilu** movement. Moshe came to Palestine with his parents in 1906. Their first home was in the Arab village of Ein Sinia, in the hills of Samaria. That experience left him with fluency in the Arabic language and a deep appreciation for Arab customs. In 1910 the family moved to Jaffa and became one of the founding families of Ahuzat Bayit, the earliest nucleus of what was to become the city of Tel Aviv. Moshe studied at the Herzliya Gymnasium, the first Hebrew high school in the country, and was in its first graduating class. He studied law in Constantinople and, with the outbreak of World War I, he joined the Turkish army as an interpreter.

After the war, Sharett returned to **Eretz Israel** and joined **Ahdut Ha'avoda** when it was founded in 1919. In 1920 he went to study at the London School of Economics and was active in the city's **Poalei Zion** organization. Sharett returned to Eretz Israel in 1925 and became the associate editor of the **Histadrut** daily, *Davar* ("The Word"). In 1931, upon the recommendation of the head of **Jewish Agency**'s Political Department, **Haim Arlosoroff**, Sharett was appointed secretary and succeeded Arlosoroff after his assassination in 1933. From then until the establishment of the State of Israel, he was the primary negotiator on behalf of Zionism with the British mandatory officials.

Sharett pushed for the establishment of Jewish Supernumerary Police during the Arab riots of 1936–1939. Although he promoted the recruitment of Jews to the British army during World War II and was active in the establishment of the **Jewish Brigade**, Sharett was arrested by the British along with other **Jewish Agency** officials in 1946, on "Black Saturday," and was incarcerated in Latrun Prison for four months. In 1947 he was present at the United Nations General Assembly during the debate over partition, and he was one of the signatories on Israel's Declaration of Independence.

Sharett served as Israel's first foreign minister in 1949 and when **David Ben-Gurion** first retired as prime minister in January 1954, Sharett succeeded him. When Ben-Gurion returned to politics and reassumed the position of prime minister in November 1955, Sharett remained foreign minister until June 1956, when he resigned due to irreconcilable differences with Ben-Gurion. The conflicts between them had emerged many years earlier, with Sharett siding with **Chaim Weizmann** in the latter's disputes with Ben-Gurion.

After leaving government service, Sharett became head of the Am Oved, Mapai's publishing house, and chairman of Beit Berl College. In 1960 he was elected chairman of the **World Zionist Organization** and the Jewish Agency. His feud with Ben-Gurion intensified during the controversy over the Lavon Affair, when Sharett was one of Ben-Gurion's staunchest opponents.

SHAW COMMISSION. After three days of Palestinian Arab violence in the summer of 1929, which claimed 133 Jewish lives, the British government appointed a Royal Commission, headed by longtime Colonial Office official Walter Shaw, to investigate the causes of the disturbances.

Shaw and the commission's other three members stayed in Palestine from October through December 1929 and heard testimony from Jewish, Arab, and British representatives. The commission's final report, issued in March 1930, argued that Jewish immigration and land purchases had provoked the Arab violence. It also charged that during World War I, the British had made contradictory promises to the Jews and the Arabs concerning Palestine's future, thereby further complicating the situation.

The Shaw Commission's report, which was praised by Arab leaders and criticized by the Zionists, urged the British government to issue a clear statement of its intentions in Palestine; to prevent "excessive immigration" to Palestine by the Jews; to reaffirm that the Zionist movement does not "share in any degree in the government of Palestine"; and to undertake a scientific study of Palestine's cultivation methods in order to regulate future land purchases. Acting on these recommendations, the British dispatched a study team headed by Sir John Hope-Simpson to Palestine later that year. *See also* WHITE PAPERS.

SHERTOK, MOSHE. *See* **SHARETT (SHERTOK), MOSHE.**

SILVER, ABBA HILLEL (1893–1963). American Zionist leader Abba Hillel Silver was born in Lithuania but raised on New York City's Lower East Side. There he was attracted to the Zionist movement at an early age. As a teenager, he co-founded the Dr. Herzl Zion Club, one of the first Zionist youth groups in America, in 1904. Inspired by the mesmerizing lectures of Zvi Hirsch Masliansky, the most influential Zionist preacher of that era, Silver soon developed a reputation of his own as an eloquent orator in Yiddish, Hebrew, and English. He addressed the national **Federation of American Zionists (FAZ)** convention when he was just fourteen.

A graduate of the Cincinnati-based Hebrew Union College, the rabbinical seminary of Reform Judaism, Silver was hired in 1917 as the spiritual leader of Cleveland's The Temple, one of the country's most prominent Reform congregations. There he attracted public attention as an outspoken defender of labor unions and frequently sparred with groups such as the Daughters of the American Revolution, which denounced him as a dangerous radical.

Reinvigorated by a visit to British-administered Palestine in the summer of 1919, Silver began speaking throughout the United States on behalf of the Zionist movement, attracting large audiences and rave reviews. As leader of Cleveland's Zionists—who comprised one of the largest districts of the **Zionist Organization of America (ZOA)**—Silver spearheaded protests against British restrictions on Jewish immigration to Palestine and organized boycotts of products from Nazi Germany.

The escalating Nazi persecution of Jews, the apathetic response of the Roosevelt administration to news of Hitler's atrocities, and Great Britain's refusal to open Palestine to refugees from Hitler stimulated a mood of growing militancy in the American Jewish community during the late 1930s and early 1940s. Silver both symbolized American Jewish militancy and helped encourage its spread. His speech at the August 1943 **American Jewish Conference**, urging endorsement of Jewish statehood, was greeted with waves of thunderous applause that said as much about Silver's popularity as it did about the American Jewish mood. **Rabbi Stephen Wise**, who until then had been widely regarded as the most powerful leader of the American Jewish community, was compelled to accept Silver as co-chair of the **American Zionist Emergency Council (AZEC)**, a coalition of the leading U.S. Zionist groups. Silver's rise launched a bitter political and personal rivalry between the two men that would endure for years.

Under Silver's leadership, American Zionism assumed a vocal new role in Washington. Mobilized by the AZEC, grassroots Zionists deluged Capitol Hill with calls and letters in early 1943 and late 1944, urging the passage of a congressional resolution declaring U.S. support for the creation of a Jewish national home in Palestine. The opposition of the War and State Departments stalled the resolution in committee but did not deter Silver from campaigning, in the summer of 1944, for the inclusion of pro-Zionist planks in the election platforms of the Republican and Democratic parties that summer. Silver's ability to maneuver the two parties into competition for Jewish electoral support was a testimony to his political sophistication even if, much to Wise's chagrin, the Republican platform went beyond what AZEC requested by denouncing Franklin D. Roosevelt for not challenging Britain's pro-Arab tilt in Palestine.

During the postwar period, Silver and the AZEC stepped up their pressure on the Harry S. Truman administration with a fresh barrage of protest rallies, newspaper advertisements, and educational campaigns. Silver's effort in early 1946 to link postwar U.S. loans to British policy in Palestine collapsed when Wise broke ranks to lobby against linkage. More successful were Silver's behind-the-scenes efforts to mobilize non-Jewish Americans on behalf of the Zionist cause. The AZEC sponsored the American Christian Palestine Committee, which activated grassroots **Christian Zionists** nationwide, and the Christian Council on Palestine, which spoke for nearly three thousand pro-Zionist Christian clergymen.

Although the Truman administration wavered in its support for the 1947 United Nations plan to partition Palestine into Jewish and Arab states, a torrent of protest activity spearheaded by Silver and the AZEC helped convince the president to recognize the new State of Israel just minutes after its creation. Silver's protests against the U.S. arms embargo on the Middle East, however, were consistently rebuffed by the administration.

In the aftermath of Israel's birth, Silver pressed for a clear separation between the new state and the Zionist movement, insisting that Israel should not control the **World Zionist Organization** or other **Diaspora** agencies. His position led to a split with **Prime Minister David Ben-Gurion**, who then helped a faction of disgruntled ZOA members to oust Silver from power in 1949. Silver resumed full-time rabbinical duties at

The Temple, with only an occasional foray into the political arena when he could utilize his Republican contacts to lobby on Israel's behalf. He turned his attention to religious scholarship, reading voraciously and authoring several well-received books on Judaism. He passed away in 1963, at age seventy.

Silver's reign marked a political coming of age for American Jewry. His lobbying victories infused the Jewish community with confidence and a sense that the Jewish agenda was a legitimate part of American political culture—no mean feat for a community composed largely of immigrants and children of immigrants. The Silver years left their mark on the American political scene as well. After the inclusion of Palestine in the 1944 party platforms, Zionist concerns assumed a permanent place in American electoral politics. In addition, the swift U.S. recognition of Israel in 1948, a decision made in large measure with an eye toward American Jewish opinion, was a first major step in cementing the U.S.–Israel friendship that has endured ever since.

SMILANSKY, MOSHE (1874–1953). Zionist author and activist Moshe Smilansky was born to a family of tenant farmers in the Ukraine. He went on *aliya* in 1890 and was one of the founders of Hadera. In 1893 he settled in Rehovot. Smilansky considered himself a student of **Ahad Ha'am**. Beginning his literary career in 1898, Smilansky wrote extensively in the Hebrew press in Russia on the problems of agricultural settlement in **Eretz Israel**. He was a founder of *Ha-omer* ("The Sheaf"), a literary journal; an early contributor to the periodical *Hapoel Hazair* ("The Young Worker"); and the author of stories about the lives of Arab and Bedouin farmers in Eretz Israel. During World War I, he headed the Federation of Moshavot in Judea (Hitahdut Hamoshavot Biyehuda). After a stint in the Jewish Legion in 1918, Smilansky participated in the founding of the Farmers' Federation (Hitahdut Ha-ikarim), which he headed. He also edited the federation's periodical, *Bustanai* ("The Orchard Owner") from 1929 to 1939.

Smilansky was active in numerous efforts to promote Arab–Jewish relations, and his opposition to the **Hebrew Labor** campaign infuriated the **Histadrut**. In 1936 Smilansky participated in secret talks with Palestinian Arab leaders about the future of Eretz Israel. His support, in 1937, for the **Peel Commission** partition plan brought him close to the **Labor Zionist** movement, and he became an avid supporter of the notion of a national economy. His political views were generally akin to those of **Chaim Weizmann**, and he opposed the Jewish armed revolt against the British during the 1940s. The *moshav* Nir Moshe, in the northern Negev, is named for him.

SMOLENSKIN, PERETZ (1842–1885). A prominent Hebrew writer of the Haskala period and advocate of Jewish nationalism and a return to Zion, Peretz Smolenskin was born in Monastyrshchina, in the province of Mogilev (Mahilyow, Mohilev) in eastern Belarus (White Russia). He founded the noted Hebrew monthly *Hashahar* in 1868 and was its editor until his death. Following the pogroms of 1881, Smolenskin concluded that the only hope for the future of Jews was to return to their homeland where they would establish themselves economically, politically, and spiritually, toward the goal of creating a Jewish state.

SNEH (KLEINBAUM), MOSHE (1909–1972). A Haganah leader who later became a prominent figure in the Israeli Communist Party, Moshe Sneh was born Moshe Kleinbaum in Radzyn, Poland, to a family that was part of **Hovevei Zion**. Sneh studied medicine at the University of Warsaw and in 1930 was elected head of Yardeniah, a Zionist student union. He also became close to **Yitzhak Gruenbaum** and joined the radical faction of the **General Zionists**. Elected to the central committee of the Polish Zionist Federation in 1932, Gruenbaum became its chairman two years later. Between 1933 and 1935, he was editor of a Polish Jewish weekly, and in 1935 he was appointed the political editor of the popular and influential daily, *Heint* ("Today"). He also became an accredited physician that same year.

Sneh was a founder in 1935 of the General Zionists (A), the group that was formed as the result of the merger of the **Radical Zionists** and a faction of the General Zionists. As a delegate to the 18th **Zionist Congress** and as a member of the steering committee of the 19th Zionist Congress, Sneh was allied with Gruenbaum and the Radical Zionists in opposition to **Chaim Weizmann**, accusing him of being too compromising with the British mandatory authorities.

Sneh was an officer in the Polish army in 1939 and, when Poland fell to the Nazis, he fled to Palestine and settled there in 1940. In June of that year, he was recruited to the **Haganah** command, and between 1941 and 1946 he was chief of the National Command (Rosh Mateh Arzi). In 1945 Sneh became a member of the **Jewish Agency** Executive. In 1946 he eluded a British dragnet and fled to Europe, where he presented to the entire administration of the **World Zionist Organization** his arguments for continued struggle with the British, in opposition once again to Weizmann. When Sneh's arguments were rejected, he resigned his position with the Haganah command. Subsequently, he was appointed the Jewish Agency's European representative and concentrated on managing the political aspects of winning support for the establishment of a state, as well as on underground immigration activities.

Sneh's political views turned sharply leftward in 1947. At the end of that year, he resigned from the Jewish Agency Executive over an argument concerning the international orientation of the Zionist leadership and shortly thereafter joined the new Socialist Mapam party. He was elected to its leadership and served as editor of its organ, *Al Hamishmar* ("On the Watch"). Except for the Sixth Knesset, he was a member of Knesset in every Knesset until his death. In 1953, he resigned his membership in Mapam after it refused to explicitly support the prosecution of the Slansky Trial in Prague, which alleged a worldwide Zionist conspiracy to sabotage Communist countries. He established the Israeli Socialist-Left Party, which in 1954 merged with the Israel Communist Party (Maki).

After joining Maki, Sneh became editor of its newspaper, *Kol Ha'am* ("The People's Voice") and head of its Knesset faction. In 1965 the Israeli Communist Party split—the Rakah faction remained loyal to the Union of Soviet Socialist Republics, while Maki, including Sneh, reasserted its basic Jewish character and opposed the anti-Israel policy of the Soviet Union and the Arab states. Following the Six-Day War, Sneh emerged as one of the earliest advocates of Palestinian Arab control of the administered territories.

SOCIALIST ZIONISM. As a result of precarious socioeconomic circumstances, there emerged among nineteenth-century European Jewry a variety of socialist approaches to the problem of the Jewish condition. Some of these were explicitly anti-Zionist, while others were Zionists who believed that the Jewish national reawakening could not be achieved without a central focus on social justice and the creation of a Jewish working class. There developed three major approaches within socialist Zionist thought; one emanating from the work of **Ber Borochov**, another from that of **Nahman Syrkin**, and a third, which was in fact not quite socialist, that of **Aharon David Gordon**. The precursor of them all, however, was **Moses Hess**.

A prominent figure in the German radical movement, Moses Hess was among the first German Communists. Though not a Marxist, he was deeply impressed with and influenced by *The Communist Manifesto* (1848) by Karl Marx and Friedrich Engels. Accordingly, Hess argued for the elimination of the existing exploitative economic system and its replacement by a system of free labor. As a student of modern nationalist movements seeking the liberation of the oppressed classes, Hess also argued for Jewish national liberation with the same passion that he held for other persecuted nations.

Ber Borochov (1881–1917) was an unorthodox Marxian who saw national struggles and class conflict as interwoven. As for Jews, he viewed **Diaspora** life as aberrant because it perpetuated Jewish economic and political subordination. Jewish life in the Diaspora would improve only when the Jewish proletariat succeeded in achieving national and economic independence in its historic homeland. In 1906 Borochov established the Jewish Social Democratic Workers' Party, **Poalei Zion**, and during the controversy over the **Uganda Plan**, he joined those who opposed any territory other than Eretz Israel.

Nahman Syrkin (1868–1924) was a member of **Hovevei Zion** from his youth onward and was one of the first thinkers to formulate a synthesis of Zionism and socialism. He asserted that the plight of the Jewish proletariat would improve only through Zionism, and he was critical of Borochov for being overly Marxist. He was a Hebraist who viewed Hebrew as the national language of the Jewish people. In 1903–1905, when the Uganda Plan was debated at the Sixth and Seventh **Zionist Congresses**, Syrkin was a staunch supporter of **Theodor Herzl**. For a while he left the **World Zionist Organization** and was a leader of the Jewish **Territorialist movement**. Following his immigration to the United States in 1907, he rejoined the Zionist Organization and went on to become the leader of Poalei Zion in the United States.

Aharon David Gordon (1856–1922) was not actually a socialist. In fact, he argued that the Jewish proletariat should not formally affiliate with the broader socialist movement because the Jewish condition was unique. He was, however, a philosophical radical who, like Henry David Thoreau, believed in the inherent goodness of man and the spiritual value of physical labor as a means of uniting man and nature. For Gordon, the highest form of labor was that involving the soil. There are, in his writings, various references to the "Religion of Labor." Physical labor on the soil is what maintains the group's ties to the homeland. Without that labor, the group is uprooted from its natural environment and inevitably loses control over its homeland. When the Jews lost their homeland, they lost their authentic Jewish culture. Gordon's view of Diaspora Jewish life was among the most deprecating of the Zionist ideologists. Although he regarded himself as a socialist, Aharon David Gordon's philosophy was actually at variance with many aspects of standard socialist belief. He was the spiritual leader of **Hapoel Hatzair**, the non-Marxist socialist Zionist organization, and is viewed as the father of the **kibbutz** movement.

Officially, the Israeli Labor Party subscribes to the principles of socialism, although a variety of social and political factors have tempered Labor's ability to fully implement those principles when it has been the governing party in Israel (1948–1977, 1992–1996, and 1999 to the present).

Although the powerful Labor-affiliated **Histadrut** trade union has retained its dominant role in Israeli economic affairs, there has been a gradual shift away from the highly centralized and government-directed economy that was typical of the 1950s and 1960s, especially during the Likud governments of 1977–1984 and 1996–1999.

In recent years, a number of major government-owned corporations have been privatized, and other efforts have been made to increase competition. In addition, Israel's modernization and urbanization have inevitably led to the adoption of many economic practices common to the West. The collapse of the Soviet Union has discredited socialism in the eyes of many Israelis, and some Labor Party activists have urged their party to formally abandon its socialist symbols, such as May Day celebrations. The party leadership has so far resisted making any far-reaching changes.

With agriculture constituting an ever-smaller role in the gross national product, the traditional Israeli glorification of farming, settlement pioneering, and **kibbutz** life has given way to a greater preoccupation with materialism, individualism, and other trends typical of the modern Western world. One result of this cultural transformation has been a marked erosion of interest in the country's once-venerated socialist youth movements. Their ethos of simplicity, community commitment, equality, and collectivism is now regarded by many Israelis as outdated. A significant segment of young Israelis raised on kibbutzim opt to live elsewhere, forcing many kibbutzim to engage in practices once considered unthinkable, such as the use of foreign workers. The traditional view of the Socialist Zionist pioneers as patriotic state-builders has come under vehement attack by advocates of **post-Zionism**. Most Israelis, however, reject the post-Zionists' unsympathetic view of Israel's founding fathers. *See also* AHDUT HA'AVODA; AMERICANS FOR PROGRESSIVE ISRAEL; HASHOMER HATZAIR; LABOR ZIONISM; MAPAI.

SOKOLOW, NAHUM (1859–1936). Russian Zionist leader Nahum Sokolow was born in Wyszogrod, Poland, to a family with a rabbinic heritage. He was given a strong traditional Jewish as well as a secular education. He had a love of languages and literature and, in addition to Yiddish and Hebrew, he developed linguistic competence in Polish, Russian, German, French, Spanish, Italian, and English. Sokolow married at age seventeen and began writing while he continued his studies. He became a regular journalistic contributor to the Hebrew periodical *Hazefirah* ("The Siren") in 1876 and eventually became its editor and publisher. Sokolow's first book, on scientific topics, appeared in 1878. After moving to Warsaw two years later, he wrote several books on Jewish themes. It was in Warsaw that Sokolow's interest in Zionism developed. In 1901 he published a volume, *Lemaranan Ulerabbanan* ("To Our Teachers and Rabbis"), in which he attempted to alleviate the fears of Orthodox Jews and to bring them closer to the Zionist movement despite its secular leadership. Sokolow also translated **Theodor Herzl**'s *Altneuland* ("Old-New Land") into Hebrew under the title *Tel Aviv.*

Sokolow became secretary general of the **Zionist Organization** in 1907, was elected to the Zionist Executive in 1911, and was reelected two years later. When World War I broke out, he moved to London to work with **Chaim Weizmann**. Sokolow played a central role in preparing the political groundwork for the **Balfour Declaration** and headed the committee that drafted it. At the same time, he wrote his major work, the two-volume *History of Zionism, 1600–1918,* which caused some controversy because of its early dating of the origins of the movement. The evidence of the deep attachments of Jews to **Eretz Israel**, as well as the support of many prominent non-Jews for their return, was an implicit legitimization of the Balfour Declaration and the cultural, practical, and political perspectives of Zionism.

Sokolow headed the Zionist delegation at the Paris Peace Conference in 1919 and was elected chairman of the Zionist Executive in 1921. After Weizmann resigned the presidency of the Zionist Organization in 1931, Sokolow succeeded him. Upon Weizmann's return to the presidency in 1935, Sokolow was elected honorary president of the Zionist Organization and the **Jewish Agency**, as well as chairman of the Zionist Organization's Department of Education and Culture. He was also named chairman of Mosad Bialik. Sokolow died in London and in 1956 was reinterred on Mount Herzl in Jerusalem.

SONNEBORN, RUDOLPH GOLDSCHMIDT (1898–1986). The industrialist Rudolph Sonneborn is one of the unsung heroes of Israel's 1948

War of Independence. In the summer of 1945, Palestine Jewish leader **David Ben-Gurion** met with Sonneborn in New York City and asked him to recruit friends and colleagues to bankroll and equip the fight for Jewish independence. Sonneborn, a Baltimore native who managed his family's large oil and chemical business, had previously been involved in American Zionism as a young man when he participated in the 1919 **Zionist Commission** to Palestine.

Ben-Gurion's first goal was to raise money to purchase ships that could bring Holocaust survivors from Europe to Palestine, in defiance of British immigration restrictions. Sonneborn assembled a group of several dozen New York businessmen and philanthropists who pledged to discreetly finance and organize the immigration project. The group's strategy sessions were held each Thursday afternoon at midtown Manhattan's Hotel McAlpin.

Sonneborn and his friends also worked behind the scenes to purchase and develop weapons to equip the army of the Jewish state-to-be. A network of sympathizers helped them acquire large quantities of guns, ammunition, and explosives. Experts were engaged to develop, in the United States, prototypes of weapons that could be easily and cheaply mass-produced in Palestine itself.

Derelict warehouses were purchased to store machinery that the federal government was auctioning as postwar scrap metal and as storage depots for weapons and other military goods. To evade the State Department's arms embargo on Palestine, the goods were packed in crates marked "Used Machine Parts" or "Industrial Goods" prior to being shipped to the Holy Land.

In addition, the Sonneborn group provided the funds for **Haganah** agent Teddy Kollek to set up his Manhattan-based "Materials for Palestine" operation. Kollek arranged for tons of vital, but not explicitly military, materials to be shipped legally to Palestine. The supplies included sandbags to protect convoys reaching besieged parts of Jerusalem, water distillation units for frontier settlements in the Negev Desert, binoculars, compasses, telephones, printing presses, parachutes labeled "hospital supplies" (to be used in supplying outlying field hospitals, they claimed), and enough clothing to dress an army. With the constant flow of materials and the huge staff of volunteers sorting and packing them, the New York City warehouses where Kollek's goods were stored were often "busier than Sears Roebuck," one participant later recalled.

Sonneborn's funds were also used to purchase surplus World War II planes, such as C-46s and Lockheed Constellations. They were refurbished at airfields in the United States and then flown to Palestine by American air force veterans, who in many cases stayed on to become part of Israel's fledgling air force.

After the war, Sonneborn served, at various times, as an official of the **United Jewish Appeal**, the **United Israel Appeal**, and the **Zionist Organization of America**. However, he preferred to continue the anonymity that had hidden his pre-1948 efforts, and as a result, his accomplishments have remained generally unrecognized.

SOUTH AFRICAN ZIONIST FEDERATION. The South African Zionist Federation, established in 1898, was the first nationwide Jewish organization in South Africa. It consisted of South African Zionist groups from across the political spectrum, although the **Revisionist Zionists**, a significant force in the South African Jewish community, operated independently from 1937 until 1946. The federation sponsors Zionist educational and fundraising activities, assists South African immigrants to Israel, and, since 1908, has published the *Zionist Record*.

SPRINZAK, YOSEF (1885–1959). Russian Zionist activist Yosef Sprinzak was born in Moscow. His father, Dov Ber, was active in the **Hovevei Zion** and his home was a center for young Hebrew writers and Zionists. When Jews were expelled from Moscow in 1891, the family moved to Kishinev and then Warsaw. Yosef was one of the organizers, in 1903, of Hatehiyah, a Zionist group led by **Yitzhak Gruenbaum**. At the same time, he worked in Ahi-asaf, a Hebrew publishing company, and for Hebrew and Yiddish newspapers in Warsaw. In 1905 Sprinzak returned to Kishinev where he founded the Zeirei Zion movement with **Chaim Greenberg**. In 1908 Sprinzak spent several months in Constantinople, where he was in communication with a number of Zionist leaders, including Menachem Ussishkin, Nahum Sokolow, David Wolffsohn, and **Ze'ev Jabotinsky**, among others, and attempted to influence the new Young Turk regime. Later that year, he went to Beirut to study medicine at American University in Beirut but left there after only a few months to go on *aliya*, because he was asked to become secretary of **Hapoel Hazair**.

In **Eretz Israel**, Sprinzak participated in the absorption of the Yemenite *aliya* at the time. He was a delegate to the 11th and 12th **Zionist Congresses** and was the first representative of the labor movement in Eretz Israel to be elected to the Zionist Executive. At the 11th Congress, in Vienna in 1913, Sprinzak organized a faction of forty-one delegates from among members of both Hapoel Hazair and Zeirei Zion. Several years later, he was one of the founders of **Hitahdut**, the movement that actually merged those two.

During the 1920s, Sprinzak was a member of the executive committee of the **World Zionist Organization** and served as head of its Aliya Department. He was also a co-founder of the **Histadrut** and a member of the Tel Aviv municipality. In the 1930s, he was a member of the Histadrut Executive. He also played a significant role in the merger of **Ahdut Ha'avoda** and **Hapoel Hazair,** which became **Mapai**. He served as chairman of the **Zionist General Council** and general secretary of the Histadrut during the 1940s.

When the State of Israel was established in 1948, Sprinzak was elected to the Provisional State Council. Subsequently, he was elected to the Knesset in 1949, 1951, and 1955. He also served as the speaker of the Knesset during its first ten years and had a significant impact on the shaping of the new state's political system and culture.

ST. JAMES CONFERENCE. Having accepted the conclusion of the 1938 **Woodhead Commission** that partition of Palestine was unfeasible, the British government in November 1938 invited Jewish and Arab representatives to take part in a conference in London to consider possible solutions to the Palestine problem.

The conference, known as the Round Table Conference, was held in St. James Palace in London, beginning on February 7, 1939. The Zionist delegation was led by **Chaim Weizmann**. In addition, an advisory committee, composed of both Zionists and non-Zionists, remained in London throughout the talks to consult with the Jewish delegates. The Palestinian Arab delegation included both followers of Haj Amin el-Husseini, the Mufti of Jerusalem, and the rival Arab National Party. Although the British had initially threatened to exclude from the conference Arabs who had been involved in recent violence in Palestine, a number of Arabs who had been deported from Palestine because of their role in the violence were ultimately permitted to serve as delegates. The governments of Egypt, Transjordan, Saudi Arabia, Iraq, and Yemen also sent representatives. The British team at the talks was led by Colonial Secretary Malcolm Macdonald and Foreign Secretary Viscount Halifax.

The Arab delegations refused to meet directly with their Zionist counterparts, going so far as to use a separate entrance to the palace to avoid encountering the Jewish leaders. Some of the Arab delegates—but not those from Palestine—did, however, take part in three informal meetings with Jewish representatives that produced no breakthroughs. The British held a series of separate meetings with the Arab and Jewish officials, alternately conveying each side's positions to the other.

The Arab delegates refused to soften their opposition to further Jewish immigration and insisted on Palestine becoming an Arab state. The British unsuccessfully sought Jewish agreement to restrictions on immigration in exchange for postponing any decision on Palestine's final status. When it was clear that the negotiations were going nowhere, the British on March 15 presented their own proposal: a maximum of 75,000 Jewish immigrants during the next five years, subsequent immigration subject to Arab consent, and no immediate decision on the country's ultimate political status. The Jews rejected the British plan as a betrayal of the promises contained in the **Balfour Declaration**; the Arabs rejected it because it permitted additional Jewish immigration and because it put off the idea of making Palestine an independent Arab state. The conference ended without any agreement. Two months later, the British issued a **White Paper** announcing a new Palestine policy, based on the proposals they had made at the St. James Conference.

STATUS QUO AGREEMENT. The term *status quo* in this context dates back to a letter, signed by **David Ben-Gurion, Rabbi Judah Leib Fishman (Maimon)**, and **Yitzhak Gruenbaum**, in the name of the **Jewish Agency**, which was sent to leaders of **Agudat Israel** in June 1947, wherein it was agreed that in the State of Israel, religious affairs would be governed as they had been until then, with freedom of religion in the private sphere and with traditional Judaism in the public sphere. As outlined in the letter, the Jewish Sabbath, Saturday, would be a national day of rest; all kitchens in government-run buildings would adhere to the kosher dietary laws; marriages and divorces would remain in the realm of the rabbinic courts; and the various educational streams would be institutionalized within the state.

As it turned out, almost since the beginning, the Orthodox and the secular have each alleged the other side has infringed on the Status Quo Agreement. On the question of Sabbath observance, for example, the National Religious Party (NRP) has sought to have the government enact and enforce a Sabbath Law, under which all nonessential public facilities, and especially buses, trains, and El Al, Israel's national airline, would cease operation from sundown Friday until Saturday night. Some of the parties, especially Mapam, were opposed to any such restrictions, and a compromise was worked out to the effect that the Sabbath was accepted as an official day of rest, but the specifics of the law, what was and what was not forbidden, were left to the local municipalities, with the result that, except for Haifa and several other areas, there was no official operation of public buses on the Sabbath. This caused considerable discord in the country. To the Orthodox Jew, the observance of the Sabbath is one of the most basic precepts of Judaism; it is the fulfillment of a religious commandment and it serves as testimony to the very act of Creation. To many non-Orthodox, even if the Sabbath does have some religious significance, the Sabbath Law is a considerable inconvenience, if for no other reason than that Saturday is the only day that one might spend shopping or at leisure with family and friends. The unavailability of public transportation, especially if one cannot afford a car or a private taxi, may be viewed as an unjustifiable restriction of a basic freedom.

Although there are few avid supporters of the Status Quo Agreement, it is doubtful whether it will be officially rescinded in the foreseeable future, because either camp would view such a rescinding as a concession to the other, and both are vital for the formation of a solid Knesset coalition.

STERN, AVRAHAM (1907–1942). Palestine Jewish underground leader Avraham Stern was born in Suwalki, Poland, in 1907. Amid the turmoil of World War I, the Russian civil war, and the Bolshevik revolution, Stern's family was exiled to the Russian Urals region. He returned to his hometown in Poland in 1921, but soon afterward made his way to Jerusalem, where he completed high school and enrolled at **Hebrew University**.

Shaken by the Palestinian Arab violence of 1929, Stern joined the **Haganah**. Then, gradually becoming convinced of the need for more militant tactics, he joined the **Irgun Zvai Leumi (IZL)** underground in 1932. That same year he composed the poem "Nameless Soldiers," which was to become the unofficial anthem of the Zionist militants. A star student at Hebrew University, Stern won a scholarship to travel to Italy in 1933 to work on his doctoral dissertation in classical Greek literature, but before completing his studies he opted to return to Palestine to devote himself to the Irgun. He graduated from its commanders' course and was named senior aide to IZL leader Avraham Tehomi, adopting "Yair" as his nom de guerre. When the IZL was formally established as an independent underground movement in 1937, Stern became a member of its High Command. He and the IZL's new commander, **David Raziel**, composed "The Pistol," the first Hebrew-language weapons instruction manual.

On the eve of World War II, Stern and other IZL leaders were jailed by the British. From his prison cell, Stern vigorously opposed the call by **Revisionist Zionist** leader **Ze'ev Jabotinsky** to refrain from anti-British activities so long as Great Britain was at war with Nazi Germany. After his release from prison in June 1940, Stern tried, but failed, to persuade Jabotinsky to end the cease-fire. He and a minority of IZL members then broke away to establish a separate underground movement, the Irgun Zvai Leumi B'Israel, which the British called the Stern Gang. It soon changed its name to **Lohamei Herut Israel** (Fighters for the Freedom of Israel) and was popularly known by its acronym, Lehi.

In 1940–1941, prior to the onslaught of the Holocaust, Stern and his colleagues hoped to make contact with German or Italian diplomats, in the belief that the Axis powers might support a Jewish state as a means of undermining British interests in the region. The contacts were never made, however.

Numbering only several hundred and poorly armed, Lehi was limited to engaging in small-scale attacks against British forces in Palestine. In February 1942, the British police captured the unarmed Stern hiding in the Tel Aviv apartment of a Lehi sympathizer and executed him on the spot. Lehi eventually regrouped under new commanders and took part, alongside the larger Haganah and Irgun, in the Jewish revolt against the British that led to the establishment of the State of Israel.

SYRKIN, NAHMAN (1868–1924). The father of **Socialist Zionism**, Nahman Syrkin was born in Mahilyow, Belarus. His family moved to Minsk in 1884, where he joined **Hovevei Zion** and had connections with revolutionary anti-czarist groups. After being arrested for several weeks, he left for London and in 1888 went to Berlin. He studied psychology and philosophy at the University of Berlin, and there he was influenced by German social-democracy, which was at the height of its intellectual development. Syrkin was an outspoken critic of those who saw nationalism and socialism as contradictory, and he rejected **Ahad Ha'am**'s Spiritual Zionism as oblivious to social reality, especially to the reality of anti-Semitism.

Syrkin began writing at an early age. By his late teens, he had already written for *Hameliz* ("The Advocate"), Russia's first Hebrew periodical and for many years the organ of the moderate wing of the Jewish Enlightenment (*Haskala*) movement. At age twenty-two, Syrkin published an essay that attempted to refute Marx's determinism and emphasized the role of the voluntary in history. He joined **Theodor Herzl** and participated in the First **Zionist Congress** in Basle in 1897, and at the Second Zionist Congress in 1898 he sponsored a resolution for the establishment of the **Jewish National Fund**.

In 1898 he published an article that argued for the necessity of realizing the Zionist dream through cooperative mass settlement. Syrkin attacked the emergence of and increased attention given to bourgeois elements in the Zionist movement, and he also criticized Herzl's efforts to win the diplomatic recognition of what he viewed as reactionary states, such as Great Britain. He was a strong supporter of Herzl during the debate over the **Uganda Plan** and, for several years, he was a leader of the **Territorialists**. In contrast to most socialist thinkers, Syrkin was an advocate of Hebrew, rather than Yiddish, as the national language of the Jews.

Between 1901 and 1906, Syrkin worked in Germany, Austria, and Switzerland to establish Socialist Zionist clubs. In 1901 he founded a Yiddish publication, *Der Hamon* ("The Masses"), and in 1903, after it ceased to appear, he founded a Hebrew publication, *Hashahar* ("The Morning"). In both of these, as well as in his pamphlets, Syrkin rallied for *aliya* and the establishment of a Jewish state based on new social foundations. He also urged participation in Russian revolutionary movements.

Syrkin published his doctoral thesis in 1903. After being expelled from Germany in 1904, and a brief stay in Paris, he spent two years in Russia following the revolution there in 1905. Then he immigrated to the United States in 1907. Two years later, he joined **Poalei Zion** and was its leader for the remainder of his lifetime. In 1909, having concluded that there was no longer any substance to Territorialism, he rejoined the Zionist Organization.

During World War I, Syrkin helped establish the **American Jewish Congress**. He was an independent thinker and often took minority positions on significant issues. For example, he supported the notion of a **Jewish Legion** for the liberation of Palestine, in coordination with the Allies, although most **Socialist Zionists** opposed it. In 1920, when Poalei Zion was divided between those loyal to the Zionist Organization and those who instead urged secession and affiliation with the new Communist Third International, Syrkin remained firmly with the loyalists, although he was convinced that there were no inherent bases for the anti-Zionism of the Communists and that Communist anti-Zionism was the product of alienated Jews.

Syrkin represented the Committee of Jewish Delegations at the Versailles Peace Conference in 1919, after World War I. In 1920 he visited Palestine as the head of a commission established by the World Poalei

Zion Conference for the purpose of studying the implementation of the plan for cooperative mass settlement. He subsequently returned to the United States, where, in addition to his activity as head of Poalei Zion, he devoted his efforts to writing and lecturing. Syrkin never realized his dream of *aliya,* and he died in New York. He was, however, buried in Israel.

SZOLD, HENRIETTA (1860–1945). **Hadassah** founder Henrietta Szold was born in Baltimore, Maryland, one of eight daughters of Rabbi Benjamin Szold, of Congregation Oheb Shalom. She majored in Jewish studies and foreign languages. In 1877 Szold turned to teaching and journalism. In 1897 she joined the Zionist Association of Baltimore, Hebras Zion, and visited **Eretz Israel** for the first time in 1909. A year later, Szold was named secretary of the **Federation of American Zionists**. In 1912 she organized the Hadassah Chapter of Daughters of Zion, consisting of women interested in "the promotion of Jewish institutions and enterprises in Palestine." The organization's name was changed to Hadassah in 1914, and at its first convention, Szold was elected president.

In 1916 a group of prominent Zionists, including Judge Julian Mack, established a fund that provided Szold with lifetime income. In 1920 she was sent to Eretz Israel by the **American Zionist Medical Unit**, where she focused her subsequent work. Resigning as president of Hadassah in 1926, Szold went to Palestine as a member of the World Zionist Executive in charge of health and education. In 1933 she was appointed director of **Youth Aliya**, a position that she held for the rest of her life and that won her the affectionate title "Mother of the *Yishuv.*" She belonged to **Judah Magnes**'s **Ihud** group, which supported binationalism in Palestine.

In 1944 Szold was scheduled to receive an honorary doctorate from Boston University. However, her serious health condition prevented her from undertaking the trip, and the doctorate was awarded in a radio broadcast. She died the following year in Hadassah Hospital in Jerusalem.

-T-

TABENKIN, YITZHAK (1887–1971). **Labor Zionist** leader Yitzhak Tabenkin was born in Bobruysk, Belarus. He studied in a traditional Jewish primary school, *heder*, and then received a general education, primarily Russian. Tabenkin joined **Poalei Zion** in his youth and was active in self-defense efforts. He took issue with **Ber Borochov**'s materialist conception of the connection between the Jewish people and **Eretz Israel**. A strong supporter of agricultural settlement, Tabenkin went on *aliya* in 1911, worked in agricultural labor on a *moshav*, joined the defense organization **Hashomer**, and became a member of Kibbutz Kinneret. He was a delegate to every Zionist Congress from World War I on.

Tabenkin was a firm believer in the ideology of the **kibbutz**, who supported populism rather than elitism, and he advocated large kibbutzim for the masses. He was one of the founders of **Ahdut Ha'avoda** in 1919, and in 1921 he joined **Yosef Trumpeldor**'s Labor Legion (Gedud Ha'avoda). That same year, he was one of the pioneers of Kibbutz Ein Harod, which later became the nucleus of Hakibbutz Hameuhad. In 1920 he was one of the founders of the **Histadrut** and in 1930 of the Mifleget Poalei Eretz Israel (Mapai).

Tabenkin supported the merging of **Ahdut Ha'avoda** and **Hapoel Hatzair** in 1929. However, a rift in Mapai subsequently arose over relations with the Soviet regime. He advocated the notion of "**Hebrew labor**" as well as settlement, and he opposed the partition plan of 1937. He maintained a positive stance toward the Soviets and helped foster a left-wing opposition that in 1944 seceded from Mapai and, under his influence, became Hatenuah Le-Ahdut Ha'avoda. In 1948 it merged with **Hashomer Hatzair** and the Socialist League to form Mapam (Mifleget Hapoalim Hame-uhedet). Within Mapam, however, Tabenkin opposed those who called for an alliance with world Communism. When a rift developed in Mapam, Tabenkin headed those who seceded and became Ahdut Ha'avoda-Poalei Zion, which, in 1968, merged with Mapai and Rafi and became the Labor Party (*Mifleget Ha'avoda*). In contrast to most of his Labor Party colleagues, Tabenkin supported the Greater Land of Israel movement after the Six-Day War.

TERRITORIALISTS. Territorialists were those who believed that the Jewish problem would be solved when the Jewish people acquired a territory of their own, be it in **Eretz Israel** or elsewhere. Though there had been varieties of territorialism earlier, the movement crystallized in 1905, as a result of the defeat of the **Uganda Plan,** which the Territorialists supported. The most prominent Territorialist organization, the Jewish Territorialist Association, was formed under the leadership of the English writer and playwright **Israel Zangwill** (1864–1926); it seceded from the **World Zionist Organization**, but its goal of finding a territorial alternative to Eretz Israel never materialized. After the **Balfour Declaration** in November 1917, many of its members returned to the Zionist Organization and in 1925 the association was formally dissolved.

TRUMPELDOR, YOSEF (1880–1920). Zionist pioneer Yosef Trumpeldor grew up in an acculturated Russian Jewish family and only became interested in his Jewish identity after a "Jewish quota" prevented his admission to high school in the town of Rostov-na-Donu. Further inspired by the convening of the **First Zionist Congress** in 1897, Trumpeldor became an active Zionist.

In 1902 Trumpeldor was drafted into the Russian army. He fought with distinction in the Russo-Japanese war, losing his left arm in battle but insisting on returning to the front despite his injuries. The multiple honors he received made him one of the most highly decorated soldiers in all of Russia. Captured by the Japanese, Trumpeldor organized a Zionist group among the Jewish soldiers in his prisoner-of-war camp.

Together with a handful of idealistic Zionist friends, Trumpeldor settled in Palestine in 1912 and, after their own attempt at establishing a cooperative settlement failed, found work at Degania, the first **kibbutz**. During this period, he also made a return visit to Russia as a Zionist emissary, promoting the **Jewish National Fund** and encouraging Russian Jews to move to Palestine.

Like other Jewish residents of Palestine who were Russian nationals, Trumpeldor was expelled to Egypt by the Turks in 1914. There he met up with **Ze'ev Jabotinsky** and joined his efforts to persuade the British to establish a Jewish fighting force. When the British agreed to create an auxiliary military unit, the Zion Mule Corps, Trumpeldor accepted the post of deputy commander. He served with the unit in Gallipoli and was later promoted to commander.

In early 1917, Trumpeldor traveled to Russia to organize a Jewish army that he hoped would fight its way south to Palestine. Unable to secure government backing for the project, Trumpeldor devoted himself to organizing the Zionist pioneering **Hehalutz** movement in Russia and establishing Jewish self-defense groups to combat pogromists.

Trumpeldor returned to Palestine in late 1919 and volunteered to command the defense of Galilee Jewish outposts that were under Arab attack. On March 1, 1920, he was killed during a battle with Arab attackers at Tel Hai. The author **Yosef Hayim Brenner** reported and popularized Trumpeldor's stirring final words, "It is good to die for our country." Although questions have been raised as to the precise wording of Trumpeldor's final statement, there can be no doubt that Brenner's formulation accurately represented the spirit of Zionist self-sacrifice that permeated Trumpeldor's life. A statue of a roaring lion, sculpted in 1934, marks the site of Trumpeldor's grave not far from the Tel Hai battle site. To this day, many Zionist youth groups visit the cemetery on the anniversary of Trumpeldor's death. A Zionist labor battalion (*gedud avoda*) was named after Trumpeldor, as was the nearby community of Tel Yosef and the Revisionist youth movement **Betar**, which is an acronym for "Brit al-Shem Yosef Trumpeldor."

-U-

UGANDA PLAN. The Uganda Plan emerged in the summer of 1903, when the British colonial secretary Joseph Chamberlain informed the **World Zionist Organization** of Great Britain's agreement in principle that a portion of East Africa could serve as a potential Jewish homeland. At the Sixth **Zionist Congress**, which met shortly thereafter, **Theodor Herzl** presented the Uganda Plan and urged its acceptance as a temporary measure. The proposal became the subject of one of the fiercest debates in Zionist history, with those who opposed it calling themselves "Zionists of Zion" (Zionei Zion). When the proposal won a majority, the opposition, most of whom were Russian, stormed out of the congress and agreed to return only after Herzl assured them that he retained his allegiance to Palestine as the ultimate objective of Zionism. Despite their return, those who opposed the Uganda Plan lost admiration for Herzl, and he never regained the staunch support that he previously enjoyed.

After the congress, the Zionei Zion called a conference in Kharkov, at which they presented Herzl with an ultimatum to abandon the Uganda Plan. Herzl ignored the ultimatum, and the animosity between him and the Zionei Zion remained fierce until the spring of 1904, when the British government withdrew its offer. Herzl died before the Seventh **Zionist Congress** in 1905, after having read a negative report on the plan by the commission of inquiry appointed at the previous congress. The Uganda Plan was rejected by a majority of the delegates.

UNITED JEWISH APPEAL (UJA). The United Jewish Appeal was founded in 1939 as the combination of two major American Jewish overseas aid agencies, the **American Joint Distribution Committee (JDC)** and the United Palestine Appeal (UPA). The UPA was formed in 1925 by American Zionists because of their ideological disagreements with the older JDC's approach of assisting oppressed Jews in their countries. This was unacceptable to the Zionists, who argued that it was more important to encourage the oppressed Jews to go to Palestine.

The Council of Jewish Federations and Welfare Funds (CJFWF), which ran the American Jewish fundraising campaigns in the local communities, had a special reason for wishing that the two overseas aid agencies should come to some agreement: the competition between the agencies for contributors was highly inefficient. For several years after its creation, the United Jewish Appeal was unstable and its relationship with the CJFWF was precarious at best. The effort at cooperation did, however, establish a pattern of increasing coordination of fundraising activities between the CJFWF and the UJA in Jewish communities throughout the United States. As a result of these efforts, fundraising was streamlined and many more dollars were raised. The joint campaigns resulted in the CJFWF's rise to a position of dominance in domestic Jewish communal affairs.

Concurrently, the UJA became the major fundraising agency involved in overseas aid, and the United Palestine Appeal, subsequently renamed the United Israel Appeal (UIA), became the major power bloc within the UJA. In 1998 the UJA, UIA, and CJF entered into a formal partnership, the rationale for which was greater financial efficiency. However, questions have been raised as to whether this might not represent a weakening of the Zionist commitments of American Jewry.

UNITED NATIONS SPECIAL COMMITTEE ON PALESTINE (UNSCOP). Unable to resolve the Arab–Jewish conflict in Palestine, shaken by Jewish military attacks, and facing growing international criticism of its Palestine policies, Great Britain announced in February 1947 that it was referring the Palestine question to the United Nations for its consideration.

In May 1947, the UN General Assembly appointed a United Nations Special Committee on Palestine to investigate the problem and recommend possible solutions. The thirteen members of the committee, representing a variety of countries (excluding the great powers and the Arab states), heard testimony from Jewish, Arab, and British representatives in Palestine from June 16 to July 24. The crisis over the **S.S. *Exodus*** unfolded during the UNSCOP hearings, and a subcommittee of UNSCOP members visited the internment camps in Germany where the passengers were held after being turned away from Palestine by the British. The episode influenced some of the UNSCOP members to favor Jewish statehood.

UNSCOP's final report, completed in August, contained a majority recommendation, supported by eight of the members, as well as an alternative plan endorsed by three of the remaining five. The majority report proposed a two-year period of transition, followed by the partition of Palestine into Jewish and Arab states, with Jerusalem as a separate entity under international trusteeship. The Jewish state would consist of most of the Negev desert, a coastal strip, and the eastern Galilee; the Arabs would have the center of the country, the Gaza-El Arish region, and the central and western Galilee. The borders, which were determined largely in accordance with patterns of settlement, would have given the Jewish state a 53 percent Jewish majority. The minority scheme called for a three-year transition period, after which Palestine would become an "independent federal state."

On November 29, the majority plan was endorsed by the UN General Assembly by a vote of 33 to 13, with 10 abstentions. Although this international acceptance of the concept of Jewish statehood provided a significant boost for Zionist morale, it was of limited practical significance, because the UN provided no means for implementation of the plan, and the recommended borders were overrun in the subsequent invasion by Arab forces seeking to thwart the establishment of the Jewish state.

UNITED PALESTINE APPEAL. *See* UNITED JEWISH APPEAL.

USSISHKIN, MENACHEM MENDEL (1863–1941). Russian Zionist leader Menachem Ussishkin was born in Dubrovno, Russia. The family moved to Moscow when he was eight years old. Ussishkin studied at Moscow's Technological Institute, from which he graduated and was certified as an engineer in 1889. While a student, he was instrumental in establishing a Jewish students' society at the institute. Ussishkin was active in the Bnei Zion society, which was founded in Moscow in 1884, and was elected secretary of Moscow's Hovevei Zion in 1885. Two years later, he became a regular contributor to the Hebrew periodical *Hamelitz* ("The Advocate"). In 1889, he joined **Benei Moshe**, an organization founded by **Ahad Ha'am**.

Ussishkin visited **Eretz Israel** in 1891 and, upon his return, became active in Hebrew education and the promotion of Zionism. He met **Theodor Herzl** and **Max Nordau** at the opening of the **First Zionist Congress**, and though he was awed by them, he maintained reservations about Herzl's singular focus on **Political Zionism**. He was a strong believer in the importance of settlement as well as cultural activity. At the Second Zionist Congress in 1898, he was elected to the Zionist General Council, a position Ussishkin maintained until his death. In 1901, at the Fifth Zionist Congress, he proposed the establishment of the Anglo-Palestine Company in Eretz Israel as a branch of the **Jewish Colonial Trust**.

Ussishkin again visited Eretz Israel in 1903. During his four months there, he attempted to organize the *yishuv* and, to that end, convened a three-day Knesset Hagedolah ("Great Assembly") in Zikhron Ya'akov, which, however, did not achieve his objective. The following month, the Zionist movement was wracked by one of its most bitter controversies, the **Uganda Plan**. Ussishkin sharply criticized the proposal and became one of Herzl's most vocal opponents. In contrast to Herzl's Political Zionism, Ussishkin became a leader of **Practical Zionism**, which emphasized *aliya* and agricultural settlement.

Ussishkin quickly rose to prominence in the *yishuv*. By 1921, he was elected chairman of the Zionist Executive. Although, due to a rift with **Chaim Weizmann**, Ussishkin was not reelected to the Executive two years later, he was named head of the **Jewish National Fund** in 1923, a post he maintained for the rest of his life.

-V-

VA'AD LEUMI. The Va'ad Leumi, or National Council, was the executive branch of Knesset Israel, the officially recognized Jewish communal body of Mandatory Palestine. The members of the Va'ad Leumi were appointed by the **Asefat Hanivcharim**, or Elected Assembly, which served as Palestine Jewry's official representative in dealings with the British ruling authorities, supervised the *yishuv*'s annual budget, and helped oversee the community's religious, educational, and social welfare spheres. The Va'ad Leumi functioned as a sort of shadow cabinet for the Jewish state-to-be, and after Israel was established in 1948, many of the Va'ad Leumi's departments were transformed into ministries of the new Israeli government.

-W-

WARBURG, FELIX (1871–1937). A prominent member of the pre–World War II German-born American Jewish elite, Felix Warburg immigrated to the United States in 1895 after marrying Frieda Schiff, daughter of the New York Jewish banking magnate and philanthropist Jacob Schiff. Warburg became a partner in his father-in-law's investment firm, Kuhn, Loeb and Company. He was also given the task of overseeing Schiff's distribution of charity and soon made a name for himself in the world of American Jewish philanthropy. Attributing his charitable interests to his traditional upbringing, Warburg provided substantial funds—both Schiff's and his own—to assist new Jewish immigrants to the United States, as well as a wide range of nonsectarian educational, cultural, and social welfare projects.

Like most of his social peers, Warburg was initially cold to Zionism, regarding Jewish nationalism as inconsistent with the goal of becoming a fully acculturated American and fearing that the establishment of a Jewish homeland would raise questions about the loyalty of Jews to the United States. However, at the urging of **Chaim Weizmann**, Warburg paid a brief visit to Palestine at the end of a Mediterranean cruise in December 1923. The experience proved overwhelming. "I have seen what is being done and I feel like throwing myself on the ground and kissing every inch of the soil," he declared. He was particularly enamored of the budding **Hebrew University**, whose chancellor was his old friend **Judah Magnes**, formerly a prominent Reform rabbi and Zionist in New York.

Upon his return to the United States, Warburg assumed a leading role in Palestine-related business projects and charitable endeavors. Even while devoting himself to fundraising for Palestine, Warburg continued to spurn Zionist ideology and considered himself a **non-Zionist**. He believed that the Zionists' socialist ideology hampered the economic development of the Jewish homeland, and he feared Zionist propaganda was undermining Arab–Jewish relations. Warburg believed that sound business practices, under the guidance of American financial experts such as himself and divorced from ideological or political interests, could remedy Palestine's problems. Warburg worked closely with Weizmann to broker the 1929 Pact of Glory that brought a large faction of non-Zionists into the leadership of the **Jewish Agency**. When Louis Marshall, leader of the non-Zionist group, passed away shortly after the deal was signed, Warburg was chosen to replace him as chairman of the agency's Administrative Committee.

As Palestinian Arab opposition to Zionism intensified, Warburg became increasingly interested in the issue of Arab–Jewish relations. In the aftermath of the Arab riots of 1929, he urged the Zionist leadership to make conciliatory gestures to the Arabs. Yet he also initiated private contacts with Arab and British officials to explore the idea of providing financial incentives to Palestinian Arabs to relocate to Transjordan or Iraq, but died suddenly in 1937, before the plan could be realized.

WEIZMANN, CHAIM (1874–1952). International Zionist leader and future president of Israel, Chaim Weizmann was born in Motol, Belarus. He received both a Jewish and a secular education and was attracted to the physical sciences, particularly chemistry, and studied biochemistry in Germany and Switzerland. While a student, Weizmann was active in the Zionist movement in Geneva, and he also taught Hebrew. He received his doctorate in chemistry from the University of Freiburg, Switzerland, in 1899; lectured at the University of Geneva from 1901 to 1903 and then at the University of Manchester. During his student years in Berlin, Weizmann belonged to the Jewish-Russian Scientific Association (Jüdisch-Russische Wissenschaftliche Verein), among whose members were some of the major Zionist ideologists.

Weizmann was strongly influenced by **Ahad Ha'am** and **Cultural Zionism** before coming into contact with **Theodor Herzl** and the **World Zionist Organization**. He was a delegate to the Second **Zionist Congress** in 1898 and, just prior to the Fifth Zionist Congress in 1901, spearheaded the formation of the **Democratic Faction**, which placed priority on the building of socio-cultural and educational institutions in the *yishuv*. Weizmann also helped develop Synthetic Zionism, which emphasized activity in the field, the *yishuv* itself, as well as in diplomatic circles.

During the controversy over the **Uganda Plan**, Weizmann sided with **Menachem Ussishkin** and other opponents of the proposal. He moved to England in 1905, where both his scientific and Zionist careers flourished. He was elected that year to the General Zionist Council. In 1906 Weizmann met Arthur James Balfour and had the opportunity to explain to him the Jewish connection to **Eretz Israel** and the reasons for the opposition to the Uganda Plan. That meeting and the subsequent relationship between the two provided the background for the **Balfour Declaration** of 1917. Weizmann's scientific research also played a role in the process leading to the declaration, in that he directed the laboratories of the British admiralty during the war years, from 1916 to 1919, and achieved a measure of fame with his development of a synthetic acetone used in producing explosives. These scientific achievements enabled him to establish close contacts with the Allied forces in World War I and with British leaders.

In 1918 Weizmann was appointed head of the **Zionist Commission** sent by the British government to Palestine to advise the British authorities on plans for settling and developing the country. While there, he laid the cornerstone at the founding of the **Hebrew University**. He also met with a leading Arab official, Emir Faisal, and discussed the plans for Jewish settlement and prospects for the establishment of autonomous Arab and Jewish states. Later, he was among the leaders of the Zionist delegation to the Versailles Peace Conference in 1919. Weizmann was elected president of the World Zionist Organization in 1920 and served until 1931, when his unsympathetic statements on the question of a Jewish majority in Palestine aroused opposition to his continued leadership of the Zionist movement. He served again as president from 1935 to 1946. Weizmann also helped establish its fundraising branch, **Keren Hayesod**.

During the early 1930s, he established the Daniel Sieff Institute for Research, which subsequently became the Weizmann Institute of Science in Rehovot. He made Rehovot his home in 1937.

Weizmann supported the **Peel Commission** partition plan of 1937. His pro-British stance, however, undermined his position within the Zionist movement when, in May 1939, the British **White Papers** in effect halted Jewish immigration to Palestine. He was one of the architects of the American Zionist **Biltmore Program**, which called for the establishment of Palestine as a Jewish Commonwealth, and lobbied for the creation of a **Jewish Brigade** to fight alongside the Allies against the Nazis. Weizmann opposed **David Ben-Gurion**'s call for a more militant approach in Palestine, fearing that it would provoke both the British and the Arabs. Weizmann's pro-British inclinations once again undermined his position with the Zionist movement, and in 1946 he was not reelected president of the World Zionist Organization. Weizmann did, however, play a central role in persuading President Harry S. Truman to support partition at the United Nations and to have the Negev included in the Jewish state.

Named by Ben-Gurion as president of the Provisional Council, Weizmann was, in February 1949, elected as the first president of Israel, a position that he held until his death in 1952. He was buried in the garden of his home in Rehovot. Yad Chaim Weizmann, the Weizmann National Memorial, which includes his archives and library, was established on the grounds of the Weizmann Institute of Science. *See also* FAISAL-WEIZMANN AGREEMENT.

WHITE PAPERS. Official statements of British policy during the Palestine Mandate period were nicknamed "White Papers," a reference to the type of paper upon which the statements were printed. The first White Paper on Palestine, issued in June 1922, is commonly called the Churchill White Paper since it was issued by Colonial Secretary Winston Churchill, although it was authored largely by the high commissioner for Palestine, Herbert Samuel. It specified that the Jewish national home would be situated in only a part of, rather than all of, Palestine; emphasized that the Zionist movement would play no role in the governing of the country; and decreed the principle that Jewish immigration should not exceed the economic absorptive capacity of the country. The Zionists reluctantly accepted the Churchill White Paper, but the Palestinian Arab leadership unequivocally rejected it as too pro-Zionist.

The Passfield White Paper of October 1930, named after Colonial Secretary Lord Passfield (Sidney Webb), was based on the recommendations of the **Shaw Commission**, which had been sent by London to investigate the causes of the 1929 Palestinian Arab riots. Although it did not provide for any immediate practical changes in the British administration of Palestine, the Passfield White Paper announced plans to establish an elected legislative council to take part in governing the country; criticized the effect of Jewish land-purchasing activity on the Palestinian Arabs and pledged to consider restrictions on that activity; and opposed "unrestricted Jewish immigration" to Palestine. Worldwide Jewish protests convinced British prime minister J. Ramsay MacDonald to issue a letter, in early 1931, effectively repudiating the Passfield White Paper.

After the **Woodhead Commission** returned from Palestine in 1938 and declared the previous year's **Peel Commission** partition plan unfeasible, the British government issued a White Paper in November 1938 formally abandoning the Peel proposal and proposing a Jewish–Arab conference in London to consider possible solutions to the Palestine problem.

The failure of that London conference prompted the British government to issue its White Paper of May 15, 1939, also known as the MacDonald White Paper, after Colonial Secretary Malcolm MacDonald. It limited Jewish immigration to a maximum of 75,000 over the next five years; restricted Jewish land acquisitions; and proposed the creation of an independent, binational Jewish-Arab Palestine after a ten-year transitional period. Despite strong Jewish protests, the 1939 White Paper remained official British policy in Palestine until the end of the Mandate regime in 1948.

WISE, STEPHEN SAMUEL (1874–1949). American Zionist leader Stephen Wise was born in Hungary and brought to the United States as a small child. Raised in New York, Wise traveled to Vienna to study with Rabbi Adolf Jellinek, from whom he received rabbinical ordination, and later earned a Ph.D. from Columbia University.

As the rabbi of Beth Israel, a Reform synagogue in Portland, Oregon, Wise quickly gained fame both as a charismatic orator and as a social activist. One of the few Zionists in the Reform rabbinate, Wise had served as a delegate to the Second **Zionist Congress** (1898) and helped organize the Federation of American Zionists. In Oregon, he established the community's first Zionist group. Wise returned to New York in 1907 to found the Free Synagogue, a pulpit from which he spoke out forcefully on a variety of issues, including union rights, women's suffrage, race relations, and Tammany Hall corruption. He was a co-founder of the National Association for the Advancement of Colored People (1909) and the American Civil Liberties Union (1920).

When **Louis Brandeis** assumed the leadership of American Zionism in 1914, Wise returned to an active role in the movement, becoming a senior aide to Brandeis and eventually becoming chairman of the **Provisional Executive Committee for General Zionist Affairs** when Brandeis was chosen for the Supreme Court. At the same time, Wise led the movement to establish the **American Jewish Congress** as a pro-Zionist, democratically elected alternative to the existing major Jewish organizations. He also took part in the negotiations over the wording of the **Balfour Declaration**, helped secure the support of President Woodrow Wilson for Zionism, and served as a Zionist spokesman at the Paris Peace Conference after World War I.

Wise joined Brandeis in resigning from the **Zionist Organization of America (ZOA)** over Brandeis's 1921 dispute with **Chaim Weizmann** but remained close to the ZOA leadership and in 1925 was named chairman of the **United Palestine Appeal**. At the same time, Wise served as president of the American Jewish Congress and founded the Jewish Institute of Religion, an independent Reform rabbinical school that later merged with Hebrew Union College. In 1936 he established the World Jewish Congress to lead the fight against anti-Semitism internationally.

Wise's early and fervent support for Franklin D. Roosevelt and the New Deal gave him a level of access to the White House that no other Jewish leader enjoyed, but access did not equal influence. Wise was unable to persuade President Roosevelt to intervene against Great Britain's 1939 **White Paper** severely restricting Jewish immigration to Palestine. Accepting Roosevelt's position that nothing should be done to provoke controversy with the British in wartime, Wise counseled Jewish leaders to refrain from criticizing Britain's Palestine policy. He likewise opposed any public Jewish criticism of Roosevelt's policies toward Palestine and European Jewry.

As news of the Nazi genocide reached the West in 1942, grassroots American Jewish opinion increasingly turned against Wise's cautious approach. The groundswell of calls for a more activist policy by the Jewish leadership compelled Wise to accept the appointment of **Abba Hillel Silver** as co-chairman of the **American Zionist Emergency Council** in the summer of 1943. Working side by side only intensified the rivalry between the two men, which was as much personal as it was political. With popular opinion behind him, Silver effectively usurped Wise as America's most prominent Zionist spokesman. Wise's final defeat came at the 1946 Zionist Congress, when he backed **Chaim Weizmann** in a losing struggle against the activist camp led by Silver and **David Ben-Gurion**.

WOLFFSOHN, DAVID (1856–1914). Zionist leader David Wolffsohn was born in Dorbiany, Lithuania, and received a religiously traditional education, through which he studied under Rabbi Isaac Ruelf, one of the future founders of **Hibbat Zion**. In 1872–1873 he went to Memel to live with family, then he went to Lyck in East Prussia, where he met **David Gordon**, an early enthusiast of Hibbat Zion and editor of *Hamaggid* ("The Herald"), a prominent Hebrew newspaper. Wolffsohn moved to Cologne in 1888, became a wealthy businessman, and involved himself in Zionist activities.

Wolffsohn became acquainted with Max Bodenheimer when Bodenheimer gave an address in which he espoused Jewish nationalist notions that were strongly challenged by most of the audience. Wolffsohn defended Bodenheimer and subsequently became active in Hibbat Zion. The two of them established the Cologne Association for the Development of Agriculture in the Land of Israel in 1893. A few years later, when he read **Theodor Herzl**'s *Der Judenstaat,* Wolffsohn was immediately taken with the book and its author, whom he met personally in Vienna in 1896. Thereafter, he became Herzl's colleague and, because Herzl's knowledge of Judaism and Jewish life was very limited, Wolffsohn served as his unofficial adviser in these matters. It was Wolffsohn who gave Herzl the idea of blue and white as the colors for the Zionist flag, based on a blue and white prayer shawl, and he suggested the shekel, derived from the ancient Hebrew standard coin, as the Zionist Organization's membership dues. From 1897 to 1904, he was a member of the **Zionist**

Organization's Actions Committee. He was also the central figure in the establishment of the **Jewish Colonial Trust**, as well as its first president.

Wolffsohn remained a staunch loyalist to Herzl even when he may have personally disagreed with him. Throughout the debate over the **Uganda Plan**, Wolffsohn voiced no opinion on the matter, although there are indications he personally opposed it. He succeeded Herzl as president of the Zionist Organization, a position he held until the Tenth Congress in Basle in 1911. Throughout the years of his presidency, Wolffsohn sought to mediate and bridge the gap between the **"practical" Zionists** and **"political" Zionists**, an effort that frequently won him the scorn of both. His skills as a synthesizer, as well as his appealing personality, were only recognized after his death. Wolffsohn was reinterred in Israel in 1952, and his grave is next to that of Herzl, on Mount Herzl in Jerusalem.

WOODHEAD COMMISSION. Following up on the report of the 1936–1937 **Peel Commission**, which recommended partition of Palestine into separate Arab and Jewish states, the British government appointed a four-man Palestine Partition Commission led by Sir John Woodhead to visit Palestine in the spring of 1938 and propose methods for implementation of the Peel scheme.

Woodhead, formerly an official of the British administration in India, arrived in Palestine in late April and remained until July. He and his colleagues met with Zionist representatives and officials of the British Mandatory government but were boycotted by the Arabs. In their 310-page final report, presented to the government in October 1938, three of the four commission members endorsed a plan to drastically reduce the boundaries of the proposed Jewish state from what Peel had recommended. According to the Woodhead plan, only a narrow coastal strip would be included in the Jewish area, while the other territories Peel had allotted to the Jewish state, the Negev, the Galilee, and the Jezreel Valley, would be retained by the British. At the same time, the Woodhead Commission concluded that there was no feasible partition plan that could assure economic success for both the Arab and Jewish states.

In November 1938, the British government accepted the Woodhead Commission's recommendations, formally abandoned the Peel proposal, and began plans for an Arab-Jewish conference, in Great Britain, to discuss possible solutions to the Palestine problem. *See also* WHITE PAPERS.

WORLD UNION OF GENERAL ZIONISTS. *See* GENERAL ZIONISTS.

WORLD ZIONIST ORGANIZATION (WZO). Originally called simply the Zionist Organization, it was founded in 1897 at the First **Zionist Congress** in Basle, Switzerland, to be the organizational embodiment of the Zionist movement. Any Jew who subscribed to the program of the movement and paid the "shekel" fee was entitled to join the organization. The idea of the organization was **Theodor Herzl**'s, and he served as its president from its founding until 1904. During Herzl's tenure, the organization's two major financial apparatuses, the **Jewish Colonial Trust** and the **Jewish National Fund**, were established.

From its creation until the establishment of the State of Israel, the Zionist Organization was the control center for the political, economic, and settlement activities in the *yishuv*. With the state's establishment, the role of the World Zionist Organization was defined, in 1952, by Israel's Status Law: "The State of Israel recognizes the WZO as the authorized agency that will continue to operate in the State of Israel for the development and settlement of the country, the absorption of immigrants from the **Diaspora** and the coordination of the activities in Israel of Jewish institutions and organizations active in those fields."

At the first Zionist Congress to take place after the establishment of the state, the 23rd Zionist Congress in 1951, the **Jerusalem Program** was adopted, and a new Jerusalem Program was adopted at the 27th Zionist Congress in 1968.

-Y-

YERIDA. *Yerida* is a Hebrew term that, literally, means "descent." It is the term that traditional Judaism and Zionism apply to emigration from Israel, because Israel is viewed as the highest point in the value system. Ideological post-Zionists call for abandoning the term and replacing it with "emigration," and they have been joined in that call by some Israelis living abroad. The latter were particularly incensed when in 1976 the then prime minister, Yitzhak Rabin, referred to *yordim*, Israeli emigrants, as *nefolet shel nemushot* ("the droppings of ants" or "the fallen among the weaklings").

Precise figures are unavailable, but it is estimated that there are some 50,000–250,000 Israelis living in the New York metropolitan area and some 350,000–500,000 throughout the United States altogether. Israeli-Americans are no longer shunned and, in recent years, have been given official recognition as a subcommunity by national American Jewish organizations as well as by the **World Zionist Organization** and the government of Israel. Similar patterns prevail in many other countries with subcommunities of former Israelis.

YISHUV. *Yishuv*, the Hebrew term for "settlement" or "community," is commonly used to refer to the pre-1948 Jewish community of Palestine as a whole. In addition, the phrases "old *yishuv*" and "new *yishuv*" are employed to distinguish between the "old" community of Jewish residents in Palestine prior to the arrival of large numbers of Jewish settlers in the late nineteenth century and the "new" Jewish society that was developed as a result of Zionist development efforts from the late 1800s until 1948.

YOUTH ALIYA. Youth Aliya was a major department of the **Jewish Agency**, established by the **World Zionist Organization (WZO)** in 1933 for the purpose of rescuing needy Jewish children in the **Diaspora** by bringing them to **Eretz Israel** and there providing for their physical and social welfare, including education. From 1934, it was directed by **Henrietta Szold**, and it organized the immigration and absorption of thousands of young Jews in **kibbutzim**, *moshavim,* and the youth villages that it established on its own. Much of the cost of Youth Aliya was funded by the American Zionist women's organization, **Hadassah**.

During the 1940s and early state years, some segments of the religious community accused the WZO of ignoring the religious and cultural backgrounds of the children in Youth Aliya, many but not all of whom were orphans. Critics charged that Youth Aliya was more interested in building a new **Socialist Zionist** society than in rescuing Jews, and that it was therefore selective in its rescue activities and overtly intent on fostering its Zionist ideals among the youth rather than enabling youth to continue in their parents' ways. The policy officially adopted by **Jewish Agency** was that young children should be reared in the tradition of their parents, but that those older than fourteen were free to choose their own lifestyle. This policy did not pacify the critics, and the issue raged for many years and has rekindled on various occasions in recent years.

From its beginnings with a small group of boys from Germany in 1933 until 1995, approximately 300,000 children have passed through Youth Aliya's various programs. When financial pressures forced the reorganization of the Jewish Agency in the 1990s, it was transferred to the Israel Ministry of Education.

-Z-

ZANGWILL, ISRAEL (1864–1926). British Zionist activist Israel Zangwill first gained fame as the author of a series of novels about East London Jewish immigrant life, among them *Children of the Ghetto* (1892), *Ghetto Tragedies* (1893), *The King of the Schnorrers* (1894), and *Dreamers of the Ghetto* (1898). He also authored a number of plays, including "The Melting Pot" (1909), which impressed Broadway audiences with its scenes of immigrants from around the world being forged into Americans through immersion in a large cooking pot.

Zangwill was the first person **Theodor Herzl** contacted when Herzl made his initial visit to Great Britain in late 1895 to seek support for Zionism. Zangwill arranged Herzl's London appearances and in 1897 joined the pilgrimage to Palestine by members of the British Zionist group, the **Order of Ancient Maccabeans**. Zangwill also attended the First **Zionist Congress** at Basle in 1897.

A strong supporter of the plan to establish a temporary Jewish refugee in East Africa, Zangwill broke from the Zionist movement when the Seventh **Zionist Congress** rejected the East Africa scheme in 1905. He then established the **Jewish Territorial Organization (JTO)**, to seek land outside of Palestine for the settlement of Jewish refugees. After the **Balfour Declaration** in 1917, Zangwill returned to the Zionist movement, where he stirred controversy with his proposal to "make the Arabs trek," that is, to encourage Arab residents of Palestine, especially those who had recently entered the country, to resettle in Arab lands.

ZIONEI ZION. *See* UGANDA PLAN.

ZIONIST COMMISSION. The Zionist Commission was a delegation of Jewish leaders from Allied countries, most of them Zionist activists from Great Britain, assembled at the initiative of **Chaim Weizmann** in early 1918. It arrived in Palestine in April 1918, intending to assume responsibility for the practical work of developing the Jewish homeland. The commission's specific tasks, as authorized by the British Foreign Office, included arranging for the repatriation of Jews who had been expelled by the Turks and provision of humanitarian aid to war-ravaged parts of the country; facilitating Jewish development projects; establishing friendly relations with the local Arabs; laying the groundwork of the establishment of **Hebrew University**; and serving as a liaison between

Palestine Jewry and the British authorities. Weizmann chaired the commission.

The British initially prevented Jewish land purchases and prohibited immigration except for the repatriation of exiles, so the commission during its first year focused on refugee relief, improvement of the country's health standards, and the development of Hebrew University. It also took over the political work of the **World Zionist Organization**'s Palestine Office in Jaffa. During this period, Weizmann held his first meeting with the Emir Faisal. After the British civil administration replaced the military occupation regime in the summer of 1920, the Zionist Commission took an active role in land purchases, settlement projects, immigrant absorption, and expansion of the educational system.

At the 12th **Zionist Congress** (1921), the Zionist Commission was officially replaced by the Palestine Zionist Executive. *See also* FAISAL-WEIZMANN AGREEMENT.

ZIONIST CONGRESS. The Zionist Congress, a periodic assembly of representatives of Zionist organizations from around the world, is the supreme policy-making agency of the World Zionist movement. Thirty-three congresses have been held since the inaugural gathering in 1897. The First Zionist Congress, which opened on August 29, 1897, was organized by **Theodor Herzl**, the charismatic Viennese journalist who had assumed the leadership of the infant Zionist movement. The congress was originally planned for Munich, but Herzl shifted it to Basle, Switzerland, after German Jewish leaders protested that their loyalty to Germany could be impugned by such an event. As Herzl explained in his keynote address to the 202 delegates, the purpose of the first congress was "to lay the foundation of the house which is to shelter the Jewish nation."

The congress established the **World Zionist Organization (WZO)**, elected Herzl its president, and composed its platform, later known as the **Basle Program**, which defined Zionism's aim as the attainment of "a legally secured home in Palestine for the Jewish people." It called for settlement of Palestine, international Jewish unity, and efforts to strengthen Jewish identity. The congress also authorized efforts to secure "the consent of the various governments" for the establishment of a Jewish national home. "In Basle, I founded the Jewish State," Herzl wrote in his diary.

Herzl was reelected president at each of the subsequent five congresses. Few rumblings of dissent were heard within the movement until the Fifth Zionist Congress, held in Basle in December 1901. The assembly included the first distinct ideological faction in the Zionist movement, called the **Democratic Faction**, led by **Chaim Weizmann** and **Leon Motzkin**. The Democratic group succeeded in persuading the congress to undertake a scientific study of conditions in the Holy Land but failed in its attempt to have the WZO assume an active role in the shaping of a secular Zionist culture. The debate that the Democratic Faction provoked during and after the Fifth Zionist Congress on the cultural question helped galvanize the establishment of the **Mizrachi** party by religious members of the World Zionist Organization.

Controversy wracked the Sixth Zionist Congress in Basle in August 1903, as the delegates battled over a British offer to establish a Jewish refuge in East Africa. The recent Kishinev pogrom in Russia strengthened the arguments of Herzl and others who favored creating a *nachtasyl,* or temporary shelter, in Uganda and adjacent territories. The congress voted, 295 to 178, to support Herzl's proposal to send a commission to investigate the viability of the East Africa region. Herzl's death cast a pall over the Seventh Zionist Congress, which was held in Basle in August 1905. A large majority of the 497 delegates unequivocally rejected the **Uganda Plan**, prompting a minority, led by **Israel Zangwill**, to secede and establish the **Jewish Territorial Organization** to seek land for a Jewish refuge outside Palestine.

David Wolffsohn, a German Jewish businessman and Herzl confidante, was elected chairman of the Zionist Executive and therefore became president of the WZO. A major step to advance practical development projects in Palestine was taken at the Eighth Zionist Congress in the Hague in August 1907, when the delegates voted to establish a Palestine Office in Jaffa, under the direction of **Arthur Ruppin**. Another critical decision was made by the 11th Zionist Congress in Vienna in September 1913, which resolved to establish a **Hebrew University** in Palestine.

After eight years without a Zionist congress, because of the upheavals caused by World War I, the 12th Zionist Congress was held in Carlsbad in September 1921. **Chaim Weizmann** was elected president of the WZO, and **Nahum Sokolow** was chosen to chair the Zionist Executive. The 512 delegates also voted to approve the purchase of land in the Jezreel Valley. Weizmann led the successful effort to convince the 16th Zionist Congress, meeting in Zurich in August 1929, to enlarge the **Jewish Agency** to give leadership roles to prominent American and European **non-Zionists**, thereby bringing in major new sources of funding for the movement. Opponents of the expansion feared the inclusion of non-Zionists would result in a diminution of the movement's Zionist ideology.

Political turmoil consumed the 17th Zionist Congress, held in Basle in July 1931. The assembly was held in the shadow of the 1929 Arab pogroms in Palestine and the subsequent Passfield **White Paper**, which called for restrictions on Jewish immigration and land purchases. A proposal by Revisionist leader **Ze'ev Jabotinsky** that the congress declare statehood as its goal was defeated, and the **Revisionist** delegation left the congress hall in protest. The congress was also wracked by controversy over a remark by Chaim Weizmann that he did not share the goal of a Jewish majority in Palestine. As a result, Nahum Sokolow was elected to replace Weizmann as WZO president. In addition, **Labor Zionist** official **Haim Arlosoroff** was elected head of the WZO's Political Department, the movement's de facto foreign ministry.

The 18th Zionist Congress convened in Prague in August 1933, just two months after the assassination, in Palestine, of Arlosoroff. After a tumultuous election campaign dominated by Labor's charges of Revisionist complicity in the Arlosoroff murder, the number of Revisionist delegates elected to the congress was sharply reduced from that of the previous congress, and the Labor share significantly increased. The 318 delegates to the congress elected Labor's **Moshe Shertok** to replace Arlosoroff as chief of the WZO Political Department. The 18th Congress was the first to be held after the rise of Adolf Hitler to power in Germany, and many of its debates dealt with the fate of German Jewry and plans for the resettlement of German Jews in Palestine.

When the delegates to the 19th Zionist Congress, meeting in Lucerne in August 1935, failed to endorse the goal of sovereign Jewish statehood, the Revisionist delegates walked out of the congress, setting the stage for their subsequent secession from the WZO. Chaim Weizmann was once again elected president of the WZO. The 484 delegates to the 20th Zionist Congress, held in Zurich in August 1937, grappled with the British **Peel Commission**'s proposal to partition western Palestine into Jewish and Arab states. After a stormy debate, the delegates voted, 300 to 158, to declare the Peel plan "unacceptable" while authorizing the Zionist Executive to "conduct negotiations" with the British to "clarify" the details of the proposal.

In August 1939, just days before the eruption of World War II, the 21st Zionist Congress convened in Geneva. The 527 delegates formally rejected the May 1939 British **White Paper**, which severely restricted Jewish immigration and land purchases in Palestine. In the aftermath of the

Holocaust and the rapidly escalating conflict in Palestine between Jewish rebels and the British authorities, the 386 delegates to the 22nd Zionist Congress met in Basle in December 1946. Those favoring a more activist approach, led by **Abba Hillel Silver** and **David Ben-Gurion**, challenged what they regarded as the excessively cautious policy of Chaim Weizmann's administration. Great Britain's invitation to the Zionists to take part in another conference with Arab representatives, which Weizmann favored, was rejected by a vote of 171 to 154. Weizmann then resigned. The delegates decided to leave the office of the presidency vacant, with governing power in the hands of Ben-Gurion as chairman of the Zionist Executive and Silver as chairman of the newly formed American Section of the **Jewish Agency**.

The 23rd Zionist Congress, which opened in August 1951, was the first to be held in Jerusalem. The 449 delegates voted to adopt the **Jerusalem Program** as the Zionist movement's official platform. It replaced the outdated Basle Program, adopted at the First Zionist Congress, which had focused on the need to establish a Jewish homeland. That aim having been accomplished, the new Jerusalem Program summarized the purpose of Zionism as "the strengthening of the State of Israel, the ingathering of the exiles in Eretz Israel, and the fostering of the unity of the Jewish people." Berl Locker was elected chairman of the WZO in Jerusalem, with **Nahum Goldmann** as chairman in New York.

The Jerusalem Program was somewhat expanded at the 27th Zionist Congress, meeting in Jerusalem in June 1968, which was the first congress after the Six-Day War. The new text read: "The aims of Zionism are: The unity of the Jewish people and the centrality of Israel in Jewish life; the ingathering of the Jewish people in its historic homeland **Eretz Israel** through *aliya* from all countries; the strengthening of the State of Israel which is based on the prophetic vision of justice and peace; the preservation of identity of the Jewish people through the fostering of Jewish and Hebrew education and of Jewish spiritual and cultural values; the protection of Jewish rights everywhere." It remains to this day the official credo of the world Zionist movement.

In the decades since Israel's establishment, the Zionist Congresses have functioned largely as forums for debate. Differences between Israeli and **Diaspora** perspectives on Zionism sparked controversy at the 28th Zionist Congress, meeting in Jerusalem in January 1972. Israeli youth delegates succeeded in winning passage of a resolution requiring Diaspora Zionist leaders to emigrate to Israel within two years or resign their offices. Angry Diaspora delegates stormed out of the congress hall, and the congress leadership, taken by surprise, hurried to find a parliamentary loophole to nullify the resolution.

Another sharp controversy arose at the 30th Zionist Congress, in Jerusalem in December 1982, when the delegates rejected a proposal by left-wing parties to prohibit the expenditure of WZO funds in areas beyond Israel's pre-1967 borders.

The issue of religious pluralism has garnered the increasing attention of Zionist Congresses in recent years. The delegates to the 29th Zionist Congress, held in Jerusalem in February 1978, vigorously debated a proposal that the WZO provide equal funding to Orthodox and non-Orthodox educational programs. The motion passed. At the 31st Zionist Congress, held in Jerusalem in December 1987, the Reform and Conservative delegations for the first time outnumbered the Orthodox, a trend that continued at subsequent congresses. *See also* PROTESTRABBINER.

ZIONIST FEDERATION OF GREAT BRITAIN AND IRELAND. The British Zionist Federation was established in 1899 as a coalition of local Zionist societies and **Hovevei Zion** chapters. Support for the fledgling British Zionist movement was to be found largely among British Jewry's Eastern European immigrant community.

Under the leadership, as of 1917, of **Chaim Weizmann**, the British Zionist Federation assumed an increasingly active role in attempting to win British public opinion and government officials to the Zionist cause. Negotiations between Weizmann and his colleagues and members of the British cabinet resulted in the **Balfour Declaration**.

The British Zionist Federation worked closely with the international Zionist movement, especially after 1920, when London became the center of world Zionism with the election of Weizmann as president of the **World Zionist Organization (WZO)** and his colleague **Nahum Sokolow** as chairman of the WZO's Zionist Executive. From a membership of 4,000 in 1917, the British Zionist Federation grew to 30,000 members and 74 member-organizations by the early 1920s. Its women's affiliate, the Federation of Women Zionists of Great Britain and Ireland, was established in 1918.

In common with Zionist movements in other parts of the world, the British Zionist movement—renamed the Zionist Federation of Great Britain and Ireland in 1928—declined significantly in the late 1920s but experienced an upsurge in public support following the Palestinian Arab violence of 1929 and the rise of Nazism in Germany in 1933. During the late 1930s and early 1940s, the Zionist Federation lobbied against

British restrictions on Jewish immigration to Palestine, sought to persuade the British public and government to support implementation of the Balfour Declaration's promise of a Jewish national home, and supported the establishment of a Jewish armed force to fight alongside the Allies against the Nazis. At the same time, the federation assumed an increasingly prominent role in the British Jewish community, and its growing role in the Board of Deputies of British Jews led, in 1943, to the formal severing of the partnership between the board and its longtime non-Zionist ally, the Anglo-Jewish Association, as well as the board's formal endorsement in 1944 of the goal of Jewish statehood.

The Zionist Federation today continues to function as the umbrella for Great Britain's wide range of Zionist organizations and seeks to strengthen Israeli–British relations through lobbying, public information campaigns, fundraising, rallies, and publications, including its monthly *Zionist Review* and the annual *Zionist Year Book.*

ZIONIST GENERAL COUNCIL. Originally known as the Greater Actions Committee, the Zionist General Council is the supreme governing body of the **World Zionist Organization (WZO)** between **Zionist Congresses**. The council decides on all matters except those under the authority of the congress itself, including budgetary questions and amendments to the WZO constitution. The members of the council are elected by each Zionist Congress, with each faction permitted to nominate one council member per five delegates.

ZIONIST ORGANIZATION. *See* WORLD ZIONIST ORGANIZATION.

ZIONIST ORGANIZATION OF AMERICA (ZOA). Fourteen local American Zionist groups, meeting in New York City in July 1898, established the **Federation of American Zionists (FAZ)**, the first national Zionist organization in the United States. Professor Richard Gottheil of Columbia University was elected president. Beginning in 1901, the FAZ published a monthly magazine, *The Maccabean,* edited by **Louis Lipsky**.

Embracing both **Political Zionism** and **Practical Zionism**, the FAZ undertook a variety of educational endeavors, including the promotion of the Hebrew language, as well as activities aimed specifically at providing direct aid to the *yishuv,* such as selling shares of the **Jewish Colonial Trust** and soliciting contributions to the **Jewish National Fund**. The FAZ's insurance organization, **B'nai Zion**, was created in 1907. The FAZ's youth movement, Young Judea, was organized in 1909; it later evolved into the Intercollegiate Zionist Association, then **Avukah**, and finally Masada. In 1912 its women's division, **Hadassah**, was established.

Shortly after the outbreak of World War I in 1914, the FAZ set up a **Provisional Executive Committee for General Zionist Affairs** to serve temporarily as the central Zionist authority in place of the Zionist movement's Berlin headquarters, which because of the war was cut off from Jewish communities in the Allied countries. The acceptance by the prominent attorney **Louis D. Brandeis** of the chairmanship of the Provisional Committee proved to be a turning point in American Zionist history. Brandeis's leadership of American Zionism, especially after he was named to the United States Supreme Court in 1916, helped make the movement acceptable to many American Jews who had previously feared that Zionism could compromise their status as American citizens. Brandeis also attracted to the movement a coterie of talented businessmen and attorneys who used their organizational acumen to channel American Jewish sympathy for the plight of Jews in wartime Europe into practical support for the American Zionist movement. This, combined with the enthusiasm surrounding the issuance of the **Balfour Declaration** and the conquest of Palestine by the British, swelled the FAZ's membership ranks.

In 1918 the FAZ and its affiliates merged with the Provisional Committee to become the Zionist Organization of America. After visiting Palestine in 1919, Brandeis became convinced that the ZOA should focus exclusively on raising funds for specific development projects in **Eretz Israel**. This put Brandeis and his followers at odds with a substantial segment of ZOA activists, led by **Louis Lipsky**, who favored continuing traditional Zionist political and cultural activities in the **Diaspora** and preferred the leadership of **World Zionist Organization** president **Chaim Weizmann**. A showdown between the two sides at the 1921 ZOA convention resulted in the resignation of Brandeis and his supporters from the organization's leadership positions.

The departure of the Brandeis faction was only the beginning of the ZOA's problems. With Great Britain pledged to facilitate the creation of a Jewish homeland and a peaceful climate between Arabs and Jews in Palestine during most of the 1920s, many American Jews no longer saw the need for an American Zionist movement. The ZOA's membership ranks dwindled steadily. The organization did, however, score a significant political victory in 1922 when it persuaded both Congress and President Warren Harding to endorse the **Balfour Declaration**.

The Palestinian Arab riots of 1929 and the subsequent Passfield **White Paper,** which was unfriendly to Zionism, sparked the return of the Brandeis faction to the ZOA. At the organization's 1930 convention, the Lipsky administration was ousted in favor of a group dominated by Brandeis loyalists. The ZOA's ranks swelled as the rise of Nazism in Germany aroused increased sympathy for Zionism in the American Jewish community during the 1930s.

When World War II erupted in 1939, American Zionist leaders established an **Emergency Committee for Zionist Affairs (ECZA)** to serve as the world Zionist movement's temporary center. But the ECZA remained largely inactive during its first two years, due to American Zionist leaders' reluctance to criticize Britain during wartime and fear of accusations that they were trying to drag the United States into overseas conflicts. Under growing pressure from the activist-minded ZOA grass roots, the ZOA leadership organized the 1942 **Biltmore Conference.** The gathering adopted more forceful language in its articulation of Zionist demands and contributed to the emerging militant mood in the American Zionist community. As news of the Holocaust reached the United States, ZOA leaders who still favored a more cautious, and less anti-British, approach were voted out in favor of an activist group headed by **Rabbi Abba Hillel Silver.**

Silver led a nationwide political action effort that mobilized a large segment of the American Jewish community on behalf of the demand for Jewish statehood. By the late 1940s, the ZOA's membership had reached an all-time high of some 250,000. Silver's lobbying efforts won widespread support for Zionism in the U.S. Congress, increased the pressure on Britain to leave Palestine, and helped win over the Truman administration to support the 1947 United Nations plan to partition Palestine into Jewish and Arab states. Although unsuccessful in its bid to end the U.S. arms embargo on the Middle East, the ZOA's pressure campaign did play a role in President Harry S. Truman's decision to extend American recognition to the new State of Israel.

In common with other American Zionist organizations, the ZOA began to decline, in both membership and political influence, after the creation of Israel. With the movement's primary goal achieved, many American Jews lost interest in Zionist activities. In addition, the emergence of the **American Israel Public Affairs Committee (AIPAC)** in 1954 and the **Conference of Presidents of Major American Jewish Organizations** in 1955 usurped the ZOA's previous position as the Jewish community's voice in Washington. While continuing its pro-Israel information activities and Zionist education programs, the ZOA devoted an increasing share of its attention to its philanthropic projects in Israel, such as ZOA House, a cultural center in Tel Aviv (est. 1953), and Kfar Silver, a vocational training campus near Ashkelon (est. 1955).

The ZOA experienced a revival in the mid-1990s, after adopting activist tactics and focusing on the issue of Palestinian Arab violations of the Israel–PLO accords. This approach attracted new members and gained the organization growing influence in Washington.

ZIONIST SUPREME COURT. The creation of an internal judicial body for the Zionist movement originated at the Fifth **Zionist Congress** in 1901, which authorized the establishment of what it called a Congress Court. Later, the 1921 constitution of the **World Zionist Organization (WZO)** provided for two separate bodies, the Congress Court and the Court of Honor. The WZO's new constitution in 1960 merged the two into a single Congress Tribunal. Its name was changed in 1979 to the Zionist Supreme Court.

The court consists of a maximum of thirty judges, including its president and six deputy presidents. Each serves a term spanning two congress periods, each period consisting of the years between congresses. The judges are chosen by a nine-member Nominations Committee, four of whose members are elected by the Zionist Congress. The Zionist Supreme Court interprets the WZO constitution, decides the legality of internal Zionist organizational actions, arbitrates disputes between Zionist agencies, and rules on matters involving the elections to the Zionist Congress.

Appendix 1: Biblical Roots

And God said to Abram: "Leave your country, and your birthplace, and your father's house and go to the land that I will show you. And I will make you into a great nation, and I will bless you, and I will make your name great, and in you shall all of the families on earth be blessed. . . . Unto your seed will I give this land." (Genesis 12:1–7)

And God spoke to Moses saying: "Command the Children of Israel and say unto them: 'When you come to the land of Canaan, this is the land that will fall to you as an inheritance, the land of Canaan according to its borders.'" (Numbers 34:1–2)

And God said unto him [Moses]: "This is the land which I promised to Abraham, Isaac, and Jacob, saying: 'Unto your children shall I give it.'" (Deuteronomy 34:4)

Appendix 2: "Hatikvah" (The Hope)

> As long as deep in the heart
> The soul of a Jew yearns,
> And towards the East
> An eye looks to Zion,
> Our hope is not yet lost:
> The hope of two thousand years
> To be a free people in our land,
> The land of Zion and Jerusalem.

Also see dictionary entry HATIKVAH.

Appendix 3: Basle Program

Zionism strives to create for the Jewish people a home in Palestine secured by public law. For the attainment of this aim the Congress envisages the following means:

1. The promotion, on suitable lines, of the settlement of Palestine by Jewish agriculturists, artisans, and tradesmen.
2. The organization and unification of the whole of Jewry by means of appropriate local and general institutions in accordance with the laws of each country.
3. The strengthening of Jewish national sentiment and national consciousness.
4. Preparatory steps toward securing the consent of governments, which is necessary to attain the aim of Zionism.

Appendix 4: Balfour Declaration

Foreign Office

November 2nd, 1917

Dear Lord Rothschild,

I have much pleasure in conveying to you, on behalf of His Majesty's Government, the following declaration of sympathy with Jewish Zionist aspirations which has been submitted to, and approved by, the Cabinet.

"His Majesty's Government view with favour the establishment in Palestine of a national home for the Jewish people, and will use their best endeavours to facilitate the achievement of this object, it being clearly understood that nothing shall be done which may prejudice the civil and religious rights of existing non-Jewish communities in Palestine, or the rights and political status enjoyed by Jews in any other country."

I should be grateful if you would bring this declaration to the knowledge of the Zionist Federation.

Yours sincerely,

Arthur James Balfour

Appendix 5: League of Nations Mandate

"The Council of the League of Nations

"Whereas the Principal Allied Powers have agreed, for the purpose of giving effect to the provisions of Article 22 of the Covenant of the League of Nations, to entrust to a Mandatory selected by the said Powers the administration of the territory of Palestine, which formerly belonged to the Turkish Empire, within such boundaries as may be fixed by them; and

Whereas the Principal Allied Powers have also agreed that the Mandatory should be responsible for putting into effect the declaration originally made on November 2nd, 1917, by the Government of His Britannic Majesty, and adopted by the said Powers, in favour of the establishment in Palestine of a national home for the Jewish people, it being clearly understood that nothing should be done which might prejudice the civil and religious rights of existing non-Jewish communities in Palestine, or the rights and political status enjoyed by Jews in any other country; and

Whereas recognition has thereby been given to the historical connection of the Jewish people with Palestine and to the grounds for reconstituting their national home in that country; and

Whereas the Principal Allied Powers have selected His Britannic Majesty as the Mandatory for Palestine; and

Whereas the mandate in respect of Palestine has been formulated in the following terms and submitted to the Council of the League for approval; and

Whereas His Britannic Majesty has accepted the mandate in respect of Palestine and undertaken to exercise it on behalf of the League of Nations in conformity with the following provisions; and

Whereas by the afore-mentioned Article 22 (paragraph 8), it is provided that the degree of authority, control or administration to be exercised by the Mandatory, not having been previously agreed upon by the Members of the League, shall be explicitly defined by the Council of the League of Nations;

"Confirming the said mandate, defines its terms as follows:

Article 1.
"The Mandatory shall have full powers of legislation and of administration, save as they may be limited by the terms of this mandate.

Article 2.
"The Mandatory shall be responsible for placing the country under such political, administrative and economic conditions as will secure the establishment of the Jewish national home, as laid down in the preamble, and the development of self-governing institutions, and also for safeguarding the civil and religious rights of all the inhabitants of Palestine, irrespective of race and religion.

Article 3.
"The Mandatory shall, so far as circumstances permit, encourage local autonomy.

Article 4.
"An appropriate Jewish agency shall be recognised as a public body for the purpose of advising and co-operating with the Administration of Palestine in such economic, social and other matters as may affect the establishment of the Jewish national home and the interests of the Jewish population in Palestine, and, subject always to the control of the Administration, to assist and take part in the development of the country.

The Zionist organisation, so long as its organisation and constitution are in the opinion of the Mandatory appropriate, shall be recognised as such agency. It shall take steps in consultation with His Britannic Majesty's Government to secure the cooperation of all Jews who are willing to assist in the establishment of the Jewish national home.

Article 5.
"The Mandatory shall be responsible for seeing that no Palestine territory shall be ceded or leased to, or in any way placed under the control of, the Government of any foreign Power.

Article 6.
"The Administration of Palestine, while ensuring that the rights and position of other sections of the population are not prejudiced, shall facilitate Jewish immigration under suitable conditions and shall encourage, in co-operation with the Jewish agency referred to in Article 4, close settlement by Jews, on the land, including State lands and waste lands not required for public purposes.

Article 7.
"The Administration of Palestine shall be responsible for enacting a nationality law. There shall be included in this law provisions framed so as to facilitate the acquisition of Palestinian citizenship by Jews who take up their permanent residence in Palestine.

Article 8.
"The privileges and immunities of foreigners, including the benefits of consular jurisdiction and protection as formerly enjoyed by Capitulation or usage in the Ottoman Empire, shall not be applicable in Palestine.

Unless the Powers whose nationals enjoyed the afore-mentioned privileges and immunities on August 1st, 1914, shall have previously renounced the right to their re-establishment, or shall have agreed to their non-application for a specified period, these privileges and immunities shall, at the expiration of the mandate, be immediately re-established in their entirety or with such modifications as may have been agreed upon between the Powers concerned.

Article 9.
"The Mandatory shall be responsible for seeing that the judicial system established in Palestine shall assure to foreigners, as well as to natives, a complete guarantee of their rights.
Respect for the personal status of the various peoples and communities and for their religious interests shall be fully guaranteed. In particular, the control and administration of Wakfs shall be exercised in accordance with religious law and the dispositions of the founders.

Article 10.
"Pending the making of special extradition agreements relating to Palestine, the extradition treaties in force between the Mandatory and other foreign Powers shall apply to Palestine.

Article 11.
"The Administration of Palestine shall take all necessary measures to safeguard the interests of the community in connection with the development of the country, and, subject to any international obligations accepted by the Mandatory, shall have full power to provide for public ownership or control of any of the natural resources of the country or of the public works, services and utilities established or to be established therein. It shall introduce a land system appropriate to the needs of the country, having regard,

among other things, to the desirability of promoting the close settlement and intensive cultivation of the land.

The Administration may arrange with the Jewish agency mentioned in Article 4 to construct or operate, upon fair and equitable terms, any public works, services and utilities, and to develop any of the natural resources of the country, in so far as these matters are not directly undertaken by the Administration. Any such arrangements shall provide that no profits distributed by such agency, directly or indirectly, shall exceed a reasonable rate of interest on the capital, and any further profits shall be utilised by it for the benefit of the country in a manner approved by the Administration.

Article 12.
"The Mandatory shall be entrusted with the control of the foreign relations of Palestine and the right to issue exequaturs to consuls appointed by foreign Powers. He shall also be entitled to afford diplomatic and consular protection to citizens of Palestine when outside its territorial limits.

Article 13.
"All responsibility in connection with the Holy Places and religious buildings or sites in Palestine, including that of preserving existing rights and of securing free access to the Holy Places, religious buildings and sites and the free exercise of worship, while ensuring the requirements of public order and decorum, is assumed by the Mandatory, who shall be responsible solely to the League of Nations. in all matters connected herewith, provided that nothing in this article shall prevent the Mandatory from entering into such arrangements as he may deem reasonable with the Administration for the purpose of carrying the provisions of this article into effect; and provided also that nothing in this mandate shall be construed as conferring upon the Mandatory authority to interfere with the fabric or the management of purely Moslem sacred shrines, the immunities of which are guaranteed.

Article 14.
"A special Commission shall be appointed by the Mandatory to study, define and determine the rights and claims in connection with the Holy Places and the rights and claims relating to the different religious communities in Palestine. The method of nomination, the composition and the functions of this Commission shall be submitted to the Council of the League for its approval, and the Commission shall not be appointed or enter upon its functions without the approval of the Council.

Article 15.
"The Mandatory shall see that complete freedom of conscience and the free exercise of all forms of worship, subject only to the maintenance of public order and morals, are ensured to all. No discrimination of any kind shall be made between the inhabitants of Palestine on the ground of race, religion or language. No person shall be excluded from Palestine on the sole ground of his religious belief.

The right of each community to maintain its own schools for the education of its own members in its own language, while conforming to such educational requirements of a general nature as the Administration may impose, shall not be denied or impaired.

Article 16.
"The Mandatory shall be responsible for exercising such supervision over religious or eleemosynary bodies of all faiths in Palestine as may be required for the maintenance of public order and good government. Subject to such supervision, no measures shall be taken in Palestine to obstruct or interfere with the enterprise of such bodies or to discriminate against any representative or member of them on the ground of his religion or nationality.

Article 17.
"The Administration of Palestine may organise on a voluntary basis the forces necessary for the preservation of peace and order, and also for the defence of the country, subject, however, to the supervision of the Mandatory, but shall not use them for purposes other than those above specified save with the consent of the Mandatory. Except for such purposes, no military, naval or air forces shall be raised or maintained by the Administration of Palestine.

Nothing in this article shall preclude the Administration of Palestine from contributing to the cost of the maintenance of the forces of the Mandatory in Palestine.

The Mandatory shall be entitled at all times to use the roads, railways and ports of Palestine for the movement of armed forces and the carriage of fuel and supplies.

Article 18.
"The Mandatory shall see that there is no discrimination in Palestine against the nationals of any State Member of the League of Nations (including companies incorporated under its laws) as compared with those of the

Mandatory or of any foreign State in matters concerning taxation, commerce or navigation, the exercise of industries or professions, or in the treatment of merchant vessels or civil aircraft. Similarly, there shall be no discrimination in Palestine against goods originating in or destined for any of the said States, and there shall be freedom of transit under equitable conditions across the mandated area.

Subject as aforesaid and to the other provisions of this mandate, the Administration of Palestine may, on the advice of the Mandatory, impose such taxes and customs duties as it may consider necessary, and take such steps as it may think best to promote the development of the natural resources of the country and to safeguard the interests of the population. It may also, on the advice of the Mandatory, conclude a special customs agreement with any State the territory of which in 1914 was wholly included in Asiatic Turkey or Arabia.

Article 19.
"The Mandatory shall adhere on behalf of the Administration of Palestine to any general international conventions already existing, or which may be concluded hereafter with the approval of the League of Nations, respecting the slave traffic, the traffic in arms and ammunition, or the traffic in drugs, or relating to commercial equality, freedom of transit and navigation, aerial navigation and postal, telegraphic and wireless communication or literary, artistic or industrial property.

Article 20.
"The Mandatory shall co-operate on behalf of the Administration of Palestine, so far as religious, social and other conditions may permit, in the execution of any common policy adopted by the League of Nations for preventing and combating disease, including diseases of plants and animals.

Article 21.
"The Mandatory shall secure the enactment within twelve months from this date, and shall ensure the execution of a Law of Antiquities based on the following rules. This law shall ensure equality of treatment in the matter of excavations and archaeological research to the nations of all States Members of the League of Nations.

(1) 'Antiquity' means any construction or any product of human activity earlier than the year A.D. 1700.
(2) The law for the protection of antiquities shall proceed by encouragement rather than by threat.

Any person who, having discovered an antiquity without being furnished with the authorisation referred to in paragraph 5, reports the same to an official of the competent Department, shall be rewarded according to the value of the discovery.

(3) No antiquity may be disposed of except to the competent Department, unless this Department renounces the acquisition of any such antiquity.

No antiquity may leave the country without an export licence from the said Department.

(4) Any person who maliciously or negligently destroys or damages an antiquity shall be liable to a penalty to be fixed.

(5) No clearing of ground or digging with the object of finding antiquities shall be permitted, under penalty of fine, except to persons authorised by the competent Department.

(6) Equitable terms shall be fixed for expropriation, temporary or permanent, of lands which might be of historical or archaeological interest.

(7) Authorisation to excavate shall only be granted to persons who show sufficient guarantees of archaeological experience. The Administration of Palestine shall not, in granting these authorisations, act in such a way as to exclude scholars of any nation without good grounds.

(8) The proceeds of excavations may be divided between the excavator and the competent Department in a proportion fixed by that Department. If division seems impossible for scientific reasons, the excavator shall receive a fair indemnity in lieu of a part of the find.

Article 22.
"English, Arabic and Hebrew shall be the official languages of Palestine. Any statement or inscription in Arabic on stamps or money in Palestine shall be repeated in Hebrew, and any statement or inscription in Hebrew shall be repeated in Arabic.

Article 23.
"The Administration of Palestine shall recognise the holy days of the respective communities in Palestine as legal days of rest for the members of such communities.

Article 24.
"The Mandatory shall make to the Council of the League of Nations an annual report to the satisfaction of the Council as to the measures taken

during the year to carry out the provisions of the mandate. Copies of all laws and regulations promulgated or issued during the year shall be communicated with the report.

Article 25.
"In the territories lying between the Jordan and the eastern boundary of Palestine as ultimately determined, the Mandatory shall be entitled, with the consent of the Council of the League of Nations, to postpone or withhold application of such provisions of this mandate as he may consider inapplicable to the existing local conditions, and to make such provision for the administration of the territories as he may consider suitable to those conditions, provided that no action shall be taken which is inconsistent with the provisions of Articles 15, 16 and 18.

Article 26.
"The Mandatory agrees that, if any dispute whatever should arise between the Mandatory and another Member of the League of Nations relating to the interpretation or the application of the provisions of the mandate, such dispute, if it cannot be settled by negotiation, shall be submitted to the Permanent Court of International Justice provided for by Article 14 of the Covenant of the League of Nations.

Article 27.
"The consent of the Council of the League of Nations is required for any modification of the terms of this mandate.

Article 28.
"In the event of the termination of the mandate hereby conferred upon the Mandatory, the Council of the League of Nations shall make such arrangements as may be deemed necessary for safeguarding in perpetuity, under guarantee of the League, the rights secured by Articles 13 and 14, and shall use its influence for securing, under the guarantee of the League, that the Government of Palestine will fully honour the financial obligations legitimately incurred by the Administration of Palestine during the period of the mandate, including the rights of public servants to pensions or gratuities. The present instrument shall be deposited in original in the archives of the League of Nations and certified copies shall be forwarded by the Secretary-General of the League of Nations to all Members of the League.

Done at London the twenty-fourth day of July, one thousand nine hundred and twenty-two."

Appendix 6: Israel's Declaration of Independence

"ERETZ-ISRAEL was the birthplace of the Jewish people. Here their spiritual, religious and political identity was shaped. Here they first attained to statehood, created cultural values of national and universal significance and gave to the world the eternal Book of Books.

After being forcibly exiled from their land, the people kept faith with it throughout their Dispersion and never ceased to pray and hope for their return to it and for the restoration in it of their political freedom.

"Impelled by this historic and traditional attachment, Jews strove in every successive generation to re-establish themselves in their ancient homeland. In recent decades they returned in their masses. Pioneers, *ma'pilim* (immigrants coming to Eretz-Israel in defiance of restrictive legislation) and defenders, they made deserts bloom, revived the Hebrew language, built villages and towns, and created a thriving community controlling its own economy and culture, loving peace but knowing how to defend itself, bringing the blessings of progress to all the country's inhabitants, and aspiring towards independent nationhood.

"In the year 5657 (1897), at the summons of the spiritual father of the Jewish State, Theodore Herzl, the First Zionist Congress convened and proclaimed the right of the Jewish people to national rebirth in its own country.

"This right was recognized in the Balfour Declaration of the 2nd November, 1917, and re-affirmed in the Mandate of the League of Nations which, in particular, gave international sanction to the historic connection between the Jewish people and Eretz-Israel and to the right of the Jewish people to rebuild its National Home.

"The catastrophe which recently befell the Jewish people—the massacre of millions of Jews in Europe—was another clear demonstration of the urgency of solving the problem of its homelessness by re-establishing in Eretz-Israel the Jewish State, which would open the gates of the homeland wide to every Jew and confer upon the Jewish people the status of a fully privileged member of the comity of nations.

"Survivors of the Nazi holocaust in Europe, as well as Jews from other parts of the world, continued to migrate to Eretz-Israel, undaunted by difficulties, restrictions and dangers, and never ceased to assert their right to a life of dignity, freedom and honest toil in their national homeland.

"In the Second World War, the Jewish community of this country contributed its full share to the struggle of the freedom- and peace-loving nations against the forces of Nazi wickedness and, by the blood of its soldiers and its war effort, gained the right to be reckoned among the peoples who founded the United Nations.

"On the 29th November, 1947, the United Nations General Assembly passed a resolution calling for the establishment of a Jewish State in Eretz-Israel; the General Assembly required the inhabitants of Eretz-Israel to take such steps as were necessary on their part for the implementation of that resolution. This recognition by the United Nations of the right of the Jewish people to establish their State is irrevocable.

"This right is the natural right of the Jewish people to be masters of their own fate, like all other nations, in their own sovereign State.

"ACCORDINGLY WE, MEMBERS OF THE PEOPLE'S COUNCIL, REPRESENTATIVES OF THE JEWISH COMMUNITY OF ERETZ-ISRAEL AND OF THE ZIONIST MOVEMENT, ARE HERE ASSEMBLED ON THE DAY OF THE TERMINATION OF THE BRITISH MANDATE OVER ERETZ-ISRAEL AND, BY VIRTUE OF OUR NATURAL AND HISTORIC RIGHT AND ON THE STRENGTH OF THE RESOLUTION OF THE UNITED NATIONS GENERAL ASSEMBLY, HEREBY DECLARE THE ESTABLISHMENT OF A JEWISH STATE IN ERETZ-ISRAEL, TO BE KNOWN AS THE STATE OF ISRAEL.

"WE DECLARE that, with effect from the moment of the termination of the Mandate being tonight, the eve of Sabbath, the 6th Iyar, 5708 (15th May, 1948), until the establishment of the elected, regular authorities of the State in accordance with the Constitution which shall be adopted by the Elected Constituent Assembly not later than the 1st October 1948, the People's Council shall act as a Provisional Council of State, and its executive organ, the People's Administration, shall be the Provisional Government of the Jewish State, to be called "Israel."

"THE STATE OF ISRAEL will be open for Jewish immigration and for the Ingathering of the Exiles; it will foster the development of the country for the benefit of all its inhabitants; it will be based on freedom, justice and peace as envisaged by the prophets of Israel; it will ensure complete equality of social and political rights to all its inhabitants irrespective of religion, race or sex; it will guarantee freedom of religion, conscience, language, education and culture; it will safeguard the Holy Places of all religions; and it will be faithful to the principles of the Charter of the United Nations.

"THE STATE OF ISRAEL is prepared to cooperate with the agencies and representatives of the United Nations in implementing the resolution of the General Assembly of the 29th November, 1947, and will take steps to bring about the economic union of the whole of Eretz-Israel.

"WE APPEAL to the United Nations to assist the Jewish people in the building-up of its State and to receive the State of Israel into the comity of nations.

"WE APPEAL—in the very midst of the onslaught launched against us now for months—to the Arab inhabitants of the State of Israel to preserve peace and participate in the upbuilding of the State on the basis of full and equal citizenship and due representation in all its provisional and permanent institutions.

"WE EXTEND our hand to all neighbouring states and their peoples in an offer of peace and good neighbourliness, and appeal to them to establish bonds of cooperation and mutual help with the sovereign Jewish people settled in its own land. The State of Israel is prepared to do its share in a common effort for the advancement of the entire Middle East.

"WE APPEAL to the Jewish people throughout the Diaspora to rally round the Jews of Eretz-Israel in the tasks of immigration and upbuilding and to stand by them in the great struggle for the realization of the age-old dream—the redemption of Israel.

"PLACING OUR TRUST IN THE ALMIGHTY, WE AFFIX OUR SIGNATURES TO THIS PROCLAMATION AT THIS SESSION OF THE PROVISIONAL COUNCIL OF STATE, ON THE SOIL OF THE HOMELAND, IN THE CITY OF TEL-AVIV, ON THIS SABBATH EVE, THE 5TH DAY OF IYAR, 5708 (14TH MAY, 1948)."

David Ben-Gurion

Daniel Auster	Eliyahu Dobkin	Meir David
Mordekhai Bentov	Meir Wilner-Kovner	Loewenstein
Izhak Ben Zvi	Zerach Wahrhaftig	Zvi Luria
Eliyahu Berligne	Herzl Vardi	Golda Myerson
Fritz Bernstein	Rachel Cohen	Nachum Nir
Rabbi Wolf Gold	Rabbi Kalman Kahana	Zvi Segal
Meir Grabovsky	Saadia Kobashi	Rabbi Yehuda Leib
Yitzhak Gruenbaum	Rabbi Yitzhak Meir	Hacohen Fishman
Dr. Abraham Granovsky	Levin	David Zvi Pinkas

Aharon Zisling	Felix Rosenblueth	Ben Zion Sternberg
Moshe Kolodny	David Remez	Bekhor Shitreet
Eliezer Kaplan	Berl Repetur	Moshe Shapira
Abraham Katznelson	Mordekhai Shattner	Moshe Shertok

Bibliography

In addition to the English-language literature on Zionism listed herein, there is a vast literature of Zionism in Hebrew. Almost everything published on the subject, in Hebrew as well as in other languages, may be found at the National Library in Jerusalem. Likewise, most university libraries in Israel, as well as many public libraries, have extensive holdings on the subject of Zionism.

University libraries throughout the world, as well as libraries of Jewish educational institutions and communal agencies, maintain significant collections concerning the history of Zionism. The catalogues of many of these libraries can be located on the Internet. Two valuable Internet sites for research on Zionism are www.maven.co.il and www.us-israel.org/jsource/zion.html

Scholarly journals that focus on Zionism include, in Hebrew, *Hazionut, Zion, Kivunim, Cathedra, Iyunim Bitkumat Israel, Te-oria U-bikoret,* among others and, in English, the *Journal of Israeli History* (formerly *Studies in Zionism*). Its final issue of each year includes a wide-ranging bibliography of the previous year's articles on Zionism published in Hebrew and English. Other Israel-related journals, such as *Israel Affairs* and *Israel Studies,* include some material on Zionism but place more emphasis on events in Israeli history. *American Jewish History* and *American Jewish Archives* are scholarly journals that focus on the American Jewish experience and thus often include material on the history of American Zionism.

Those seeking an introduction to the history of Zionism would do well to begin with biographies of several of the giants of the movement: Shabtai Teveth's biographies of Ben-Gurion, Jehuda Reinharz's study of Chaim Weizmann, and Shmuel Katz's biography of Vladimir Ze'ev Jabotinsky, *Lone Wolf.* These biographies help the reader understand not only the most prominent leaders of Zionism, but also the parties they headed and the events they shaped. To understand religious Zionism, the reader may want to consult Aviezer Ravitzky's study *Messianism, Zionism, and Jewish Religious Radicalism;* Gary Schiff's analysis *Tradition and Politics;* as well as the collection on Religious Zionism by Shubert Spero and Yitzchak Pessin.

Another noteworthy biography is *Abba Hillel Silver,* by Marc Lee Raphael, which surveys both the life of one of the most important leaders of American Zionism as well as the trials and tribulations of the movement itself. Two good overviews of the major trends in Zionist philosophy are Shlomo Avineri's *The Making of Modern Zionism: Intellectual Origins of the Jewish State* and *The Emergence of Zionist Thought* by Monty Penkower. Also useful is Arthur Hertzberg's *The Zionist Idea,* a collection of excerpts from significant documents that illustrate the major developments in Zionist history and thought.

The Jewish struggle for independence during the British Mandate period is ably recounted by J. Bowyer Bell in *Terror Out of Zion,* while Menachem Begin's *The Revolt* offers an insider's perspective. A good survey of the diplomatic battles over Palestine is Michael Cohen's *Palestine and the Great Powers, 1945–1948.* Dalia Ofer's *Escaping the Holocaust* is a scholarly account of the illegal immigration of the 1930s–1940s, while Ehud Avriel's *Open the Gates!* and William Perl's *The Four-Front War* approach the history of Aliya Bet from the perspective of those who helped organize it.

BIBLIOGRAPHY CONTENTS

BIOGRAPHIES AND AUTOBIOGRAPHIES

Aberbach, David. *Bialik.* New York: Grove Press, 1988.
Adler, Cyrus. *I Have Considered the Days.* Philadelphia: Jewish Publication Society of America, 1941.

Avi-Hai, Avraham. *Ben-Gurion, State Builder; Principles and Pragmatism, 1948–1963*. New York: Wiley, 1974.

Avineri, Shlomo. *Arlosoroff*. New York: Grove Weidenfeld, 1990.

———. *Moses Hess, Prophet of Communism and Zionism*. New York: New York University Press, 1985.

Barnard, Harry. *The Forging of an American Jew: The Life and Times of Judge Julian W. Mack*. New York: Herzl Press, 1974.

Bein, Alex. *Theodore Herzl, A Biography*. Philadelphia: Jewish Publication Society of America, 1941.

———, ed. *Arthur Ruppin: Memoirs, Diaries, Letters*. New York: Herzl Press, 1971.

Ben-Gurion, David. *Memoirs*. Tel Aviv: Am Oved, 1987.

———. *Rebirth and Destiny of Israel*. New York: Philosophical Library, 1954.

———. *Israel; A Personal History*. New York: Funk & Wagnalls, 1971.

———. *Ben-Gurion Looks Back in Talks with Moshe Pearlman*. New York: Schocken, 1970.

Ben-Horin, Meir. *Max Nordau: Philosopher of Human Solidarity*. London: London Jewish Society, 1956.

Bentwich, Norman. *For Zion's Sake; A Biography of Judah L. Magnes, First Chancellor and First President of the Hebrew University of Jerusalem*. Philadelphia: Jewish Publication Society of America, 1954.

Brandeis, Louis D. *Brandeis on Zionism: A Collection of Addresses and Statements by Louis D. Brandeis*. New York: Zionist Organization of America, 1942.

Brinner, William, and Rischin, Moses, eds. *Like All the Nations? The Life and Legacy of Judah L. Magnes*. Albany: State University of New York Press, 1987.

Chernow, Ron. *The Warburgs, The Twentieth-Century Odyssey of a Remarkable Jewish Family*. New York: Random House, 1993.

Christman, Henry M. *This Is Our Strength: The Selected Papers of Golda Meir*. New York: Macmillan, 1962.

Cohen, Michael J., ed. *The Letters and Papers of Chaim Weizmann*. New Brunswick, N.J.: Transaction Books and Israel Universities Press, 1979.

Cohen, Naomi W. *A Dual Heritage; The Public Career of Oscar S. Straus*. Philadelphia: Jewish Publication Society of America, 1969.

Crossman, Richard H. S. *A Nation Reborn: A Personal Report on the Roles Played by Weizmann, Bevin and Ben-Gurion in the Story of Israel*. New York: Atheneum, 1960.

Dash, Joan. *Summoned to Jerusalem: The Life of Henrietta Szold*. New York: Harper & Row, 1979.

Eban, Abba. *Abba Eban: An Autobiography*. New York: Random House, 1977.

Elon, Amos. *Herzl*. New York: Holt, Rinehart and Winston, 1975.

Farrer, David. *The Warburgs: The Story of a Family*. New York: Stein and Day, 1975.

Fineman, Irving. *Woman of Valor; The Story of Henrietta Szold, 1860–1645*. New York: Simon and Schuster, 1961.

Friesel, Evyatar, ed. *Certain Days: Zionist Memoirs and Selected Papers of Julius Simon.* Jerusalem: Israel Universities Press, 1971.

Goldmann, Nahum. *The Autobiography of Nahum Goldmann; Sixty Years of Jewish Life.* New York: Holt, Rinehart & Winston, 1969.

———. *The Jewish Paradox,* translated by Steve Cox. New York: Grosset & Dunlap, 1978.

———. *Autobiography: America, Europe, Israel.* London: Weidenfeld and Nicolson, 1985.

Goren, Arthur A. *Dissenter in Zion: From the Writings of Judah L. Magnes.* Cambridge, Mass.: Harvard University Press, 1982.

Ha-am, Ahad. *Essays-Letters-Memoirs,* translated by Leon Simon. Oxford: East and West Library, 1946.

———. *Selected Essays,* translated by Leon Simon. Philadelphia: Jewish Publication Society, 1948.

———. *Ten Essays on Zionism and Judaism,* translated by Leon Simon. New York: Arno, 1973.

Haber, Julius. *The Odyssey of an American Zionist; Fifty Years of Zionist History.* New York: Twayne, 1956.

Herzl, Theodor. *Complete Diaries,* 5 vols., translated by Harry Zohn. New York: Herzl Press and Thomas Yoseloff, 1960.

———. *Zionist Writings: Essays and Addresses,* 2 vols., translated by Harry Zohn. New York: Herzl Press, 1973, 1975.

———. *The Jewish State,* translated by Harry Zohn. New York: Herzl Press, 1970.

Hoffman, Leon S. *Ideals and Illusions: The Story of an Ivy League Woman in 1920's Israel.* New York: SPI Books, 1992.

Ish Shalom, Binyamin. *Rav Avraham Itzhak HaCOhen Kook: Between Rationalism and Mysticism.* Albany: State University of New York Press, 1993.

Kabakoff, Jacob, ed. *Master of Hope: Selected Writings of Naphtali Herz Imber.* New York and Madison, N.J.: Herzl Press and Fairleigh Dickinson University Press, 1985.

Kallen, Horace M. *Zionism and World Politics: A Study in History and Social Psychology.* Garden City, N.Y.: Doubleday, Page and Co., 1921

Katz, Shmuel. *Lone Wolf: A Biography of Vladimir (Ze'ev) Jabotinsky,* 2 vols. New York: Barricade Books, 1996.

Katzman, Jacob. *Commitment: The Labor Zionist Life-Style in America: A Personal Memoir.* New York: Labor Zionist Letters, 1975.

Keren, Michael. *Ben-Gurion and the Intellectuals: Power, Knowledge, and Charisma.* DeKalb: Northern Illinois University Press, 1983.

Kling, Simcha. *Nachum Sokolow, Servant of His People.* New York: Herzl Press, 1960.

Kohn, Hans, ed. *Nationalism and the Jewish Ethic; Basic Writings of Ahad Ha'am.* New York: Schocken Books, 1962.

Kook, Abraham Isaac. *The Lights of Penitence, Lights of Holiness, the Moral Principles, Essays, Letters, and Poems.* New York: Paulist Press, 1978.

Kornberg, Jacques. *Theodor Herzl: From Assimilation to Zionism.* Bloomington: Indiana University Press, 1993.

Kornberg, Jacques, ed. *At the Crossroads: Essays on Ahad Ha-am.* Albany: State University of New York Press, 1973.

Krausz, Ernest, ed. *The Sociology of the Kibbutz.* New Brunswick, N.J.: Transaction, 1983.

Kutnick, Jerome M. "Non-Zionist Leadership: Felix M. Warburg 1929–1937." Ph.D. dissertation, Brandeis University, 1983.

Levin, Alexandra, ed. *Henrietta Szold and Youth Aliyah: Family Letters, 1934–1944.* New York: Herzl Press, 1986.

Liebman, Charles S., and Don-Yehiya, Eliezer. *Civil Religion in Israel: Traditional Judaism and Political Culture in the Jewish State.* Berkeley: University of California Press, 1983.

Lindheim, Irma L. *Parallel Quest, A Search of a Person and a People.* New York: Thomas Yoseloff, 1962.

Lipstadt, Deborah E. *The Zionist Career of Louis Lipsky 1900–1921.* New York: Arno Press, 1982.

Lowenthal, Marvin. *Henrietta Szold, Life and Letters.* New York: Viking Press, 1942.

Luz, Ehud. *Parallels Meet: Religion and Nationalism in the Early Zionist Movement (1882–1904).* Philadelphia: Jewish Publication Society, 1988.

Mack, Julian W. *Americanism and Zionism.* New York: Zionist Organization of America, 1919.

Malone, Bobbie. *Rabbi Max Heller: Reformer, Zionist, Southerner, 1860–1929.* Tuscaloosa: University of Alabama Press, 1997.

Meir, Golda. *A Land of Our Own: An Oral Biography.* New York: Putnam, 1973.

Meir, Menahem. *My Mother Golda Meir: A Son's Evocation of Life with Golda Meir.* New York: Arbor House, 1983.

Metzger, Alter B. Z. *Rabbi Kook's Philosophy of Repentance: A Translation of Orot Ha-Teshuvah.* New York: Yeshiva University Press, 1968.

Neumann, Emanuel. *In the Arena.* New York: Herzl Press, 1978.

Nordau, Anna. *Max Nordau: A Biography of Anna and Maxa Nordau.* New York: Nordau Committee, 1943.

Pawel, Ernst. *The Labyrinth of Exile: A Life of Theodor Herzl.* New York: Farrar, Straus & Giroux, 1989.

Perlmutter, Amos. *The Life and Times of Menachem Begin.* Garden City, N.Y.: Doubleday, 1987.

Pinsker, Lev Semenovich. *Road to Freedom.* New York: Scopus, 1944.

Polier, Justine Wise, and James Waterman Wise. *The Personal Letters of Stephen S. Wise.* Boston: Beacon Press, 1956.

Proskauer, Joseph M. *A Segment of My Times.* New York: Farrar, Straus, 1950.

Raider, Mark A., Jonathan D. Sarna, and Ronald W. Zweig. *Abba Hillel Silver and American Zionism.* London: Frank Cass, 1997.

Reinharz, Jehuda. *Chaim Weizmann: The Making of a Zionist Leader*—Volume 1. New York: Oxford University Press, 1985.

Reinharz, Jehuda. *Chaim Weizmann: The Making of a Statesman*—Volume 2. New York: Oxford University Press, 1993.

Rosenblatt, Bernard A. *Two Generations of Zionism*. New York: Shengold, 1976.

Rosenstock, Morton. *Louis Marshall, Defender of Jewish Rights*. Detroit, Mich.: Wayne State University Press, 1965.

Raphael, Marc Lee. *Abba Hillel Silver*. New York: Holmes & Meier, 1989.

Rose, Herbert H. *The Life and Thought of A. D. Gordon: Pioneer, Philosopher, and Prophet of Modern Israel*. New York: Bloch, 1964.

Ruppin, Arthur. *Memoirs, Diaries, Letters*. New York: Herzl Press, 1971.

Sarig, Mordechai, ed. *The Political and Social Philosophy of Ze'ev Jabotinsky: Selected Writings*. Ilford, Essex: Valentine Mitchell, 1999.

Schechtman, Joseph B. *Rebel and Statesman: The Jabotinsky Story—The Early Years, 1880–1923*. New York: Thomas Yoseloff, 1956.

———. *Fighter and Prophet: The Jabotinsky Story—The Last Years, 1923–1940*. New York: Thomas Yoseloff, 1961.

Schmidt, Sarah L. *Horace M. Kallen: Prophet of American Zionism*. Brooklyn, N.Y.: Carlson, 1997.

Scult, Mel. *Judaism Faces the Twentieth Century: A Biography of Mordecai M. Kaplan*. Detroit, Mich.: Wayne State University Press, 1993.

Shamir, Yitzhak. *Summing Up: An Autobiography*. Boston: Little, Brown, 1994.

Shapira, Anita. *Berl: The Biography of a Socialist Zionist*. New York: Cambridge University Press, 1984.

Shargel, Baila Round. *Lost Love: The Untold Story of Henrietta Szold*. Philadelphia: Jewish Publication Society of America, 1997.

———. *Practical Dreamer: Israel Friedlaender and the Shaping of American Judaism*. New York: Jewish Theological Seminary of America, 1985.

Shilony, Zvi. *Ideology and Settlement: The Jewish National Fund, 1897–1914*. Jerusalem: Magnes Press, 1998

Silver, Abba Hillel. *Vision and Victory*. New York: Zionist Organization of America, 1949.

Simon, Leon. *Ahad Ha-am: A Biography*. Philadelphia: Jewish Publication Society of America, 1986.

Sokolow, Florian. *Nahum Sokolow: Life and Legend*. London: Jewish Chronicle Publications, 1975.

St. John, Robert T. *Tongue of the Prophets: The Life Story of Eliezer Ben Yehuda*. New York: Doubleday, 1952.

———. *Ben-Gurion: A Biography*. Garden City, N.Y.: Doubleday, 1971.

Stewart, Desmond. *Theodor Herzl: Artist and Politician*. Garden City, N.Y.: Doubleday, 1974.

Strum, Philippa. *Louis D. Brandeis: Justice for the People*. Cambridge, Mass.: Harvard University Press, 1984.

Syrkin, Marie. *Nachman Syrkin: Socialist Zionist.* New York: Herzl Press, 1961.
———. *Golda Meir,* rev. ed. New York: Putnam, 1969.
Teveth, Shabtai. *Ben-Gurion and the Palestinian Arabs: From Peace to War.* New York: Oxford University Press, 1985.
———. *Ben-Gurion: The Burning Ground, 1886–1948.* Boston: Houghton Mifflin, 1987.
Urofsky, Melvin I. *A Voice That Spoke for Justice: The Life and Times of Stephen S. Wise.* Albany: State University of New York Press, 1982.
———. *Louis D. Brandeis and the Progressive Tradition.* Boston: Little, Brown, 1981.
——— and David W. Levy, eds. *Letters of Louis D. Brandeis—Volume III 1913–1915: Progressive and Zionist.* Albany: State University of New York Press, 1973.
———. *Letters of Louis D. Brandeis—Volume IV 1916–1921: Mr. Justice Brandeis.* Albany: State University of New York Press, 1975.
———. *Letters of Louis D. Brandeis—Volume V 1929–1941: Elder Statesman.* Albany: State University of New York Press, 1978.
Voss, Carl Hermann, ed. *Stephen S. Wise: Servant of the People. Selected Letters.* Philadelphia: Jewish Publication Society of America, 1969.
———. *Rabbi and Minister: The Friendship of Stephen S. Wise and John Haynes Holmes.* Cleveland: World Publishing, 1964.
Waldman, Morris. *Nor by Power.* New York: International Universities Press, 1953.
Weinstein, Jacob J. *Solomon Goldman: A Rabbi's Rabbi.* New York: Ktav, 1973.
Weisgal, Meyer, ed. *Letters and Papers of Chaim Weizmann.* 26 vols. New Brunswick, N.J.: Transaction Books, 1983.
Weizmann, Chaim. *Trial and Error.* 2 vols. Philadelphia: Jewish Publication Society of America, 1949.
Wise, Stephen S. *As I See It.* New York: Jewish Opinion Publishing, 1947.
Wohlgelernter, Maurice. *Israel Zangwill; A Study.* New York: Columbia University Press, 1964.
Yaron, Zvi. *The Philosophy of Rabbi Kook.* Jerusalem: World Zionist Organization, 1991.
Zeitlin, Rose. *Henrietta Szold: A Record of a Life.* New York: Dial Press, 1952.
Zertal, Idith. *From Catastrophe to Power: Holocaust Survivors and the Emergence of Israel.* Berkeley: University of California Press, 1998.
Zipperstein, Steven J. *Elusive Prophet: Ahad Ha'am and the Origins of Zionism.* Berkeley: University of California Press, 1992.

GENERAL HISTORY OF ZIONISM

Adler, Joseph. *Restoring the Jews to Their Homeland: Nineteen Centuries in the Quest for Zion.* Northvale, N.J.: Jason Aronson, 1997.

Avineri, Shlomo. *The Making of Modern Zionism: Intellectual Origins of the Jewish State.* New York: Basic Books, 1981.

Ben-Zvi, Itzhak. *The Exiled and the Redeemed.* Philadelphia: Jewish Publication Society of America, 1963.

Bentwich, Norman. *Fulfilment in the Promised Land, 1917–1937.* Westport, Conn.: Hyperion Press, 1976.

Buber, Martin. *On Zion: The History of an Idea.* New York: Schocken Books, 1973.

Chertoff, Mordecai S., ed. *Zionism: A Basic Reader.* New York: Herzl Press, 1975.

Cohen, Mitchell. *Zion & State: Nation, Class, and the Shaping of Modern Israel.* New York: Basil Blackwell, 1987.

Davis, Moshe, ed. *Zionism in Transition.* New York: Herzl Press, 1990.

Feuer, Leon I. *Why a Jewish State.* New York: R. R. Smith, 1942.

Fisch, Harold. *The Zionist Revolution: A New Perspective.* London: Weidenfeld and Nicolson, 1978.

Frankenstein, Ernst. *Justice for My People.* New York: Dial, 1944.

Gilbert, Martin. *Exile and Return: The Struggle for a Jewish Homeland.* Philadelphia: J. B. Lippincott, 1978.

Gorny, Yosef. *The State of Israel in Jewish Public Thought: The Quest for Collective Identity.* New York: New York University Press, 1994.

Gottheil, Richard J. H. *Zionism.* Philadelphia: Jewish Publication Society of America, 1914.

Halpern, Ben. *The Idea of the Jewish State,* 2d ed. Cambridge, Mass.: Harvard University Press, 1969.

———. *A Clash of Heroes M. Brandeis, Weizmann, and American Zionism.* New York: Oxford University Press, 1987.

Heller, Joseph. *The Zionist Idea.* New York: Schocken Books, 1949.

Hertzberg, Arthur. *The Zionist Idea.* Philadelphia: Jewish Publication Society, 1959.

Heymann, Michael, ed. *The Minutes of the Zionist General Council; The Uganda Controversy.* 2 vols. Jerusalem: Israel Universities Press, Institute for Zionist Research at Tel-Aviv University, 1970.

Kallen, Horace M. *Utopians at Bay: Essays toward the Adjustment of Judaism to Modernity.* New York: Arno, 1972.

———. *"Of Them which Say They Are Jews," and Other Essays on the Jewish Struggle for Survival.* New York: Bloch, 1954.

Kaplan, Mordecai M. *A New Zionism.* New York: Theodor Herzl Foundation, 1955.

Kark, Ruth, ed. *The Land That Became Israel: Studies in Historical Geography.* New Haven: Yale University Press, 1990.

Katz, Jacob. *Jewish Emancipation and Self-Emancipation.* Philadelphia: Jewish Publication Society, 1986.

Katz, Yossi. *Between Jerusalem and Hebron: Jewish Settlement in the Pre-State Period.* Ramat Gan: Bar-Illan University Press, 1992.

Kellerman, Aharon. *Society and Settlement: Jewish Land of Israel in the Twentieth Century.* Albany: State University of New York Press, 1993.

Laqueur, Walter. *A History of Zionism.* New York: Holt, Rinehart and Winston, 1972.

Menuhin, Moshe. *The Decadence of Judaism in Our Time,* 2d ed. Beirut: Institute for Palestine Studies, 1969.

Noah, Mordecai Manuel. *Discourse on the Restoration of the Jews: Delivered at the Tabernacle, Oct. 28 and Dec. 2, 1844.* New York: Harper, 1845.

O'Brien, Conor Cruise. *The Siege: The Saga of Israel and Zionism.* New York: Simon and Schuster, 1986.

Oppenheim, Israel. *The Struggle of Jewish Youth for Productivization: The Zionist Youth Movement in Poland.* Boulder, Colo.: East European Monographs/ Columbia University Press, 1989.

Penkower, Monty Noam. *The Emergence of Zionist Thought.* Millwood, N.Y.: Associated Faculty Press, 1986.

Penslar, Derek J. *Zionism and Technocracy: The Engineering of Jewish Settlement in Palestine, 1870–1918.* Bloomington: Indiana University Press, 1987.

Petuchowski, Jakob J. *Zion Reconsidered.* New York: Twayne, 1966.

Reinharz, Jehuda, and Anita Shapira. *Essential Papers on Zionism.* New York: New York University Press, 1996.

Sachar, Howard M. *A History of Israel: From the Rise of Zionism to Our Time.* New York: Alfred A. Knopf, 1979.

Schweid, Eliezer. *The Land of Israel: National Home or Land of Destiny,* translated by Deborah Greniman. New York and Rutherford, N.J.: Herzl Press and Associated Universities Press, 1985.

Selzer, Michael, ed. *Zionism Reconsidered: The Rejection of Jewish Normalcy.* New York: Macmillan, 1970

Shimoni, Gideon. *Jews and Zionism: The South African Experience (1910–1967).* Cape Town: Oxford University Press, 1980.

———. *The Zionist Ideology.* Hanover, N.H.: Brandeis University Press/University Press of New England, 1995.

Sofer, Sasson. *Zionism and the Foundations of Israeli Diplomacy.* New York: Cambridge University Press, 1998.

Sokolow, Nahum. *History of Zionism, 1600–1918.* New York: Ktav, 1969.

Spiro, Melford E. *Kibbutz: Venture in Utopia.* Cambridge, Mass.: Harvard University Press, 1956.

———. *Children of the Kibbutz.* New York: Schocken, 1965.

Vital, David. *Zionism: The Formative Years.* New York: Oxford University Press, 1988.

———. *The Origins of Zionism.* Oxford: Oxford University Press, 1975.

———. *Zionism: The Formative Years.* Oxford: Oxford University Press, 1982.

Zertal, Idith. *From Catastrophe to Power: Holocaust Survivors and the Emergence of Israel.* Berkeley: University of California Press, 1998.

CULTURE AND RELIGION

Almog, Shmuel, Jehuda Reinharz, and Anita Shapira, eds. *Zionism and Religion*. Hanover, N.H.: Brandeis University Press and University Press of New England, 1998.

Berkowitz, Michael. *Zionist Culture and West European Jewry before the First World War*. Chapel Hill: University of North Carolina Press, 1996.

———. *Western Jewry and the Zionist Project, 1914–1933*. Cambridge: Cambridge University Press, 1997.

Bernstein, Deborah S. *Pioneers and Homemakers: Jewish Women in Pre-State Israel*. Albany: State University of New York Press, 1992.

———. *The Struggle for Equality: Urban Women Workers in Pre-state Israeli Society*. Westport, Conn.: Praeger, 1987.

Eisenstadt, S. N. *The Transformation of Israeli Society: An Essay in Interpretation*. Boulder, Colo.: Westview, 1986.

———. *Israeli Society*. New York: Basic Books, 1967.

Evron, Boas. *Jewish State or Israeli Nation?* Bloomington: Indiana University Press, 1995.

Fishman, Aryei, ed. *Religious Kibbutz Movement; The Revival of the Jewish Religious Community*. Jerusalem: Religious Section of the Youth and Hehalutz Dept. of the Zionist Organization, 1957.

———. *Judaism and Modernization on the Religious Kibbutz*. New York: Cambridge University Press, 1992.

Halpern, Ben, and Jehuda Reinharz. *Zionism and the Creation of a New Society*. New York: Oxford University Press, 1998.

Herman, Simon N. *Israelis and Jews; The Continuity of an Identity*. Philadelphia: Jewish Publication Society, 1970.

Horowitz, Dan, and Moshe Lissak. *Origins of the Israeli Polity: Palestine Under the Mandate*. Chicago: University of Chicago Press, 1978.

Lewittes, Mendell. *Religious Foundations of the Jewish State*. Northvale, N.J.: Jason Aronson, 1994.

Liebman, Charles S., and Eliezer Don-Yehiya. *Civil Religion in Israel: Traditional Judaism and Political Culture in the Jewish State*. Berkeley: University of California Press, 1983.

Luz, Ehud. *Parallels Meet: Religion and Nationalism in the Early Zionist Movement (1882–1904)*. Philadelphia: Jewish Publication Society, 1988.

Marmorstein, Emile. *Heaven at Bay: The Jewish Kulturkampf in the Holy Land*. London: Oxford University Press, 1969.

Ravitzky, Aviezer. *Messianism, Zionism, and Jewish Religious Radicalism*. Chicago: University of Chicago Press, 1996.

Schiff, Gary S. *Tradition and Politics: The Religious Parties of Israel*. Detroit, Mich.: Wayne State University Press, 1977.

Silberstein, Laurence J. *The Postzionism Debates: Knowledge and Power in Israeli Culture*. New York and London: Routledge, 1999.

Spero, Shubert, and Yitzchak Pessin, eds. *Religious Zionism: After 40 Years of Statehood.* Jerusalem: Mesilot, World Movement of Mizrachi-Hapoel Hamizrachi and World Zionist Organization, Dept. for Torah Education and Culture in the Diaspora, 1989.
Zerubavel, Yael. *Recovered Roots: Collective Memory and the Making of the Israeli National Tradition.* Chicago: University of Chicago Press, 1995.

MILITARY AND DIPLOMATIC STRUGGLES

Avriel, Ehud. *Open the Gates! A Personal Story of "Illegal" Immigration to Israel.* New York: Atheneum, 1975.
Bauer, Yehuda. *From Diplomacy to Resistance: A History of Jewish Palestine 1930–1945.* Philadelphia: Jewish Publication Society of America, 1970.
Begin, Menachem. *The Revolt.* Los Angeles: Nash, 1972.
Bell, J. Bowyer. *Terror Out of Zion: Irgun Zvai Leumi, LEHI, and the Palestine Underground, 1929–1949.* New York: St. Martin's Press, 1977.
Ben-Ami, Yitshaq. *Years of Wrath, Days of Glory: Memoirs from the Irgun.* New York: Shengold, 1983.
Bethell, Nicholas. *The Palestine Triangle: The Struggle for the Holy Land, 1935–48.* New York: G. P. Putnam's Sons, 1979.
Clarke, Thurston. *By Blood and Fire: The Attack on the King David Hotel.* New York: G. P. Putnam's Sons, 1981.
Cohen, Michael J. *Palestine and the Great Powers, 1945–1948.* Princeton, N.J.: Princeton University Press, 1982.
Cohen, Naomi W. *The Year after the Riots: American Responses to the Palestine Crisis of 1929–30.* Detroit, Mich.: Wayne State University Press, 1988.
Cornfield, Giveon. *Zion Liberated.* Malibu, Calif.: Pangloss Press, 1990.
Crossman, Richard. *Palestine Mission.* New York: Harper and Bros., 1947.
Crum, Bartley C. *Behind the Silken Curtain.* New York: Simon and Schuster, 1947.
Dekel, Ephraim. *Shai; The Exploits of Hagana Intelligence.* New York: Thomas Yoseloff, 1959.
ESCO Foundation for Palestine. *Palestine: A Study of Jewish, Arab and British Policies.* 2 vols. New Haven, Conn.: Yale University Press, 1947.
Frank, Gerold. *The Deed.* New York: Simon and Schuster, 1963.
Friedman, Isaiah. *The Question of Palestine, 1914–1918.* New York: Schocken Books, 1973.
Gal, Allon. *David Ben-Gurion and the American Alignment for a Jewish State.* Bloomington: Indiana University Press, 1991.
Galnoor, Itzhak. *The Partition of Palestine: Decision Crossroads in the Zionist Movement.* Albany: State University of New York Press, 1995.
Gitlin, Jan. *The Conquest of Acre Fortress.* Tel Aviv: Hadar, 1962.
Golan, Zev. *Free Jerusalem.* Jerusalem: Sdan Press and Historical Society of Israel, 1998.

Gorny, Joseph. *The British Labour Movement and Zionism 1917–1948*. London: Frank Cass, 1983.

Halamish, Aviva. *The Exodus Affair: Holocaust Survivors and the Struggle for Palestine*. Syracuse, N.Y.: Syracuse University Press, 1998.

Heller, Joseph. *The Stern Gang: Ideology, Politics, and Terror, 1940–1949*. London: Frank Cass, 1995.

Heller, Tzila Amidror. *Behind Prison Walls: A Jewish Woman Freedom Fighter for Israel's Independence*. Hoboken, N.J.: Ktav, 1999.

Hochstein, Joseph M., and Murray S. Greenfield. *The Jews' Secret Fleet*. Jerusalem: Gefen, 1987.

Hoffmann, Bruce. *The Failure of British Military Strategy within Palestine, 1939–1947*. Ramat Gan: Bar-Ilan University Press, 1983.

Hurewitz, J. C. *The Struggle for Palestine*. New York: Norton, 1950.

Katz, Doris. *The Lady Was a Terrorist, During Israel's War of Liberation*. New York: Shiloni, 1953.

Katz, Shmuel. *Days of Fire*. Jerusalem: Steimatzky's, 1968.

Lankin, Eliahu. *To Win the Promised Land: Story of a Freedom Fighter*. Walnut Creek, Calif.: Benmir Books, 1992.

Levine, Daniel. *The Birth of the Irgun Zvai Leumi—A Jewish Liberation Movement*. Jerusalem: Gefen, 1991.

Mardor, Munya M. *Haganah*. New York: New American Library, 1957.

Marton, Kati. *A Death in Jerusalem*. New York: Pantheon, 1994.

McDonald, James G. *My Mission in Israel, 1948–1951*. New York: Simon and Schuster, 1951.

Monroe, Elizabeth. *Britain's Moment in the Middle East, 1914–1956*. Baltimore: Johns Hopkins University Press, 1963.

Ofer, Dalia. *Escaping the Holocaust: Illegal Immigration to the Land of Israel, 1939–1944*. New York: Oxford University Press, 1990.

Penkower, Monty Noam. *The Holocaust and Israel Reborn: From Catastrophe to Sovereignty*. Urbana and Chicago: University of Illinois Press, 1994.

Perl, William R. *The Four-Front War: From the Holocaust to the Promised Land*. New York: Crown, 1978.

Postal, Bernard, and Henry W. Levy. *And the Hills Shouted for Joy; The Day Israel Was Born*. New York: McKay, 1973.

Reinharz, Jehuda. *Zionism and the Great Powers: A Century of Foreign Policy*. New York: Leo Baeck Institute, 1994.

Stein, Leonard. *The Balfour Declaration*. New York: Simon and Schuster, 1961.

Tavin, Eli, and Yonah Alexander. *Psychological Warfare and Propaganda: Irgun Documentation*. Wilmington, Del.: Scholarly Resources, 1982.

Taylor, Alan R. *Prelude to Israel: An Analysis of Zionist Diplomacy, 1897–1947*. New York: Philosophical Library, 1959.

Weisbord, Robert G. *African Zion; The Attempt to Establish a Jewish Colony in the East Africa Protectorate, 1903–1905*. Philadelphia: Jewish Publication Society of America, 1969.

Zadka, Saul. *Blood in Zion: How the Jewish Guerrillas Drove the British Out of Palestine.* London: Brassey's, 1995.

ARAB–JEWISH RELATIONS

Avnery, Uri. *Israel without Zionists: A Plea for Peace in the Middle East.* New York: Macmillan, 1968.

Buber, M., J. L. Magnes, and E. Simon, eds. *Towards Union in Palestine, Essays on Zionism and Jewish–Arab Cooperation.* Jerusalem: Ihud Association, 1947.

Caplan, Neil. *Futile Diplomacy—Volume 1: Early Arab-Zionist Negotiation Attempts, 1913–1931.* London: Frank Cass, 1983.

———. *Futile Diplomacy—Volume 2: Arab-Zionist Negotiations and the End of the Mandate.* London: Frank Cass, 1986.

Eisenberg, Laura Zittrain. *My Enemy's Enemy: Lebanon in the Early Zionist Imagination, 1900–1948.* Detroit, Mich.: Wayne State University Press, 1994.

Haim, Yehoyada. *Abandonment of Illusions: Zionist Political Attitudes Toward Palestinian Arab Nationalism, 1936–1939.* Boulder, Colo.: Westview Press, 1983.

Hattis, Susan Lee. *The Bi-National Idea in Palestine during Mandatory Times.* Haifa: Shikmona, 1970.

Kamen, Charles S. *Little Common Ground: Arab Agriculture and Jewish Settlement in Palestine, 1920–1948.* Pittsburgh: University of Pittsburgh Press, 1991.

Mandel, Neville J. *The Arabs and Zionism before World War I.* Berkeley: University of California Press, 1976.

Medoff, Rafael. *Zionism and the Arabs: An American Jewish Dilemma, 1898–1948.* Westport, Conn.: Praeger, 1997.

Morris, Benny. *The Birth of the Palestinian Refugee Problem, 1947–1949.* London: Cambridge University Press, 1988.

Porath, Yehoshua. *The Emergence of the Palestinian-Arab National Movement, 1918–1929.* London: Frank Cass, 1974.

———. *The Palestinian Arab National Movement, 1929–1939.* London: Frank Cass, 1977.

Shapira, Anita. *Land and Power: The Zionist Resort to Force, 1881–1948.* New York: Oxford University Press, 1992.

Stein, Kenneth W. *The Land Question in Palestine, 1917–1939.* Chapel Hill: University of North Carolina Press, 1984.

Teveth, Shabtai. *Ben-Gurion and the Palestinian Arabs: From Peace to War.* New York: Oxford University Press, 1985.

AMERICA–HOLY LAND RELATIONS

Brown, Michael. *The Israeli–American Connection: Its Roots in the Yishuv, 1914–1945.* Detroit, Mich.: Wayne State University Press, 1996.

Clifford, Clark M., Eugene V. Rostow, and Barbara W. Tuchman. *The Palestine Question in American History.* New York: Arno Press, 1978.

Cohen, Michael J. *Truman and Israel.* Berkeley: University of California Press, 1990.

Davis, Moshe, and Yehoshua Ben-Arieh, eds. *With Eyes toward Zion—III: Western Societies and the Holy Land.* New York: Praeger, 1991.

DeNovo, John A. *American Interests and Policies in the Middle East, 1900–1939.* Minneapolis, Minn.: Minneapolis University Press, 1963.

Evensen, Bruce J. *Truman, Palestine, and the Press: Shaping Conventional Wisdom at the Beginning of the Cold War.* Westport, Conn.: Greenwood, 1992.

Grose, Peter. *Israel in the Mind of America.* New York: Random House, 1981.

Knee, Stuart E. *The Concept of Zionist Dissent in the American Mind, 1917–1941.* New York: Robert Speller & Sons, 1979.

Lowdermilk, Walter C. *Palestine, Land of Promise.* New York: Harper and Bros., 1944.

Manuel, Frank E. *The Realities of American–Palestine Relations.* Washington, D.C.: Public Affairs Press, 1949.

Oder, Irwin. "The United States and the Palestine Mandate, 1920–1948: A Study of the Impact of Interest Groups on Foreign Policy," Ph.D. dissertation, Columbia University, 1956.

Polk, William R. *The United States and the Arab World.* Cambridge, Mass.: Harvard University Press, 1969.

Schechtman, Joseph B. *The United States and the Jewish State Movement: The Crucial Decade, 1939–1949.* New York: Herzl Press, 1966.

Schoenbaum, David. *The United States and the State of Israel.* New York: Oxford University Press, 1993.

Vogel, Lester I. *To See a Promised Land: Americans and the Holy Land in the Nineteenth Century.* University Park: Pennsylvania State University Press, 1993.

Zaar, Isaac. *Rescue and Liberation: America's Part in the Birth of Israel.* New York: Bloch, 1954.

AMERICAN ZIONISM

Altman, Sima, et al., *Pioneers from America: 75 Years of Hehalutz, 1905–1980.* Tel Aviv: Bogrei Hehalutz America, 1980.

Berman, Aaron. *Nazism, the Jews and American Zionism, 1933–1948.* Detroit, Mich.: Wayne State University Press, 1990.

Cohen, Naomi W. *American Jews and the Zionist Idea.* New York: Ktav Publishing House, 1975.

———. *Not Free to Desist; The American Jewish Committee, 1906–1966.* Philadelphia: Jewish Publication Society of America, 1972.

Feinstein, Marnin. *American Zionism, 1884–1904.* New York: Herzl Press, 1965.

Frommer, Morris. "The American Jewish Congress: A History, 1914–1950," Ph.D. dissertation, Ohio State University, 1978.

Gal, Allon, ed. *Envisioning Israel: The Changing Ideals and Images of North American Jews*. Jerusalem and Detroit, Mich.: Magnes Press and Wayne State University Press, 1996.

Ganin, Zvi. *Truman, American Jewry, and Israel, 1945–1948*. New York: Holmes and Meier, 1979.

Halkin, Hillel. *Letters to an American Jewish Friend: A Zionist's Polemic*. Philadelphia: Jewish Publication Society of America, 1977.

Halperin, Samuel. *The Political World of American Zionism*. Detroit, Mich.: Wayne State University Press, 1961.

Halpern, Ben. *The American Jew: A Zionist Analysis*. New York: Herzl Press, 1961.

Jaffe, Eliezer, D. *Letters to Yitz*. New York: Herzl Press, 1981.

Kaufman, Menahem. *An Ambiguous Partnership: Non-Zionists and Zionists in America, 1939–1948*. Jerusalem and Detroit: Magnes Press and Wayne State University Press, 1991.

Kenen, I. L. *Israel's Defense Line: Her Friends and Foes in Washington*. Buffalo, N.Y.: Prometheus Books, 1981.

Kleiman, Aaron, and Adrian L. Klieman, eds. *American Zionism: A Documentary History*. New York: Garland, 1987.

Kolsky, Thomas A. *Jews against Zionism: The American Council for Judaism, 1942–1948*. Philadelphia: Temple University Press, 1990.

Lesser, Allen. *Israel's Impact, 1950–51*. Lanham, Md.: University Press of America, 1984.

Levin, Marlin. *It Takes a Dream: The Story of Hadassah*. Jerusalem: Gefen, 1997.

Meyer, Isidore S., ed. *Early History of Zionism in America*. New York: Herzl Press, 1958.

Miller, Donald H. "A History of Hadassah 1912–1935." Ph.D. dissertation, New York University, 1968.

Neustadt-Noy, Isaac. "The Unending Task: Efforts to Unite American Jewry from the American Jewish Congress to the American Jewish Conference." Ph.D. dissertation, Brandeis University, 1976.

Polish, David. *Renew Our Days: The Zionist Issue in Reform Judaism*. Jerusalem: World Zionist Organization, 1976.

Sandler, Bernard I. "The Jews of America and the Resettlement of Palestine 1908–1934: Efforts and Achievements," Ph.D. dissertation, Bar Ilan University, 1979.

Shapiro, Yonathan. *Leadership of the American Zionist Organization, 1897–1930*. Chicago: University of Illinois Press, 1971.

Shpiro, David H. *From Philanthropy to Activism: The Political Transformation of American Zionism in the Holocaust Years, 1933–1945*. New York: Pergamon Press, 1994.

Silverberg, Robert. *If I Forget Thee O Jerusalem: American Jews and the State of Israel*. New York: Morrow, 1970.

Slater, Leonard. *The Pledge*. New York: Simon and Schuster, 1970.

Stevens, Richard P. *American Zionism and U.S. Foreign Policy, 1942–1947.* New York: Pageant Press, 1962.

Urofsky, Melvin I., ed. *Essays in American Zionism—Herzl Year Book, Volume VIII.* New York: Herzl Press, 1978.

Urofsky, Melvin I. *We Are One!* Garden City, N.Y.: Anchor Press/Doubleday, 1978.

———. *American Zionism from Herzl to the Holocaust.* Garden City, N.Y.: Anchor Press/Doubleday, 1975.

Waxman, Chaim I. *American Aliya: Portrait of an Innovative Migration Movement.* Detroit, Mich.: Wayne State University Press, 1989.

———. *America's Jews in Transition.* Philadelphia: Temple University Press, 1983.

REVISIONIST ZIONISM

Rapoport, Louis. *Shake Heaven & Earth: Peter Bergson and the Struggle to Rescue the Jews of Europe.* Jerusalem and New York: Gefen, 1999.

Rosenblum, Howard Isaac. "A Political History of Revisionist Zionism, 1925–1938." Ph.D. dissertation, Columbia University, 1986.

Saidel, Joanna Maura. "Revisionist Zionism in America: The Campaign to Win American Public Support, 1939–1948." Ph.D. dissertation, University of New Hampshire, 1994.

Schechtman, Joseph B., and Yehuda Benari. *History of the Revisionist Movement—Volume I: 1925–1930.* Tel Aviv: Hadar, 1970.

Shapiro, Yonathan. *The Road to Power: Herut Party in Israel.* Albany: State University of New York Press, 1991.

Shavit, Yaacov. *Jabotinsky and the Revisionist Movement, 1925–1948.* London: Frank Cass, 1988.

Weinbaum, Laurence. *A Marriage of Convenience: The New Zionist Organization and the Polish Government 1936–1939.* Boulder, Colo.: East European Monographs/Columbia University Press, 1993.

LABOR/SOCIALIST ZIONISM

Frankel, Jonathan. *Prophecy and Politics: Socialism, Nationalism, and the Russian Jews, 1862–1917.* New York: Cambridge University Press, 1981.

Gal, Allon. *Socialist-Zionism.* Cambridge: Schenkman, 1973.

Goldberg, J. J., and Elliot King, eds. *Builders and Dreamers: Habonim Labor Zionist Youth in North America.* New York: Herzl Press and Cornwall Books, 1993.

Hurwitz, Ariel, ed. *Against the Stream: Seven Decades of Hashomer Hatzair in North America.* Givat Haviva, Israel: Association of North American Shomrim and Yad Yaari, 1994.

Katzman, Jacob. *Commitment: The Labor Zionist Life-style in America.* New York: Labor Zionist Letters, 1975.

Leon, Dan. *The Kibbutz; A New Way of Life.* Oxford: Pergamon Press, 1969.

Near, Henry. *Frontiersmen and Halutzim: The Image of the Pioneer in North America and Pre-State Jewish Palestine.* Haifa: University of Haifa and Kibbutz University Center, 1987.

Raider, Mark A. *The Emergence of American Zionism.* New York: New York University Press, 1998.

Sternhell, Zeev. *The Founding Myths of Israel: Nationalism, Socialism, and the Making of the Jewish State,* translated by David Maisel. Princeton, N.J.: Princeton University Press, 1998.

CHRISTIAN ZIONISM

Ariel, Yaakov. *On Behalf of Israel: American Fundamentalist Attitudes Toward Jews, Judaism, and Zionism, 1865–1945.* Brooklyn, N.Y.: Carlson, 1991.

Fox, Richard. *Reinhold Niebuhr: A Biography.* San Francisco: Harper and Row, 1987.

Merkley, Paul C. *The Politics of Christian Zionism, 1891–1948.* London: Frank Cass, 1998.

Minerbi, Sergio I. *The Vatican and Zionism: Conflict in the Holy Land, 1895–1925.* New York: Oxford University Press, 1990.

Rausch, David A. *Zionism within Early American Fundamentalism, 1878–1918: A Convergence of Two Traditions.* New York: Edwin Mellen Press, 1979.

Wilken, Robert L. *The Land Called Holy: Palestine in Christian History and Thought.* New Haven, Conn.: Yale University Press, 1992.

REFERENCE BOOKS

Encyclopedia Judaica. Jerusalem: Keter, 1971.

Patai, Raphael, ed. *Encyclopedia of Zionism and Israel.* New York: Herzl Press, 1971.

Reich, Bernard. *Historical Dictionary of Israel.* Metuchen, N.J.: Scarecrow, 1992.

Rolef, Susan Hattis. *Political Dictionary of the State of Israel.* New York: Macmillan, 1993.

Simon, Reeva S., Philip Mattar, and Richard W. Bulliet, eds. *Encyclopedia of the Modern Middle East.* New York: Macmillan, 1996.

Wigoder, Geoffrey, ed. *New Encyclopedia of Zionism and Israel.* New York: Herzl Press, 1994.

About the Authors

Rafael Medoff is visiting scholar in Jewish studies at Purchase College, the State University of New York. His previous books include *Zionism and the Arabs: An American Jewish Dilemma* (1997) and *The Deafening Silence: American Jewish Leaders and the Holocaust, 1933–1945* (1987). Dr. Medoff is a member of the editorial boards of *American Jewish History* (of which he is also associate book review editor), *Southern Jewish History, Shofar,* and *Menorah Review,* as well as a member of the Academic Council of the American Jewish Historical Society. His essays and reviews have appeared in numerous encyclopedias and other reference volumes, as well as scholarly journals such as *Studies in Zionism,* the *Journal of Israeli History, Holocaust and Genocide Studies, Holocaust Studies Annual, Modern Judaism, Judaism, American Jewish History,* and *American Jewish Archives.* He authored the essay "New Yorkers and the Birth of Israel," which was featured in the 1998 *New York Times* supplement commemorating the fiftieth anniversary of the establishment of Israel.

Chaim I. Waxman is professor of sociology and Jewish studies at Rutgers University and a widely published author. His books include *The Stigma of Poverty: A Critique of Poverty Theories and Policies* (1977; second edition, 1983); *America's Jews in Transition* (1983); and *American Aliya* (1989). He has also edited more than a half-dozen books, including *The End of Ideology Debate* (1969), *Israel as a Religious Reality* (Jason Aronson, 1984), and, with Roberta R. Farber, *Jews in America: A Contemporary Reader* (University Press of New England, 1999).

His newest book, *Jewish Baby Boomers: A Communal Perspective,* will be published in 2000 by State University of New York Press. It is based largely on data from the 1990 National Jewish Population Survey and analyzes American Jewish baby boomers in detail, comparing them with baby boomers of other religious and ethnic groups in the United States. Professor Waxman is editor of the *Israel Studies Bulletin,* the periodical of the

Association for Israel Studies, and is a member of the editorial board of the journal *Israel Studies*. For more than three decades, he has served in various consultant and leadership positions with a variety of educational and Israel-oriented organizations.